The Poems of Emily Dickinson

THE POEMS OF

Emily Dickinson

READING EDITION

EDITED BY

R. W. FRANKLIN

The Belknap Press of Harvard University Press

Cambridge, Massachusetts, and London, England · 1999

First Harvard University Press paperback edition, 2005

Library of Congress Cataloging-in-Publication Data

Dickinson, Emily, 1830–1886.
    [Poems]
    The poems of Emily Dickinson / edited by R. W. Franklin. —
Reading ed.
        p.   cm.
    Includes index.
    ISBN 0-674-67624-6 (cloth)
    ISBN 0-674-01824-9 (pbk.)
    I. Franklin, R. W. (Ralph William), 1937– .   II. Title.
PS1541.A1   1999
811'.4—DC21   ˙99-11821

Contents

Introduction

Emily Dickinson wrote poems nearly all her life, most of them in the Dickinson Homestead on Main Street in Amherst, Massachusetts, where she was born in December 1830, lived in virtual seclusion as an adult, and, in May 1886, died. She may already have been at work in 1845 when, still fourteen years old, she confided to a friend that "poetical" was "what young ladys aim to be now a days." She was then residing on North Pleasant Street, where her father had removed the family in 1840, the Homestead having passed out of Dickinson ownership. Her earliest known verse, a high-spirited valentine implying a practiced if youthful hand, dates from 1850, when she was nineteen. Other early poems, now lost, may be inferred from her correspondence in the early 1850s, but only four (1-4) survive from before 1858, a landmark year when Dickinson, aged twenty-seven, back in the Homestead, set about accumulating her poems by copying them onto folded sheets of stationery and binding them into handmade volumes, commonly called fascicles. She was most active in 1862 (227 poems), 1863 (295), 1864 (98), and 1865 (229), much of the latter two years while—under the care of a Boston ophthalmologist— she was sharing living arrangements in Cambridgeport with her Norcross cousins, Louise and Frances.

She wrote poems every year thereafter—in 1877 averring that she had "no other Playmate"—but the number was never large, fewer than a dozen in some years, usually about twenty or thirty, occasionally more than forty. Although ill in the 1880s, she persevered to the end of life, the art of poetry having become an essential part of her personal expression and communication. The last two poems are from April 1886, incorporated into a letter to her literary friend Thomas Wentworth Higginson, who had already received a good many others. The final lines were a tribute to Helen Hunt Jackson (1685), a celebrated friend from childhood, who had died a few months earlier, as Dickinson, yet unknown, was to do the next.

> Of Glory not a Beam is left
> But her Eternal House -
> The Asterisk is for the Dead,
> The Living, for the Stars -

Dickinson's workshop in 1860 and in 1865 looked quite different from the mass of manuscripts she left behind at her death. By summer 1860, after two years of work, there were eight fascicles, carefully copied and bound, containing about 170 poems. This fine array constituted nearly everything in her possession, because she systematically destroyed drafts when she transcribed them to a later form. First came composition in pencil; then a neater copy, also in pencil, which, though it might contain alternative readings still pending, carried forward what she wanted to retain from the initial draft; then the fascicle record in ink, in the early years always a fair copy, all readings resolved. Because of her rules for destruction, the eight fascicles of completed poems were about all she had at hand in mid-1860.

This careful order ended in the second half of the year, when Dickinson temporarily stopped making fascicles, and remained in doubt in 1861 and early 1862, a period of apparent personal crisis for her, when fascicle sheets lay unbound for some time and poems were copied in ink individually instead of in groups. Though revived in 1861, her fascicle effort was less comprehensive, with the result that some poems never entered the fascicles or did so only years later. Other copying was divergent, in that individual manuscripts in ink, including a few for poems already in fascicles, appeared anomalously among her papers. From this time onward, miscellaneous manuscripts, in pencil or in ink, would be present in addition to the little volumes. But the most fundamental change in 1861 was textual: alternative readings, previously confined to the first two manuscript states, were now sometimes brought into the fascicles, a pattern that continued as long as she made them.

Dickinson restored order during 1862, perhaps under the steadying attention of Higginson, a new correspondent. She bound up the fascicle sheets remaining from 1861 and, with her muse fully engaged, increased the number of new poems at an extraordinary rate. She composed, copied, and bound relentlessly, so that by early 1864, after two further years of work, she had a total of forty fascicles, containing over eight hundred poems in various states of completion, from fair copies to mere transcriptions of rough worksheets. Besides a somewhat larger pool of miscellaneous manuscripts, which continued to grow that year while she was away for eye treatments, she had a few leftover fascicle sheets. These odds and ends of her process remained always unbound (such are now called *sets*).

The next year marked an important change, anticipated by those leftover sheets: she ceased binding fascicle sheets entirely, leaving them to their separate ways, even though she made enough to have assembled nine or ten more gatherings. She was energetic, if not quite exhaustive, in reducing the number of preliminary working drafts in her possession by transcribing them into these sets of 1865, which contain poems from as early as 1861, along with others known to have come from 1862, 1863, and 1864. At the end of 1865, about forty miscellaneous manuscripts remained, some of them duplicate, others of ambiguous status. Meanwhile, the number of poems on fascicle sheets, bound or unbound, had reached nearly eleven hundred.

Over the last twenty years of her life, as if some form of entropy governed this workshop, she copied few fascicle sheets, stringing them out between 1871 and 1875, with none in 1866-70 or in her last decade. Most of the poems of these twenty years survive on scraps of discarded household paper—incoming letters, abandoned envelopes, advertising flyers, wrapping paper—in the second draft or, increasingly, the first. Step by step, she had abandoned the system established in 1858, though the principle of accumulation remained in force, as it had not before 1858. The complex mass of manuscripts found after her death contained forty fascicles, ninety-eight unbound sheets, and seven or eight hundred individual manuscripts, from quite rough to quite finished.

Additional manuscripts had been sent to friends and family. Oddly perhaps, none went to her father, mother, or sister, with whom she shared the Homestead, but about 250 poems, by far the largest number, went to Susan Dickinson, her sister-in-law, who lived next door. At greater distance, Higginson received about a hundred, her Norcross cousins, seventy-one, with substantial numbers also going to longtime friends Samuel and Mary Bowles and Elizabeth and Josiah Gilbert Holland. About six hundred manuscripts of poems were sent to some forty recipients in what may resemble scribal publication, since the manuscripts were at times passed on to others. Not necessarily beautiful in appearance, these manuscripts were nevertheless fair copies, the text always consisting of one set of readings, without alternatives. Because such copies usually derived from her working manuscripts, often the first or second draft, Dickinson maintained a record of most poems, but because of her rules for destruction, that record, typically the fascicle, might not have been the actual source for the manuscript dispatched. She showed no interest in keeping track of the exact texts she sent out, even when derived from the fascicles, on which there is rarely an indication of later variants (though sometimes revision took place there), for she was confident that she could create another acceptable version from the text at hand. The same confidence lay behind her permitting alternative readings to enter the fascicles: one need not make a choice until one needed to make a choice.

Dickinson usually kept no record of what may be called impromptu verse. Such lines, sometimes woven into letters or notes, may be brief and epigrammatic, like these in a letter to Higginson, the only source (499):

> Best Gains - must have the Losses' test -
> To constitute them - Gains.

and these in a letter to Samuel Bowles, the influential editor of the *Springfield Republican,* also the only source (186):

> The Juggler's *Hat* her Country is -
> The Mountain Gorse - the *Bee's* -

Although Dickinson may have felt such lines to be undeserving of further record, she wrote them out as verse, and a few of similar character, unattested in a letter, did enter the fascicles (31, 206):

> To him who keeps an Orchis' heart -
> The swamps are pink with June.

and

> Least Rivers - docile to some sea.
> My Caspian - thee.

A few longer ones, not at all epigrammatic, also exist outside of the fascicles and not otherwise in Dickinson's possession, including lines of reassurance in 1860 for Louise and Frances Norcross, eighteen and twelve years old, on the death of their mother (130):

> "Mama" never forgets her birds -
> Though in another tree.
> She looks down just as often
> And just as tenderly,
> As when her little mortal nest
> With cunning care she wove -
> If either of her "sparrows fall",
> She "notices" above.

    Emily Dickinson wrote nearly eighteen hundred poems, 1,789 at present count, each of them represented in this reading edition. They exist in multiple versions and survive in about 2,500 textual sources, generally holographs, but also, given the hazards of history, in a number of secondary sources—transcripts by various hands and publication in various places. Although Dickinson sent poems to others as a personal act, she did not publish, or "print" as she was inclined to call it. Still, her poems got around, and at least ten of them appeared in her lifetime, anonymously, mostly in newspapers, having been supplied by admiring friends and never seen through the press by the poet. She is known to have complained only once—about a question mark in "A narrow fellow in the grass" (1096) that stopped a line whose thought should have continued into the next. She said nothing adverse about typography or its effects on her poems. A good citizen of the age of print, she was a committed reader of newspapers, magazines, and books but could not undertake the commercial, impersonal, and fundamentally exposing act of publishing her work. This is the poet who, knowing her boundaries, said, "I do not cross my Father's ground to any House or Town." "Publication," she wrote in 1863, her most prolific year, "is the Auction / Of the Mind of Man," a "Disgrace of Price" (788):

> Poverty - be justifying
> For so foul a thing
>
> Possibly - but We - would rather
> From Our Garret go
> White - unto the White Creator -
> Than invest - Our Snow -

This reading edition is based on *The Poems of Emily Dickinson* (1998), a rendering of the entire corpus of textual sources, prepared by the present editor and published by The Belknap Press of Harvard University Press. A three-volume set, *Poems* (1998) presents the full text of each of the 2,500 source documents, often giving several versions of the same poem. It traces their particular histories, including the identification of recipients, and describes the relationships and variants among the versions. There is an account of physical lineation, which includes word division, and of emendation by the editor to restore damaged texts, correct slips of the pen, or, in the case of secondary sources, undo uncharacteristic habits of transcriber or publisher. The overall organization is chronological, reflecting a new dating and employing a new numbering. In addition to detailed publishing histories, this three-volume edition is outfitted with fourteen appendixes and an extensive introduction that provides an overview of the early publishing history and a detailed account of the Dickinson workshop. The appendixes are specialized tables and lists, including, among others, poems published in Dickinson's lifetime, poems attributed to her, titles and other characterizations she gave to them, recipients and the poems they received, word division, and emendation. One appendix, a tabulation of the number of poems per year, is reproduced as Appendix 1 in this reading edition.

The numbering here is that introduced by *Poems* (1998), from which the texts also derive, both the transcription and the emendation. The editorial discourse and apparatus have been omitted, and the multiplicity of texts has been reduced to a single reading version for each poem—a fair copy—as Dickinson did when sending poems to others. Readers interested in further background, or in additional readings or versions, or in the texts before the policies of the present edition were applied may consult *Poems* (1998), which serves as a primary resource.

About three fourths of the poems exist in a single source. For the rest, with from two to seven sources, the policy has been to choose the latest version of the entire poem, thereby giving to the poet, rather than the editor, the ownership of change. Dickinson many times copied or used her poems in part, writing out a few lines, or sending a single stanza to a friend, or weaving fragments into letters. While these might be considered complete poems, arguably so for those sent out of the house to an audience, they are here not regarded as independent of the rest, nor as the extent of the poem to which Dickinson was committed. Although in 1861 she incorporated three lines of "'Tis anguish grander than delight" (192) into a note to Susan Dickinson,

I'm thinking on that other morn -

When Cerements - let go -
And Creatures - clad in Victory -
Go up - by two - and two!

she transcribed the whole into Set 7 in 1865:

'Tis Anguish grander than Delight
'Tis Resurrection Pain -
The meeting Bands of smitten Face
We questioned to, again -

'Tis Transport wild as thrills the Graves
When Cerements let go
And Creatures clad in Miracle
Go up by Two and Two -

The set version is both later and fuller, but there are instances in which the last is a fragment. For such, an earlier full copy has been selected, as for "Her spirit rose to such a hight" (1527). In a few instances, when Dickinson settled on a shorter version, after a longer one, the choice has been the last copy of the shorter version, typically the latest itself. "Further in summer than the birds" (895), which began as seven stanzas, was recast into four, a length that survives in four copies, the last of which is the one in this reading edition.

Such selection is—at first—indifferent as to whether the document is a fair copy or a working draft, a holograph or a secondary source, though additional considerations may shift the choice. A holograph, for example, takes precedence over a transcript when they are substantively identical or when, though variant, the sequence of the holograph and the other source is indefinite. Earlier manuscripts have also become the choice—again, all things being substantively equal—if the manuscript otherwise to be chosen, perhaps roughly made or miswritten, has a lapse in form, as with "Nobody knows this little rose" (11).

An earlier version has been accepted when, compared to the others, the latest was customized for a particular circumstance. The last line of a poem incorporated into a letter to Samuel Bowles (1432)

> I have no Life but this -
> To lead it here -
> Nor any Death - but lest
> Dispelled from there -
> Nor tie to Earths to come,
> Nor Action new
> Except through this Extent
> The love of you.

which in earliest draft read

> The loving you -

was changed for a more distant relationship with Higginson

> The Realm of you -

when Dickinson prepared a version for him. In another instance, she adjusted the opening words of "He lived the life of ambush" (1571) in order to fit the poem into a letter to Samuel Bowles the younger.

A Tree your Father gave me, bore this priceless flower.
Would you accept it because of him

> Who abdicated Ambush
> And went the way of Dusk,
> And now against his subtle name
> There stands an Asterisk
> As confident of him as we -
> Impregnable we are -
> The whole of Immortality
> Secreted in a Star -

The opening lines in this version do not stand alone, so bound are they syntactically to the particular context.

Appendix 2 records the choices among multiple documents, identified by poem number and alphabetic designation. The texts may be readily traced to the larger edition. Also in this appendix is a record of the adoption of Dickinson's revisions and alternative readings. The policy has been to retain the primary readings, those in the line, unless Dickinson indicated a different preference. Revisions have been adopted when Dickinson cancelled the primary readings in favor of the change; revisions have not been adopted when, without cancellation, she left them only as words to be considered. Sometimes in lieu of cancellation, Dickinson underscored the preferred reading. Although in the course of composition or revision this choice might yield to a new one, also underscored, the act of underscoring expressed her will, much as cancellation did, and has been similarly followed. There are instances when the underscoring was carried into the fascicles, shaping choices for subsequent fair copies. For the famous poem "I'm nobody! Who are you?" (260), there is no fair copy, only the fascicle appearance that includes underscored alternatives, the readings adopted in this edition.

> I'm Nobody! Who are you?
> Are you - Nobody - too?
> Then there's a pair of us!
> Dont tell! they'd banish us - you know!
>
> How dreary - to be - Somebody!   5
> How public - like a Frog -
> To tell your name - the livelong June -
> To an admiring Bog!
>
> 4 banish us] <u>advertise</u>   7 your] <u>one's</u>

Alternatives have also been selected based on Dickinson's adoption of them in other instances, either earlier or later, of the same poem. This policy reflects the understanding that Dickinson made choices when she needed to (or wanted to), as in a fair copy for a friend, and that versions with alternatives, in particular those in fascicles and sets, may follow fair copies in which she had made choices but kept no record of them. Two fair copies of "Her last Poems" (600), one sent to Susan Dickinson and one retained, were followed in the fascicle by a text with alternatives:

> Her - last Poems -
> Poets ended -   '

Silver - perished - with her Tongue -
Not on Record - bubbled Other -
Flute - or Woman - so divine - 5

Not unto it's Summer Morning -
Robin - uttered half the Tune
Gushed too full for the adoring -
From the Anglo-Florentine -

Late - the Praise - 'Tis dull - Conferring 10
On the Head too High - to Crown -
Diadem - or Ducal symbol -
Be it's Grave - sufficient Sign -

Nought - that We - No Poet's Kinsman -
Suffocate - with easy Wo - 15
What - and if Ourself a Bridegroom -
Put Her down - in Italy?

(*1*) 7 uttered] published   12 symbol -] showing - • Token -

(*2*) 6 unto] upon -   7 uttered] lavished

In both fair copies, each with variants not continued into the fascicle, Dickinson˙adopted one of the alternatives for line 12 ("showing"), as does the present edition. Though informed by Dickinson's judgment in other places, the resulting texts are not composite, derived as they have been from readings on a single document.

Unlike diaries, journals, or letters, poetry is commonly considered a public genre, to be brought editorially into line with public norms of presentation, but Dickinson's poems, never published by the poet, may be seen as a private genre—a journal of her effort, with a distribution of poems that, like letters, was a part of personal communication with individuals. As she said (1036),

The Products of my Farm are these
Sufficient for my Own
And here and there a Benefit
Unto a Neighbor's Bin.

With Dickinson's practice in her manuscripts as the standard for representing her poems, this volume follows her spelling, capitalization, punctuation, and usage.

"I spelt a word wrong in this letter," she teased her brother, Austin, in 1854, "but I know better, so you need'nt think you have caught me," and

in 1862 she acknowledged to Higginson that, in the copy of "Of tribula-
tion these are they" (328) that she was sending to him, "I spelled Ankle -
wrong" (as "Ancle"—her usual form), without in either case effecting a
reformation in her bright orthography. She was aware of external stand-
ards but did not strive to adhere to them, only slowly altering some
spellings. *Extasy* was her form until 1873, *Bethleem* until sometime after
1874 (before 1880), *opon* until 1880, *etherial, Febuary, retrogade,* and
others until the end. Her spelling can indicate how she heard the words
and thus the sound of her poems. To her ear, the final lines from "Had I
not this or this I said" (828),

> To feed opon the Retrogade -
> Enfeebles - the Advance -

included the sound of only two *r*'s, a condition concealed if her spelling is
normalized.

Her capitalization and punctuation, rendered in standard type, have
been familiar in texts since mid-twentieth century. In manuscript, Dickin-
son capitalized many words beyond usual expectation, and her sylvan
punctuation, while including commas, periods, exclamation points, and
question marks, relied mainly on dashes of varying length and position,
tilting up or down as well as extending horizontally. In the mid-1860s she
reduced the amount and force of punctuation in the poems, some, such as
"Like men and women shadows walk" (964), having none. A spaced
hyphen, rather than an en or em dash, has been used as appropriate to the
relative weight of her dashes in most of the poems. The apostrophes in
many contractions are misplaced, as in *hav'nt* and *did'nt* (perhaps indica-
tive of how her ear divided the sounds), or not used at all, as in *dont,
wont,* and *cant* (no division). In certain possessive forms, apostophes
appear by analogy: *her's, your's, it's.* The single form *it's* served her as
both a possessive pronoun and a contraction of "it is."

Although the early Dickinson editors not only regularized such ele-
ments of her style but also altered texts to effect rhyme, smooth rhythm,
clarify sense, and adjust irregular usage, the trend since mid-twentieth
century has been to accept Dickinson's substantives as they are, preserv-
ing manner as well as sound and sense. This edition continues this trend,
not changing, for example, as Martha Dickinson Bianchi did in *Poems*
(1930), the nominative to the objective case in the final word of "My
wheel is in the dark!" (61):

> Some with new - stately feet -
> Pass royal thro' the gate -

Flinging the problem back
At you and I!

If the orthography, capitalization, punctuation, and usage should seem problematical, they are nonetheless Dickinson's, not the editor's or the publisher's, not, except indirectly, society's—agents with whom she conducted no negotiation toward public norms for her poetry. In this reading edition—a printed codex, a form familiar to her—the basic editorial choice has been either to follow her private intentions and characteristics, presenting the poems as well as transcription and the custom of typography can, or to lay onto the poems social conventions and judgments that were not hers. Although there can be various kinds of reading editions, with different technological bases or with greater intervention in the interests of editorial taste or recognized convention, the present one follows her own practice, selecting versions that focus on her latest full effort, adopting revisions and alternative readings for which she indicated a choice, and deferring to her custom in presentation and usage. The entry into her poetry is through her idiom.

1   Awake ye muses nine, sing me a strain divine,
     unwind the solemn twine, and tie my Valentine!

Oh the Earth was *made* for lovers, for damsel, and hopeless swain,
for sighing, and gentle whispering, and *unity* made of *twain,*
all things do go a courting, in earth, or sea, or air,
God hath made nothing single but *thee* in his world so fair!
The *bride,* and then the *bridegroom,* the *two,* and then the *one,*
Adam, and Eve, his consort, the moon, and then the sun;
the life doth prove the precept, who obey shall happy be,
who will not serve the sovreign, be hanged on fatal tree.   10
The high do seek the lowly, the great do seek the small,
none cannot find who *seeketh* on this terrestrial ball;
The bee doth court the flower, the flower his suit receives,
and they make a merry wedding, whose guests are hundred leaves;
the wind doth woo the branches, the branches they are won,
and the father fond demandeth the maiden for his son.
The storm doth walk the seashore humming a mournful tune,
the wave with eye so pensive, looketh to see the moon,
their spirits meet together, they make them solemn vows,
no more he singeth mournful, her sadness she doth lose.   20
The *worm* doth woo the *mortal,* death claims a living bride,
night unto day is married, morn unto eventide;
Earth is a merry damsel, and *Heaven* a knight so true,
and Earth is quite coquettish, and he seemeth in vain to sue.
Now to the *application,* to the reading of the roll,
to bringing thee to justice, and marshalling thy soul;
thou art a *human* solo, a being cold, and lone,
wilt have no kind companion, thou *reap'st* what thou hast *sown.*
Hast never silent hours, and minutes all too long,
and a deal of sad reflection, and *wailing* instead of song?   30
There's *Sarah,* and *Eliza,* and *Emeline* so fair,
and *Harriet,* and *Susan,* and she with *curling hair!*
Thine eyes are sadly blinded, but yet thou mayest see
six true, and comely maidens sitting opon the tree;
approach that tree with caution, then up it boldly climb,
and seize the one thou lovest, nor care for *space,* or *time!*

Then bear her to the greenwood, and build for her a bower,
and give her what she asketh, jewel, or bird, or flower;
and bring the fife, and trumpet, and beat opon the drum -
and bid the world Goodmorrow, and go to glory home! 40

2   Sic transit gloria mundi
     "How doth the busy bee"
     Dum vivamus vivamus
     I stay mine enemy! —

     Oh veni vidi vici!   5
     Oh caput cap-a-pie!
     And oh "memento mori"
     When I am far from thee

     Hurrah for Peter Parley
     Hurrah for Daniel Boone   10
     Three cheers sir, for the gentleman
     Who first observed the moon —

     Peter put up the sunshine!
     Pattie arrange the stars
     Tell Luna, tea is waiting   15
     And call your brother Mars —

     Put down the apple Adam
     And come away with me
     So shal't thou have a pippin
     From off my Father's tree!   20

     I climb the "Hill of Science"
     I "view the Landscape o'er"
     Such transcendental prospect
     I ne'er beheld before! —

     Unto the Legislature   25
     My country bids me go,
     I'll take my india rubbers
     In case the wind should blow.

     During my education
     It was announced to me   30
     That gravitation stumbling
     Fell from an apple tree —

                                                    □

The Earth opon it's axis
Was once supposed to turn
By way of a gymnastic
In honor to the sun —

35

It was the brave Columbus
A sailing o'er the tide
Who notified the nations
Of where I would reside

40

Mortality is fatal
Gentility is fine
Rascality, heroic
Insolvency, sublime

Our Fathers being weary
Laid down on Bunker Hill
And though full many a morn'g
Yet they are sleeping still

45

The trumpet sir, shall wake them
In streams I see them rise
Each with a solemn musket
A marching to the skies!

50

A coward will remain, Sir,
Until the fight is done;
But an immortal hero
Will take his hat and run.

55

Good bye Sir, I am going
My country calleth me
Allow me Sir, at parting
To wipe my weeping e'e

60

In token of our friendship
Accept this "Bonnie Doon"
And when the hand that pluck'd it
Hath passed beyond the moon

The memory of my ashes
Will consolation be
Then farewell Tuscarora
And farewell Sir, to thee.

65

3   On this wondrous sea - sailing silently -
Ho! Pilot! Ho!
Knowest thou the shore
Where no breakers roar -
Where the storm is o'er?   5

In the silent West
Many - the sails at rest -
The anchors fast.
Thither I pilot thee -
Land! Ho! Eternity!   10
Ashore at last!

So sailors say - on yesterday -   5
Just as the dusk was brown
One little boat gave up it's strife
And gurgled down and down.

So angels say - on yesterday -
Just as the dawn was red   10
One little boat - o'erspent with gales -
Retrimmed it's masts - redecked it's sails -
And shot - exultant on!

7   Summer for thee, grant I may be
        When Summer days are flown!
        Thy music still, when Whippowil
        And Oriole - are done!

        For thee to bloom, I'll skip the tomb   5
        And row my blossoms o'er!
        Pray gather me -
            Anemone -
        Thy flower - forevermore!

8   When Roses cease to bloom, Sir,
        And Violets are done -
        When Bumblebees in solemn flight
        Have passed beyond the Sun -
        The hand that paused to gather   5
        Opon this Summer's day
        Will idle lie - in Auburn -
        Then take my flowers - pray!

9   If recollecting were forgetting,
        Then I remember not,
        And if forgetting, recollecting,
        How near I had forgot,
        And if to miss, were merry,   5
        And to mourn, were gay,

How very blithe the fingers
That gathered this, today!

10 Garlands for Queens, may be -
Laurels - for rare degree
Of soul or sword -
Ah - but remembering me -
Ah - but remembering thee -   5
Nature in chivalry -
Nature in charity -
Nature in equity -
The Rose ordained!

11 Nobody knows this little Rose -
It might a pilgrim be
Did I not take it from the ways
And lift it up to thee.
Only a Bee will miss it -   5
Only a Butterfly,
Hastening from far journey -
On it's breast to lie -
Only a Bird will wonder -
Only a Breeze will sigh -   10
Ah Little Rose - how easy
For such as thee to die!

12 I had a guinea golden -
I lost it in the sand -
And tho' the sum was simple
And pounds were in the land -
Still, had it such a value   5
Unto my frugal eye -
That when I could not find it -
I sat me down to sigh.

I had a crimson Robin -
Who sang full many a day   10

But when the woods were painted -
He - too - did fly away -
Time brought me other Robins -
Their ballads were the same -
Still, for my missing Troubadour   15
I kept the "house at hame".

I had a star in heaven -
One "Pleiad" was it's name -
And when I was not heeding,
It wandered from the same -   20
And tho' the skies are crowded -
And all the night ashine -
I do not care about it -
Since none of them are mine -

My story has a moral -   25
I have a missing friend -
"Pleiad" it's name - and Robin -
And guinea in the sand -
And when this mournful ditty
Accompanied with tear -   30
Shall meet the eye of traitor
In country far from here -
Grant that repentance solemn
May seize opon his mind -
And he no consolation   35
Beneath the sun may find.

13   There is a morn by men unseen -
        Whose maids opon remoter green
        Keep their seraphic May -
        And all day long, with dance and game,
        And gambol I may never name -   5
        Employ their holiday.

        Here to light measure, move the feet
        Which walk no more the village street -
        Nor by the wood are found -
        Here are the birds that sought the sun   10

When last year's distaff idle hung
And summer's brows were bound.

Ne'er saw I such a wondrous scene -
Ne'er such a ring on such a green -
Nor so serene array -   15
As if the stars some summer night
Should swing their cups of Chrysolite -
And revel till the day -

Like thee to dance - like thee to sing -
People opon that mystic green -   20
I ask, each new May morn.
I wait thy far - fantastic bells -
Announcing me in other dells -
Unto the different dawn!

14   As if I asked a common Alms,
      And in my wondering hand
      A Stranger pressed a Kingdom,
      And I, bewildered, stand -
      As if I asked the Orient   5
      Had it for me a Morn -
      And it should lift it's purple Dikes,
      And shatter Me with Dawn!

15   She slept beneath a tree -
      Remembered but by me.
      I touched her Cradle mute -
      She recognized the foot -
      Put on her Carmine suit   5
         And see!

16   The feet of people walking home -
      With gayer sandals go -
      The Crocus, till she rises
      The Vassal of the snow -

                                                    □

The lips at Hallelujah   5
Long years of practise bore -
Till bye and bye, these Bargemen
Walked singing, on the shore.

Pearls are the Diver's farthings -
Extorted from the sea -   10
Pinions - the Seraph's wagon -
Pedestrian once - as we -

Night is the morning's Canvas -
Larceny - *Legacy.*
Death, but our rapt attention   15
To immortality.

My figures fail to tell me
How far the village lies
Whose Peasants are the angels -
Whose Cantons dot the skies -   20

My Classics vail their faces -
My faith that dark adores -
Which from it's solemn abbeys
Such Resurrection pours -

17   It's all I have to bring today -
       This, and my heart beside -
       This, and my heart, and all the fields -
       And all the meadows wide -
       Be sure you count - sh'd I forget   5
       Some one the sum could tell -
       This, and my heart, and all the Bees
       Which in the Clover dwell.

18   Morns like these - we parted -
       Noons like these - she rose -
       Fluttering first - then firmer
       To her fair repose.

                                                                □

Never did she lisp it -   5
It was not for me -
She - was mute from transport -
I - from agony -

Till - the evening nearing
One the curtains drew -   10
Quick! A sharper rustling!
And this linnet flew!

19   So has a Daisy vanished
        From the fields today -
        So tiptoed many a slipper
        To Paradise away -
        Oozed so, in crimson bubbles   5
        Day's departing tide -
        Blooming - tripping - flowing -
        Are ye then with God?

20   If those I loved were lost
        The Crier's voice w'd tell me -
        If those I loved were found
        The bells of Ghent w'd ring -
        Did those I loved repose   5
        The Daisy would impel me.
        Philip - when bewildered
        Bore his riddle in!

21   The Gentian weaves her fringes -
        The Maple's loom is red -
        My departing blossoms
            Obviate parade.

22   A brief, but patient illness -
        An hour to prepare -
        And one below, this morning

Is where the angels are -
It was a short procession -   5
The Bobolink was there -
An aged Bee addressed us -
And then we knelt in prayer -
We trust that she was willing -
We ask that we may be -   10
Summer - Sister - Seraph!
Let us go with thee!

23   In the name of the Bee -
      And of the Butterfly -
      And of the Breeze - Amen!

24   Frequently the woods are pink -
      Frequently, are brown.
      Frequently the hills undress
      Behind my native town -
      Oft a head is crested   5
      I was wont to see -
      And as oft a cranny
      Where it used to be -
      And the Earth - they tell me
      On it's axis turned!   10
      Wonderful rotation -
      By but *twelve* performed!

25   A sepal - petal - and a thorn
      Opon a common summer's morn -
      A flask of Dew - A Bee or two -
      A Breeze - a'caper in the trees -
      And I'm a Rose!   5

26   Distrustful of the Gentian -
      And just to turn away,

The fluttering of her fringes
Chid my perfidy -
Weary for my ——   5
I will singing go -
I shall not feel the sleet - then -
I shall not fear the snow.

27   Flees so the phantom meadow
      Before the breathless Bee -
      So bubble brooks in deserts
      On ears that dying lie -
      Burn so the evening spires   5
      To eyes that Closing go -
      Hangs so distant Heaven -
      To a hand below.

28   We lose - because we win -
      Gamblers - recollecting which -
      Toss their dice again!

29   All these my banners be.
      I sow my - pageantry
      In May -
      It rises train by train -
      Then sleeps in state again -   5
      My chancel - all the plain
            Today.

30   To lose - if One can find again -
      To miss - if One shall meet -
      The Burglar cannot rob - then -
      The Broker cannot cheat.
      So build the hillocks gaily -   5
      Thou little spade of mine
      Leaving nooks for Daisy

And for Columbine -
You and I the secret
Of the Crocus know -
Let us chant it softly -
"*There* is no more snow"!

10

31   To him who keeps an Orchis' heart -
The swamps are pink with June.

32   The morns are meeker than they were -
The nuts are getting brown -
The berry's cheek is plumper -
The Rose is out of town.

The maple wears a gayer scarf -
The field a scarlet gown -
Lest I sh'd be old fashioned
I'll put a trinket on.

5

33   Whether my bark went down at sea -
Whether she met with gales -
Whether to isles enchanted
She bent her docile sails -

By what mystic mooring
She is held today -
This is the errand of the eye
Out opon the Bay.

5

34   Taken from men - this morning -
Carried by men today -
Met by the Gods with banners -
Who marshalled her away -

One little maid - from playmates -
One little mind from school -

5

There must be guests in Eden -
All the rooms are full -

Far - as the East from Even -
Dim - as the border star -　　　　　　　　　　10
Courtiers quaint, in Kingdoms
Our departed are.

35   Sleep is supposed to be
By souls of sanity
The shutting of the eye.

Sleep is the station grand
Down wh', on either hand　　　　　　　　　5
The hosts of witness stand!

Morn is supposed to be
By people of degree
The breaking of the Day.

Morning has not occurred!　　　　　　　　10

That shall Aurora be -
East of Eternity -
One with the banner gay -
One in the red array -
That is the break of Day!　　　　　　　　15

36   If I should die -
And you should live -
And time sh'd gurgle on -
And morn sh'd beam -
And noon should burn -　　　　　　　　　5
As it has usual done -
If Birds should build as early
And Bees as bustling go -
One might depart at option
From enterprise below!　　　　　　　　　10
'Tis sweet to know that stocks will stand
When we with Daisies lie -

That Commerce will continue -
And Trades as briskly fly -
It makes the parting tranquil   15
And keeps the soul serene -
That gentlemen so sprightly
Conduct the pleasing scene!

37   By Chivalries as tiny,
        A Blossom, or a Book,
        The seeds of smiles are planted -
        Which blossom in the dark.

38   I never told the buried gold
        Opon the hill - that lies -
        I saw the sun - his plunder done
        Crouch low to guard his prize.

        He stood as near   5
        As stood you here -
        A pace had been between -
        Did but a snake bisect the brake
        My life had forfeit been.

        That was a wondrous booty -   10
        I hope 'twas honest gained.
        Those were the fairest ingots
        That ever kissed the spade!

        Whether to keep the secret -
        Whether to reveal -   15
        Whether as I ponder
        "Kidd" will sudden sail -

        Could a shrewd advise me
        We might e'en divide -
        Should a shrewd betray me -   20
        Atropos decide!

39   I never lost as much but twice -
       And that was in the sod.
       Twice have I stood a beggar
       Before the door of God!

       Angels - twice descending   5
       Reimbursed my store -
       Burglar! Banker - Father!
       I am poor once more!

40   I hav'nt told my garden yet -
       Lest that should conquer me.
       I hav'nt quite the strength now
       To break it to the Bee -

       I will not name it in the street   5
       For shops w'd stare at me -
       That one so shy - so ignorant
       Should have the face to die.

       The hillsides must not know it -
       Where I have rambled so -   10
       Nor tell the loving forests
       The day that I shall go -

       Nor lisp it at the table -
       Nor heedless by the way
       Hint that within the Riddle   15
       One will walk today -

41   I often passed the Village
       When going home from school -
       And wondered what they did there -
       And why it was so still -

       I did not know the year then,   5
       In which my call would come -
       Earlier, by the Dial,
       Than the rest have gone.

                         □

46   Before the ice is in the pools -
Before the skaters go,
Or any cheek at nightfall
Is tarnished by the snow -

Before the fields have finished -   5
Before the Christmas tree,
Wonder opon wonder -
Will arrive to me!

What we touch the hems of
On a summer's day -   10
What is only walking
Just a bridge away -

That which sings so - speaks so -
When there's no one here -
Will the frock I wept in   15
Answer me to wear?

47   By such and such an offering
To Mr So and So -
The web of life is woven -
So martyrs albums show!

Harmless as Streaks of Meteor -
Opon a Planet's Bond -

Their faith the Everlasting Troth -
Their Expectation - fair -   10
The Needle to the North Degree
Wades so - through Polar Air -

188   Could *I* - then - shut the door -
      Lest *my* beseeching face - at last -
      Rejected - be - of *Her?*

189   Is it true, dear Sue?
      Are there *two?*
      I should'nt like to come
      For fear of joggling Him!
      If you could shut him up   5
      In a Coffee Cup,
      Or tie him to a pin
      Till I got in -
      Or make him fast
      To "Toby's" fist -   10
      Hist! Whist! I'd come!

190   No Rose, yet felt myself a'bloom,
      No Bird - yet rode in Ether -

191   "Morning" - means "Milking" - to the Farmer -
      Dawn - to the Teneriffe -
      Dice - to the Maid -
      Morning means just Risk - to the Lover -
      Just Revelation - to the Beloved -   5

      Epicures - date a Breakfast - by it -
      Brides - an Apocalypse -
      Worlds - a Flood -

Faint-going Lives - Their lapse from Sighing -
Faith - The Experiment of Our Lord -   10

192   'Tis Anguish grander than Delight
       'Tis Resurrection Pain -
       The meeting Bands of smitten Face
       We questioned to, again -

       'Tis Transport wild as thrills the Graves   5
       When Cerements let go
       And Creatures clad in Miracle
       Go up by Two and Two -

193   *Speech* - is a prank of *Parliament* -
       Tears - a trick of the *nerve* -
       But the Heart with the heaviest freight on -
       Does'nt - always - move -

194   Title divine, is mine.
       The Wife without the Sign -
       Acute Degree conferred on me -
       Empress of Calvary -
       Royal, all but the Crown -   5
       Betrothed, without the Swoon
       God gives us Women -
       When You hold Garnet to Garnet -
       Gold - to Gold -
       Born - Bridalled - Shrouded -   10
       In a Day -
       Tri Victory -
       "My Husband" - Women say
       Stroking the Melody -
       Is this the way -   15

195   Victory comes late -
       And is held low to freezing lips -

Too rapt with frost
To take it -
How sweet it would have tasted -   5
Just a Drop -
Was God so economical?
His Table's spread too high for Us -
Unless We dine on Tiptoe -
Crumbs - fit such little mouths -   10
Cherries - suit Robins -
The Eagle's Golden Breakfast strangles - Them -
God keep His Oath to Sparrows -
Who of little Love - know how to starve -

196   I'll send the feather from my Hat!
       Who knows - but at the sight of *that*
       My Sovereign will relent?
       As trinket - worn by faded Child -
       Confronting eyes long - comforted -   5
       Blisters the Adamant!

197   Jesus! thy Crucifix
       Enable thee to guess
       The smaller size!

       Jesus! thy second face
       Mind thee in Paradise   5
       Of our's!

198   Baby -

       Teach Him - when He makes the *names* -
       Such an one - to say -
       On his babbling - Berry - lips -
       As should sound - to me -
       Were my Ear - as near his nest -   5
       As my *thought* - today -
       As should sound -

"Forbid us not" -
Some like "Emily."

199 Tho' I get home how late - how late -
So I get home - 'twill compensate -
Better will be the Extasy
That they have done expecting me -
When night - descending - dumb - and dark - 5
They hear my unexpected knock -
Transporting must the moment be -
Brewed from decades of Agony!

To think just how the fire will burn -
Just how long-cheated eyes will turn - 10
To wonder what myself will say,
And what itself, will say to me -
Beguiles the Centuries of way!

200 The Rose did caper on her cheek -
Her Boddice rose and fell -
Her pretty speech - like drunken men -
Did stagger pitiful -

Her fingers fumbled at her work - 5
Her needle would not go -
What ailed so smart a little maid -
It puzzled me to know -

Till opposite - I spied a cheek
That bore *another* Rose - 10
Just opposite - another speech
That like the Drunkard goes -

A Vest that like her Boddice, danced -
To the immortal tune -
Till those two troubled - little Clocks 15
Ticked softly into one.

201   With thee, in the Desert -
With thee in the thirst -
With thee in the Tamarind wood -
Leopard breathes - at last!

202   "Faith" is a fine invention
For Gentlemen who *see!*
But Microscopes are prudent
In an Emergency!

203   The thought beneath so slight a film -
Is more distinctly seen -
As laces just reveal the surge -
Or Mists - the Appenine -

204   I'll tell you how the Sun rose -
A Ribbon at a time -
The Steeples swam in Amethyst -
The news, like Squirrels, ran -
The Hills untied their Bonnets -   5
The Bobolinks - begun -
Then I said softly to myself -
"That must have been the Sun"!
But how he set - I know not -
There seemed a purple stile   10
That little Yellow boys and girls
Were climbing all the while -
Till when they reached the other side -
A Dominie in Gray -
Put gently up the evening Bars -   15
And led the flock away -

205   Come slowly - Eden!
Lips unused to Thee -

Bashful - sip thy Jessamines -
As the fainting Bee -

Reaching late his flower,   5
Round her chamber hums -
Counts his nectars -
Enters - and is lost in Balms.

206   Least Rivers - docile to some sea.
         My Caspian - thee.

207   I taste a liquor never brewed -
         From Tankards scooped in Pearl -
         Not all the Frankfort Berries
         Yield such an Alcohol!

         Inebriate of air - am I -   5
         And Debauchee of Dew -
         Reeling - thro' endless summer days -
         From inns of molten Blue -

         When "Landlords" turn the drunken Bee
         Out of the Foxglove's door -   10
         When Butterflies - renounce their "drams" -
         I shall but drink the more!

         Till Seraphs swing their snowy Hats -
         And Saints - to windows run -
         To see the little Tippler   15
         Leaning against the - Sun!

208   Pine Bough -

         A feather from the Whippowil
         That everlasting sings -
         Whose Galleries are Sunrise -
         Whose Stanzas, are the Springs -

                                                             □

Whose Emerald Nest - the Ages spin -
With mellow - murmuring Thread -
Whose Beryl Egg, what School Boys hunt -
In "Recess", Overhead!   5

209   I lost a World - the other day!
Has Anybody found?
You'll know it by the Row of Stars
Around it's forehead bound!

A Rich man - might not notice it -   5
Yet - to my frugal Eye,
Of more Esteem than Ducats -
Oh find it - Sir - for me!

210   If I should'nt be alive
When the Robins come,
Give the one in Red Cravat,
A Memorial crumb -

If I could'nt thank you,   5
Being fast asleep,
You will know I'm trying
With my Granite lip!

211   I've heard an Organ talk, sometimes -
In a Cathedral Aisle,
And understood no word it said -
Yet held my breath, the while -

And risen up - and gone away,   5
A more Bernardine Girl -
Yet - knew not what was done to me
In that old Chapel Aisle.

212   A transport one cannot contain
May yet, a transport be -

Though God forbid it lift the lid,
Unto it's Extasy!

A Diagram - of Rapture!   5
A sixpence at a show -
With Holy Ghosts in Cages!
The *Universe* would go!

213   The Skies cant keep their secret!
       They tell it to the Hills -
       The Hills just tell the Orchards -
       And they - the Daffodils!

       A Bird - by chance - that goes that way -   5
       Soft overhears the whole -
       If I should bribe the little Bird -
       Who knows but *she* would tell?

       I think I wont - however -
       It's finer - not to know -   10
       If Summer were *an axiom* -
       What sorcery had *snow?*

       So keep your secret - Father!
       I would not - if I could -
       Know what the Sapphire Fellows, do,   15
       In your new-fashioned world!

214   Poor little Heart!
       Did they forget thee?
       Then dinna care! Then dinna care!

       Proud little Heart!
       Did they forsake thee?   5
       Be debonnaire! Be debonnaire!

       Frail little Heart!
       I would not break thee -
       Could'st credit *me?* Could'st credit me?

                                                          □

Gay little Heart -
Like Morning Glory!
Wind and Sun - wilt thee array!

215   I shall know why - when Time is over -
        And I have ceased to wonder why -
        Christ will explain each separate anguish
        In the fair schoolroom of the sky -

        He will tell me what "Peter" promised -   5
        And I - for wonder at his woe -
        I shall forget the drop of anguish
        That scalds me now - that scalds me now!

216   On this long storm the Rainbow rose -
        On this late morn - the sun -
        The Clouds - like listless Elephants -
        Horizons - straggled down -

        The Birds rose smiling, in their nests -   5
        The gales - indeed - were done -
        Alas, how heedless were the eyes -
        On whom the summer shone!

        The quiet nonchalance of death -
        No Daybreak - can bestir -   10
        The slow - Archangel's syllables
        Must awaken *her!*

217   The Bumble of a Bee -
        A Witchcraft, yieldeth me.
        If any ask me "Why" -
        'Twere easier to die
        Than tell!   5

        The Red opon the Hill
        Taketh away my will -
        If anybody sneer,

Take care - for God is near -
That's all!   10

The Breaking of the Day -
Addeth to my Degree -
If any ask me "how" -
Artist who drew me so -
Must tell!   15

218   You love me - you are sure -
        I shall not fear mistake -
        I shall not *cheated* wake -
        Some grinning morn -
        To find the Sunrise left -   5
        And Orchards - unbereft -
        And Dollie - gone!

        I need not start - you're sure -
        That night will never be -
        When frightened - home to Thee I run -   10
        To find the windows dark -
        And no more Dollie - mark -
        Quite none?

        Be sure you're sure - you know -
        I'll bear it better now -   15
        If you'll just tell me so -
        Than when - a little dull Balm grown -
        Over this pain of mine -
        You sting - again!

219   My River runs to Thee -
        Blue Sea - Wilt welcome me?

        My River waits reply.
        Oh Sea - look graciously!

                                                               □

I'll fetch thee Brooks   5
From spotted nooks -

Say Sea - take me?

220   It's such a little thing to weep -
        So short a thing to sigh -
        And yet - by Trades - the size of *these*
        We men and women die!

221   He was weak, and I was strong - then -
        So He let me lead him in -
        I was weak, and He was strong then -
        So I let him lead me - Home.

        'Twas'nt far - the door was near -   5
        'Twas'nt dark - for He went - too -
        'Twas'nt loud, for He said nought -
        That was all I cared to know.

        Day knocked - and we must part -
        Neither - was strongest - now -   10
        He strove - and I strove - too -
        We did'nt do it - tho'!

222   Dying! Dying in the night!
        Wont somebody bring the light
        So I can see which way to go
        Into the everlasting snow?

        And "Jesus"! Where is *Jesus* gone?   5
        They said that Jesus - always came -
        Perhaps he does'nt know the House -
        This way, Jesus, Let him pass!

        Somebody run to the great gate
        And see if Dollie's coming! Wait!   10
        I hear her feet opon the stair!
        Death wont hurt - now Dollie's here!

223 Morning - is the place for Dew -
    Corn - is made at Noon -
    After dinner light - for flowers -
    Dukes - for setting sun!

224 An awful Tempest mashed the air -
    The clouds were gaunt, and few -
    A Black - as of a spectre's cloak
    Hid Heaven and Earth from view -

    The creatures chuckled on the Roofs -   5
    And whistled in the air -
    And shook their fists -
    And gnashed their teeth -
    And swung their frenzied hair -

    The morning lit - the Birds arose -   10
    The Monster's faded eyes
    Turned slowly to his native coast -
    And peace - was Paradise!

225 I'm "wife" - I've finished that -
    That other state -
    I'm Czar - I'm "Woman" now -
    It's safer so -

    How odd the Girl's life looks   5
    Behind this soft Eclipse -
    I think that Earth feels so
    To folks in Heaven - now -

    This being comfort - then
    That other kind - was pain -   10
    But Why compare?
    I'm "Wife"! Stop there!

226 I stole them from a Bee -
    Because - Thee -

Sweet plea -
He pardoned me!

227   Two swimmers wrestled on the spar -
       Until the morning sun -
       When One - turned smiling to the land -
       Oh God! the Other One!

       The stray ships - passing -   5
       Spied a face -
       Opon the waters borne -
       With eyes in death - still begging raised -
       And hands - beseeching - thrown!

228   My eye is fuller than my vase -
       Her Cargo - is of Dew -
       And still - my Heart - my eye outweighs -
       East India - for you!

229   Musicians wrestle everywhere -
       All day - among the crowded air
       I hear the silver strife -
       And - waking - long before the morn -
       Such transport breaks opon the town   5
       I think it that "New life"!

       It is not Bird - it has no nest -
       Nor "Band" - in brass and scarlet - drest -
       Nor Tamborin - nor Man -
       It is not Hymn from pulpit read -   10
       The "Morning Stars" the Treble led
       On Time's first afternoon!

       Some - say - it is "the Spheres" - at play!
       Some say - that bright Majority
       Of vanished Dames - and Men!   15
       Some - think it service in the place

Where we - with late - celestial face -
Please God - shall ascertain!

230   For this - accepted Breath -
Through it - compete with Death -
The fellow cannot touch this Crown -
By it - my title take -
Ah, what a royal sake   5
To my nescessity - stooped down!

No Wilderness - can be
Where this attendeth me -
No Desert Noon -
No fear of frost to come   10
Haunt the perennial bloom -
But Certain June!

Get Gabriel - to tell - the royal syllable -
Get saints - with new - unsteady tongue -
To say what trance below   15
Most like their glory show -
Fittest the Crown!

231   We dont cry - Tim and I -
We are far too grand -
But we bolt the door tight
To prevent a friend -

Then we hide our brave face   5
Deep in our hand -
Not to cry - Tim and I -
We are far too grand -

Nor to dream - he and me -
Do we condescend -   10
We just shut our brown eye
To see to the end -

Tim - see Cottages -
But, Oh, so high!

Then - we shake - Tim and I -   15
And lest I - cry -

Tim - reads a little Hymn -
And we both pray,
Please, Sir, I and Tim -
Always lost the way!   20

We must die - by and by -
Clergymen say -
Tim - shall - if I - do -
I - too - if he -

How shall we arrange it -   25
Tim - was - so - shy?
Take us simultaneous - Lord -
I - "Tim" - and - me!

232   He forgot - and I - remembered -
       'Twas an everyday affair -
       Long ago as Christ and Peter -
       "Warmed them" at the "Temple fire".

       "Thou wert with him" - quoth "the Damsel"?   5
       "No" - said Peter - 'twas'nt me -
       Jesus merely "looked" at Peter -
       Could I do aught else - to Thee?

233   A Slash of Blue! A sweep of Gray!
       Some scarlet patches - on the way -
       Compose an evening sky -

       A little Purple - slipped between -
       Some Ruby Trowsers - hurried on -   5
       A Wave of Gold - a Bank of Day -
       This just makes out the morning sky!

234   I should not dare to leave my friend,
       Because - because if he should die

While I was gone - and I - too late -
Should reach the Heart that wanted me -

If I should disappoint the eyes   5
That hunted - hunted so - to see -
And could not bear to shut until
They "noticed" me - they noticed me -

If I should stab the patient faith
So sure I'd come - so sure I'd come -   10
It *listening* - listening - went to sleep -
Telling my tardy name -

My Heart would wish it broke before -
Since breaking then - since breaking then -
Were useless as next morning's sun -   15
Where midnight frosts - had lain!

235   The Flower must not blame the Bee -
       That seeketh his felicity
       Too often at her door -

       But teach the Footman from Vevay -
       Mistress is "not at home" - to say -   5
       To people - any more!

236   Some keep the Sabbath going to Church -
       I keep it, staying at Home -
       With a Bobolink for a Chorister -
       And an Orchard, for a Dome -

       Some keep the Sabbath in Surplice -   5
       I, just wear my Wings -
       And instead of tolling the Bell, for Church,
       Our little Sexton - sings.

       God preaches, a noted Clergyman -
       And the sermon is never long,   10
       So instead of getting to Heaven, at last -
       I'm going, all along.

237   What shall I do - it whimpers so -
This little Hound within the Heart -
All day and night - with bark and start -
And yet - it will not go?

Would you untie it - were you me -   5
Would it stop whining, if to Thee
I sent it - even now?

It should not teaze you - by your chair -
Or on the mat - or if it dare -
To climb your dizzy knee -   10

Or sometimes - at your side to run -
When you were willing -
May it come -
Tell Carlo - He'll tell me!

238   How many times these low feet staggered -
Only the soldered mouth can tell -
Try - can you stir the awful rivet -
Try - can you lift the hasps of steel!

Stroke the cool forehead - hot so often -   5
Lift - if you care - the listless hair -
Handle the adamantine fingers
Never a thimble - more - shall wear -

Buzz the dull flies - on the chamber window -
Brave - shines the sun through the freckled pane -   10
Fearless - the cobweb swings from the ceiling -
Indolent Housewife - in Daisies - lain!

239   Make me a picture of the sun -
So I can hang it in my room.
And make believe I'm getting warm
When others call it "Day"!

Draw me a Robin - on a stem -   5
So I am hearing him, I'll dream,

And when the Orchards stop their tune -
Put my pretense - away -

Say if it's really - warm at noon -
Whether it's Buttercups - that "skim" -   10
Or Butterflies - that "bloom"?
Then - skip - the frost - opon the lea -
And skip the Russet - on the tree -
Let's play those - never come!

240   Bound a Trouble - and Lives will bear it -
       Circumscription - enables Wo -
       Still to anticipate - Were no limit -
       Who were sufficient to Misery?

       State it the Ages - to a cipher -   5
       And it will ache contented on -
       Sing, at it's pain, as any Workman -
       Notching the fall of the even Sun -

241   What is - "Paradise" -
       Who live there -
       Are they "Farmers" -
       Do they "hoe" -
       Do they know that this is "Amherst" -   5
       And that I - am coming - too -

       Do they wear "new shoes" - in "Eden" -
       Is it always pleasant - there -
       Wont they scold us - when we're hungry -
       Or tell God - how cross we are -   10

       You are sure there's such a person
       As "a Father" - in the sky -
       So if I get lost - there - ever -
       Or do what the Nurse calls "die" -

       I shant walk the "Jasper" - barefoot -   15
       Ransomed folks - wont laugh at me -

Maybe - "Eden" a'nt so lonesome
As New England used to be!

242 It is easy to work when the soul is at play -
But when the soul is in pain -
The hearing him put his playthings up
Makes work difficult - then -

It is simple, to ache in the Bone, or the Rind -   5
But Gimblets - among the nerve -
Mangle daintier - terribler -
Like a Panther in the Glove -

243 That after Horror - that 'twas *us* -
That passed the mouldering Pier -
Just as the Granite crumb let go -
Our Savior, by a Hair -

A second more, had dropped too deep   5
For Fisherman to plumb -
The very profile of the Thought
Puts Recollection numb -

The possibility - to pass
Without a moment's Bell -   10
Into Conjecture's presence
Is like a Face of Steel -
That suddenly looks into our's -
With a metallic grin -
The Cordiality of Death -   15
Who drills his Welcome in -

244 We - Bee and I - live by the quaffing -
'Tis'nt *all Hock* - with us -
Life has it's *Ale* -
But it's many a lay of the Dim Burgundy -
We chant - for cheer - when the Wines - fail -   5

   □

Do we "get drunk"?
Ask the jolly Clovers!
Do we "beat" our "Wife"?
I - never wed -
Bee - pledges *his* - in minute flagons -   10
Dainty - as the tress - on her deft Head -

While runs the Rhine -
He and I - revel -
First - at the Vat - and latest at the Vine -
Noon - our last Cup -   15
"Found dead" - "of Nectar" -
By a humming Coroner -
In a By-Thyme!

245   God permits industrious Angels -
           Afternoons - to play -
           I met one - forgot my schoolmates -
           All - for Him - straightway -

           God calls home - the Angels - promptly -   5
           At the Setting Sun -
           I missed mine - how *dreary* - *Marbles* -
           After playing *Crown*!

246   The *Sun* - *just touched* the Morning
           The *Morning* - Happy thing -
           Supposed that He had come to *dwell* -
           And Life would all be *Spring*!

           She felt herself *supremer* -   5
           A *Raised* - *Etherial Thing*!
           Henceforth - for Her - *what Holiday*!
           Meanwhile - Her wheeling King -
           Trailed - slow - along the Orchards -
           His *haughty* - spangled Hems -   10
           Leaving a *new nescessity*!
           The *want* of *Diadems*!

                                                                            □

The Morning - *fluttered* - *staggered* -
Felt feebly - for Her *Crown* -
Her *unannointed forehead* -   15
Henceforth - Her *only* One!

247   The Lamp burns sure - within -
       Tho' Serfs - supply the Oil -
       It matters not the busy Wick -
       At her phosphoric toil!

       The Slave - forgets - to fill -   5
       The Lamp - burns golden - on -
       Unconscious that the oil is out -
       As that the Slave - is gone.

248   *One life* of so much consequence!
       Yet I - for it - would pay -
       My soul's *entire income* -
       In ceaseless - salary -

       One Pearl - to me - so signal -   5
       That I would instant dive -
       Although - I *knew* - to *take* it -
       Would *cost* me - *just a life!*

       The Sea is full - I know it!
       That - does not blur *my Gem!*   10
       It burns - distinct from all the row -
       Intact - *in Diadem!*

       The life is thick - I know it!
       Yet - not so dense a crowd -
       But *Monarchs* - are *perceptible* -   15
       Far down the dustiest Road!

249   You're right - "the way *is* narrow" -
       And "difficult the Gate" -
       And "few there be" - Correct again -
       That "enter in - thereat" -

                                                                □

'*Tis* Costly - So are *purples!*   5
'Tis just the price of *Breath* -
With but the "Discount" of *the Grave* -
Termed by the *Brokers* - "*Death*"!

And after *that* - there's Heaven -
The *Good* man's - "*Dividend*" -   10
And *Bad* men - "go to Jail" -
I guess -

250   The Court is far away -
         No Umpire - have I -
         My Sovreign is offended -
         To gain his grace - I'd die!

         I'll seek his royal feet -   5
         I'll say - Remember - King -
         Thou shalt - thyself - one day - a Child -
         Implore a *larger* - thing -

         That Empire - is of Czars -
         As small - they say - as I -   10
         Grant *me* - that day - the royalty -
         To *intercede* - for *Thee* -

251   If *He dissolve* - then - there is *nothing - more* -
         Eclipse - at *Midnight* -
         It was *dark - before* -

         Sunset - at *Easter* -
         Blindness - on the *Dawn* -   5
         Faint Star of Bethleem -
         Gone down!

         Would but some *God - inform* Him -
         Or it be *too late!*
         Say - that the pulse *just lisps* -   10
         The *Chariots wait* -

         Say - that a *little life* - for *His* -
         Is *leaking - red* -

His little Spaniel - tell Him!
Will He heed?   15

252   I think just how my shape will rise -
       When I shall be *"forgiven"* -
       Till Hair - and Eyes - and timid Head -
       Are *out of sight* - in Heaven -

       I think just how my lips will weigh -   5
       With shapeless - quivering - prayer -
       That you - *so late* - *"consider"* me -
       The *"sparrow"* of your care -

       I mind me that of Anguish - sent -
       Some drifts were moved away -   10
       Before my simple bosom - broke -
       And why not *this* - if *they?*

       And so I con that thing - *"forgiven"* -
       Until - delirious - borne -
       By my long bright - and *longer* - *trust* -   15
       I *drop* my Heart - *unshriven!*

253   I've nothing Else - to bring, You know -
       So I keep bringing These -
       Just as the Night keeps fetching Stars
       To our familiar eyes -

       Maybe, we should'nt mind them -   5
       Unless they did'nt come -
       Then - maybe, it would puzzle us
       To find our way Home -

254   A Mien to move a Queen -
       Half Child - Half Heroine -
       An Orleans in the eye
       That puts it's manner by
       For humbler Company   5
       When none are near

Even a Tear -
It's frequent Visitor -

A Bonnet like a Duke -
And yet a Wren's Peruke   10
Were not so shy
Of Goer by -
And Hands - so slight,
They would elate a sprite
With merriment -   15

A Voice that alters - Low
And on the ear can go
Like Let of Snow -
Or shift supreme -
As tone of Realm   20
On Subjects Diadem -
Too small - to fear -
Too distant - to endear -
And so Men Compromise -
And just - revere -   25

255   The Drop, that wrestles in the Sea -
        Forgets her own locality
        As I, in Thee -

        She knows herself an incense small -
        Yet small, she sighs, if all, is all,   5
        How larger - be?

        The Ocean, smiles at her conceit -
        But she, forgetting Amphitrite -
        Pleads "Me"?

256   The Robin's my Criterion for Tune -
        Because I grow - where Robins do -
        But, were I Cuckoo born -
        I'd swear by him -
        The ode familiar - rules the Noon -   5
        The Buttercup's, my whim for Bloom -

Because, we're Orchard sprung -
But, were I Britain born,
I'd Daisies spurn -

None but the Nut - October fit -   10
Because - through dropping it,
The Seasons flit - I'm taught -
Without the Snow's Tableau
Winter, were lie - to me -
Because I see - New Englandly -   15
The Queen, discerns like me -
Provincially -

257 I've known a Heaven, like a Tent -
To wrap it's shining Yards -
Pluck up it's stakes, and disappear -
Without the sound of Boards
Or Rip of Nail - Or Carpenter -   5
But just the miles of Stare -
That signalize a Show's Retreat -
In North America -

No Trace - no Figment - of the Thing
That dazzled, Yesterday,   10
No Ring - no Marvel -
Men, and Feats -
Dissolved as utterly -
As Bird's far Navigation
Discloses just a Hue -   15
A plash of Oars, a Gaiety -
Then swallowed up, of View.

258 I came to buy a smile - today -
But just a single smile -
The smallest one opon your face -
Will suit me just as well -
The one that no one else would miss   5
It shone so very small -

I'm pleading at the counter - sir -
Could you afford to sell?

I've Diamonds - on my fingers!
You know what Diamonds - are!   10
I've Rubies - like the Evening Blood -
And Topaz - like the star!
'Twould be a bargain for a Jew!
Say? May I have it - Sir?

259   A Clock stopped -
        Not the Mantel's -
        Geneva's farthest skill
        Cant put the puppet bowing -
        That just now dangled still -   5

        An awe came on the Trinket!
        The Figures hunched - with pain -
        Then quivered out of Decimals -
        Into Degreeless noon -

        It will not stir for Doctor's -   10
        This Pendulum of snow -
        The Shopman importunes it -
        While cool - concernless No -

        Nods from the Gilded pointers -
        Nods from the Seconds slim -   15
        Decades of Arrogance between
        The Dial life -
        And Him -

260   I'm Nobody! Who are you?
        Are you - Nobody - too?
        Then there's a pair of us!
        Dont tell! they'd advertise - you know!

        How dreary - to be - Somebody!   5
        How public - like a Frog -

To tell one's name - the livelong June -
To an admiring Bog!

261 I held a Jewel in my fingers -
And went to sleep -
The day was warm, and winds were prosy -
I said "'Twill keep" -

I woke - and chid my honest fingers,   5
The Gem was gone -
And now, an Amethyst remembrance
Is all I own -

262 Ah, Moon - and Star!
You are very far -
But - were no one farther than you -
Do you think I'd stop for a firmament -
Or a cubit - or so?   5

I could borrow a Bonnet - of the Lark -
And a Chamois' silver boot -
And a stirrup of an Antelope -
And leap to you - tonight!

But - Moon - and Star -   10
Though you're very far -
There is one - farther than you -
He - is more than a firmament - from me -
And I cannot go!

263 Just so - Christ - raps -
He - does'nt weary -
First at the Knocker -
And then - at the Bell -
Then - on Divinest tiptoe standing -   5
Might he but spy the hiding soul!

When he - retires -
Chilled - or weary -

It will be ample time for me -
Patient - opon the steps - until then -
Heart - I am knocking low
At thee!

10

264   Forever at His side to walk -
The smaller of the two!
Brain of His Brain -
Blood of His Blood -
Two lives - One Being - now -

5

Forever of His fate to taste -
If grief - the largest part -
If joy - to put my piece away
For that beloved Heart -

All life - to know each other

10

Whom we can never learn -
And bye and bye - a Change -
Called Heaven -
Rapt neighborhoods of men -
Just finding out - what puzzled us -

15

Without the lexicon!

265   It cant be "Summer"!
That - got through!
It's early - yet - for "Spring"!
There's that long town of White - to cross -
Before the Blackbirds sing!

5

It cant be "Dying"!
It's too Rouge -
The Dead shall go in white -
So Sunset shuts my question down
With Cuffs of Chrysolite!

10

266   What would I give to see his face?
I'd give - I'd give my life - of course -
But *that* is not enough!

Stop just a minute - let me think!
I'd give my biggest Bobolink!   5
That makes *two* - *Him* - and *Life!*
You know who *"June"* is -
I'd give *her* -
Roses a day from Zinzebar -
And Lily tubes - like wells -   10
Bees - by the furlong -
Straits of Blue -
Navies of Butterflies - sailed thro' -
And dappled Cowslip Dells -

Then I have "shares" in Primrose "Banks" -   15
Daffodil Dowries - spicy "stocks" -
Dominions - broad as Dew -
Bags of Doubloons - adventurous Bees
Brought me - from firmamental seas -
And Purple - from Peru -   20

Now - have I bought it -
"Shylock"? Say!
Sign me the Bond!
"I vow to pay
To Her - who pledges *this* -   25
One hour - of her Sovreign's face"!
Extatic Contract!
Niggard Grace!
My *Kingdom's worth* of Bliss!

267   Rearrange a "Wife's" Affection!
        When they dislocate my Brain!
        Amputate my freckled Bosom!
        Make me bearded like a man!

        Blush, my spirit, in thy Fastness -   5
        ˙ Blush, my unacknowledged clay -
        Seven years of troth have taught thee
        More than Wifehood ever may!

        Love that never leaped it's socket -
        Trust intrenched in narrow pain -   10

Constancy thro' fire - awarded -
Anguish - bare of anodyne!

Burden - borne so far triumphant -
None suspect me of the crown,
For I wear the "Thorns" till *Sunset* -   15
Then - my Diadem put on.

Big my Secret but it's *bandaged* -
It will never get away
Till the Day it's Weary Keeper
Leads it through the Grave to thee.   20

268   Why - do they shut me out of Heaven?
       Did I sing - too loud?
       But - I can say a little "minor"
       Timid as a Bird!

       Would'nt the Angels try me -   5
       Just - once - more -
       Just - see - if I troubled them -
       But dont - shut the door!

       Oh, if I - were the Gentleman
       In the "White Robe" -   10
       And they - were the little Hand - that knocked -
       Could - I - forbid?

269   Wild nights - Wild nights!
       Were I with thee
       Wild nights should be
       Our luxury!

       Futile - the winds -   5
       To a Heart in port -
       Done with the Compass -
       Done with the Chart!

       Rowing in Eden -
       Ah - the Sea!   10

Might I but moor - tonight -
In thee!

270   I shall keep singing!
        Birds will pass me
        On their way to Yellower Climes -
        Each - with a Robin's expectation -
        I - with my Redbreast -   5
        And my Rhymes -

        Late - when I take my place in summer -
        But - I shall bring a fuller tune -
        Vespers - are sweeter than matins - Signor -
        Morning - only the seed - of noon -   10

271   Over the fence -
        Strawberries - grow -
        Over the fence -
        I could climb - if I tried, I know -
        Berries are nice!   5

        But - if I stained my Apron -
        God would certainly scold!
        Oh, dear, - I guess if He were a Boy -
        He'd - climb - if He could!

272   Would you like Summer? Taste of our's -
       Spices? Buy - here!
       Ill! We have Berries, for the parching!
       Weary! Furloughs of Down!
       Perplexed! Estates of Violet - Trouble ne'er looked on!   5
       Captive! We bring Reprieve of Roses!
       Fainting! Flasks of Air!
       Even for Death - A Fairy medicine -
       But, which is it - Sir?

273   Perhaps you think Me stooping
       I'm not ashamed of that
       Christ - stooped until He touched the Grave -
       Do those at Sacrament

       Commemorate Dishonor   5
       Or love annealed of love
       Until it bend as low as Death
       Redignified, above?

274   Again - his voice is at the door -
       I feel the old *Degree* -
       I hear him ask the servant
       For such an one - as me -

       I take a *flower* - as I go -   5
       My face to *justify* -
       He never *saw* me - in *this life* -
       I might *surprise* his eye!

       I cross the Hall with *mingled* steps -
       I - silent - pass the door -   10
       I look on all this world *contains* -
       Just his face - nothing more!

       We talk in *careless* - and in *toss* -
       A kind of *plummet* strain -

Each - sounding - shily -
Just - how - deep -
The *other's* one - had been -

We *walk* - I leave my Dog - at home -
A *tender - thoughtful* Moon
Goes with us - just a little way -
And - then - we are *alone* -

Alone - if *Angels* are "alone" -
First time they *try* the *sky!*
Alone - if those "vailed faces" - be -
We cannot *count* -
On High!
I'd give - to live that hour - *again* -
The *purple - in my Vein* -
But *He* must *count the drops - himself* -
My price for *every stain!*

15

20

25

30

275   Should you but fail at - Sea -
In sight of me -
Or doomed lie -
Next Sun - to die -
Or rap - at Paradise - unheard -
I'd *harass God* -
Until He let you in!

5

276   Civilization - spurns - the Leopard!
Was the Leopard - bold?
Deserts - never rebuked her Satin -
Ethiop - her Gold -
Tawny - her Customs -
She was Conscious -
Spotted - her Dun Gown -
This was the Leopard's nature - Signor -
Need - a keeper - frown?

Pity - the Pard - that left her Asia!
Memories - of Palm -

5

10

Cannot be stifled - with Narcotic -
Nor suppressed - with Balm -

277   Going to Him! Happy letter!
Tell Him -
Tell Him the page I did'nt write -
Tell Him - I only said the Syntax -
And left the Verb and the pronoun - out -   5
Tell Him just how the fingers hurried -
Then - how they waded - slow - slow -
And then you wished you had eyes in your pages -
So you could see what moved them so -

Tell Him - it was'nt a Practised Writer -   10
You guessed - from the way the sentence toiled -
You could hear the Boddice tug, behind you -
As if it held but the might of a child -
You almost pitied it - you - it worked so -
Tell Him - No - you may quibble there -   15
For it would split His Heart, to know it -
And then you and I, were silenter.

Tell Him - Night finished - before we finished -
And the Old Clock kept neighing "Day"!
And you - got sleepy -   20
And begged to be ended -
What would it hinder so - to - say?
Tell Him - just how she sealed you - Cautious!
But - if He ask where you are hid
Until tomorrow - Happy letter!   25
Gesture Coquette - and shake your Head!

278   A word is dead, when it is said
Some say -
I say it just begins to live
That day

279   Of all the Souls that stand create -
I have Elected - One -
When Sense from Spirit - files away -
And Subterfuge - is done -
When that which is - and that which was -   5
Apart - intrinsic - stand -
And this brief Drama in the flesh -
Is shifted - like a Sand -
When Figures show their royal Front -
And Mists - are carved away,   10
Behold the Atom - I preferred -
To all the lists of Clay!

280   The World - stands - solemner - to me -
Since I was wed - to Him -
A modesty - befits the soul
That bears another's - name -
A doubt - if it be fair - indeed -   5
To wear that perfect - pearl -
The Man - opon the Woman - binds -
To clasp her soul - for all -
A prayer, that it more angel - prove -
A Whiter Gift - within -   10
To that munificence, that chose -
So unadorned - a Queen -
A Gratitude - that such be true -
It had esteemed the Dream -
Too beautiful - for Shape to prove -   15
Or posture - to redeem!

281   Me, change! Me, alter!
Then I will, when on the Everlasting Hill
A Smaller Purple grows -
At Sunset, or a lesser glow
Flickers opon Cordillera -   5
At Day's superior close!

282   We play at Paste -
        Till qualified for Pearl -
        Then, drop the Paste -
        And deem Ourself a fool -
        The Shapes, tho', were similar,   5
        And our new Hands
        Learned Gem Tactics
        Practising Sands -

283   I should have been too glad, I see -
        Too lifted - for the scant degree
        Of Life's penurious Round -
        My little Circuit would have shamed
        This new Circumference - have blamed -   5
        The homelier time behind -

        I should have been too saved - I see -
        Too rescued - Fear too dim to me
        That I could spell the Prayer
        I knew so perfect - yesterday -   10
        That scalding one - Sabacthini -
        Recited fluent - here -

        Earth would have been too much - I see -
        And Heaven - not enough for me -
        I should have had the Joy   15
        Without the Fear - to justify -
        The Palm - without the Calvary -
        So Savior - Crucify -

        Defeat whets Victory - they say -
        The Reefs in Old Gethsemane   20
        Endear the Coast beyond -
        'Tis Beggars - Banquets best define -
        'Tis Thirsting - vitalizes Wine -
        Faith bleats to understand -

284   The Zeros taught Us - Phosphorus -
        We learned to like the Fire

By handling Glaciers - when a Boy -
And Tinder - guessed - by power

Of Opposite - to equal Ought -   5
Eclipses - Suns - imply -
Paralysis - our Primer dumb
Unto Vitality -

285   The Love a Life can show Below
        Is but a filament, I know,
        Of that diviner thing
        That faints opon the face of Noon -
        And smites the Tinder in the Sun -   5
        And hinders Gabriel's Wing -

        'Tis this - in Music - hints and sways -
        And far abroad on Summer days -
        Distills uncertain pain -
        'Tis this enamors in the East -   10
        And tints the Transit in the West
        With harrowing Iodine -

        'Tis this - invites - appalls - endows -
        Flits - glimmers - proves - dissolves -
        Returns - suggests - convicts - enchants   15
        Then - flings in Paradise -

286   Dropped into the Ether Acre -
        Wearing the Sod Gown -
        Bonnet of Everlasting Laces -
        Brooch - frozen on -

        Horses of Blonde - and Coach of Silver -   5
        Baggage a strapped Pearl -
        Journey of Down - and Whip of Diamond -
        Riding to meet the Earl -

287   While it is alive
        Until Death touches it

While it and I lap one Air
Dwell in one Blood
Under one Sacrament
Show me division can split or pare -   5

Love is like Life - merely longer
Love is like Death, during the Grave
Love is the Fellow of the Resurrection
Scooping up the Dust and chanting "Live"!   10

288   My first well Day - since many ill -
        I asked to go abroad,
        And take the Sunshine in my hands
        And see the things in Pod -

        A'blossom just - when I went in   5
        To take my Chance with pain -
        Uncertain if myself, or He,
        Should prove the strongest One.

        The Summer deepened, while we strove -
        She put some flowers away -   10
        And Redder cheeked Ones - in their stead -   •
        A fond - illusive way -

        To Cheat Herself, it seemed she tried -
        As if before a Child
        To fade - Tomorrow - Rainbows held   15
        The Sepulchre, could hide.

        She dealt a fashion to the Nut -
        She tied the Hoods to Seeds -
        She dropped bright scraps of Tint, about -
        And left Brazilian Threads   20

        On every shoulder that she met -
        Then both her Hands of Haze
        Put up - to hide her parting Grace
        From our unfitted eyes -

        My loss, by sickness - Was it Loss?   25
        Or that Etherial Gain

One earns by measuring the Grave -
Then - measuring the Sun -

289   A Burdock twitched my gown
Not Burdock's blame - but mine
Who went too near the Burdock's Den -

A Bog affronts my shoe.
What else have Bogs to do -   5
The only Trade they know
The splashing men?

'Tis Minnows - should despise -
An Elephant's calm eyes
Look further on.   10

290   Let others - show this Surry's Grace -
Myself - assist his Cross -

291   *E* It sifts from Leaden Sieves -
It powders all the Wood -
It fills with Alabaster Wool
The Wrinkles of the Road -

It scatters like the Birds -   5
Condenses like a Flock -
Like Juggler's Figures situates
Upon a baseless Arc -

It traverses yet halts -
Disperses as it stays -   10
Then curls itself in Capricorn -
Denying that it was -

292   I got so I could take his name -
Without - Tremendous gain -

That Stop-sensation - on my Soul -
And Thunder - in the Room -

I got so I could walk across   5
That Angle in the floor,
Where he turned so, and I turned - how -
And all our Sinew tore -

I got so I could stir the Box -
In which his letters grew   10
Without that forcing, in my breath -
As Staples - driven through -

Could dimly recollect a Grace -
I think, they called it "God" -
Renowned to ease Extremity -   15
When Formula, had failed -

And shape my Hands -
Petition's way,
Tho' ignorant of a word
That Ordination - utters -   20

My Business - with the Cloud,
If any Power behind it, be,
Not subject to Despair -
It care - in some remoter way,
For so minute affair   25
As Misery -
Itself, too vast, for interrupting - more -

293   A single Screw of Flesh
        Is all that pins the Soul
        That stands for Deity, to mine,
        Opon my side the Vail -

        Once witnessed of the Gauze -   5
        It's name is put away
        As far from mine, as if no plight
        Had printed yesterday,

        In tender - solemn Alphabet,
        My eyes just turned to see -   10

When it was smuggled by my sight
Into Eternity -

More Hands - to hold - These are but Two -
One more new-mailed Nerve
Just granted, for the Peril's sake -   15
Some striding - Giant - Love -

So greater than the Gods can show,
They slink before the Clay,
That not for all their Heaven can boast
Will let it's Keepsake - go   20

294   A Weight with Needles on the pounds -
       To push, and pierce, besides -
       That if the Flesh resist the Heft -
       The puncture - Coolly tries -

       That not a pore be overlooked   5
       Of all this Compound Frame -
       As manifold for Anguish -
       As Species - be - for name.

295   Father - I bring thee - not myself -
       That were the little load -
       I bring thee the imperial Heart
       I had not strength to hold -

       The Heart I cherished in my own   5
       Till mine - too heavy grew -
       Yet - strangest - heavier - since it went -
       Is it too large for you?

296   Where Ships of Purple - gently toss -
       On Seas of Daffodil -
       Fantastic Sailors - mingle -
       And then - the Wharf is still!

297   This - is the land - the Sunset washes -
        These - are the Banks of the Yellow Sea -
        Where it rose - or whither it rushes -
        These - are the Western Mystery!

        Night after Night   5
        Her Purple traffic
        Strews the landing - with Opal Bales -
        Merchantmen - poise opon Horizons -
        Dip - and vanish like Orioles!

298   The Doomed - regard the Sunrise
        With different Delight -
        Because - when next it burns abroad
        They doubt to witness it -

        The Man - to die - tomorrow -   5
        Harks for the Meadow Bird -
        Because it's Music stirs the Axe
        That clamors for his head -

        Joyful - to whom the Sunrise
        Precedes Enamored - Day -   10
        Joyful - for whom the Meadow Bird
        Has ought but Elegy!

299   Did we disobey Him?
        Just one time!
        Charged us to forget Him -
        But we could'nt learn!

        Were Himself - such a Dunce -   5
        What would we - do?
        Love the dull lad - best -
        Oh, would'nt you?

300   Unto like Story - Trouble has enticed me -
        How Kinsmen fell -
        Brothers and Sisters - who preferred the Glory -

And their young will
Bent to the Scaffold, or in Dungeons - chanted -   5
Till God's full time -
When they let go the ignominy - smiling -
And Shame went still -

Unto guessed Crests, my moaning fancy, leads me,
Worn fair   10
By Heads rejected - in the lower country -
Of honors there -
Such spirit makes her perpetual mention,
That I - grown bold -
Step martial - at my Crucifixion -   15
As Trumpets - rolled -

Feet, small as mine - have marched in Revolution
Firm to the Drum -
Hands - not so stout - hoisted them - in witness -
When Speech went numb -   20
Let me not shame their sublime deportments -
Drilled bright -
Beckoning - Etruscan invitation -
Toward Light -

301   One Year ago - jots what?
         God - spell the word! I - cant -
         Was't Grace? Not that -
         Was't Glory? That - will do -
         Spell slower - Glory -   5

         Such anniversary shall be -
         Sometimes - not often - in Eternity -
         When farther Parted, than the common Wo -
         Look - feed upon each other's faces - so -
         In doubtful meal, if it be possible   10
         Their Banquet's True -

         I tasted - careless - then -
         I did not know the Wine
         Came once a World - Did you?
         Oh, had you told me so -   15

This Thirst would blister - easier - now -
You said it hurt you - most -
Mine - was an Acorn's Breast -
And could not know how fondness grew
In Shaggier Vest -   20
Perhaps - I could'nt -
But, had you looked in -
A Giant - eye to eye with you, had been -
No Acorn - then -

So - Twelve months ago -
We breathed -   25
Then dropped the Air -
Which bore it best?
Was this - the patientest -
Because it was a Child, you know -
And could not value - Air?   30

If to be "Elder" - mean most pain -
I'm old enough, today, I'm certain - then -
As old as thee - how soon?
One - Birthday more - or Ten?
Let me - choose!   35
Ah, Sir, None!

302   It's like the Light -
       A fashionless Delight -
       It's like the Bee -
       A dateless - Melody -

       It's like the Woods -
       Private - Like the Breeze -   5
       Phraseless - yet it stirs
       The proudest Trees -

       It's like the morning -
       Best - when it's done -
       And the Everlasting Clocks -   10
       Chime - Noon!

303　　　　Alone, I cannot be -
　　　　　For Hosts - do visit me -
　　　　　Recordless Company -
　　　　　Who baffle Key -

　　　　　They have no Robes, nor Names -　　　　　　5
　　　　　No Almanacs - nor Climes -
　　　　　But general Homes
　　　　　Like Gnomes -

　　　　　Their Coming, may be known
　　　　　By Couriers within -　　　　　　　　　　10
　　　　　Their going - is not -
　　　　　For they're never gone -

304　　　　The nearest Dream recedes - unrealized -
　　　　　The Heaven we chase -
　　　　　Like the June Bee - before the School Boy -
　　　　　Invites the Race -
　　　　　Stoops - to an easy Clover -　　　　　　5
　　　　　Dips - evades - teazes - deploys -
　　　　　Then - to the Royal Clouds
　　　　　Lifts his light Pinnace -
　　　　　Heedless of the Boy -
　　　　　Staring - bewildered - at the mocking sky -　　10

　　　　　Homesick for steadfast Honey -
　　　　　Ah - the Bee flies not
　　　　　That brews that rare variety!

305　　　　What if I say I shall not wait!
　　　　　What if I burst the fleshly Gate -
　　　　　And pass Escaped - to thee!

　　　　　What if I file this mortal - off -
　　　　　See where it hurt me - That's enough -　　　　5
　　　　　And wade in Liberty!
　　　　　　　　　　　　　　　　　　　　　　□

They cannot take me - any more!
Dungeons can call - and Guns implore -
Unmeaning - now - to me -

As laughter - was - an hour ago -   10
Or Laces - or a Travelling Show -
Or who died - yesterday!

306   A Shady friend - for Torrid days -
        Is easier to find -
        Than one of higher temperature
        For Frigid - hour of mind -

        The Vane a little to the East -   5
        Scares Muslin souls - away -
        If Broadcloth Hearts are firmer
        Than those of Organdy -

        Who is to blame? The Weaver?
        Ah, the bewildering thread!
        The Tapestries of Paradise   10
        So notelessly - are made!

307   A solemn thing - it was - I said -
        A Woman - white - to be -
        And wear - if God should count me fit -
        Her blameless mystery -

        A hallowed thing - to drop a life   5
        Into the purple well -
        Too plummetless - that it return -
        Eternity - until -

        I pondered how the bliss would look -
        And would it feel as big -   10
        When I could take it in my hand -
        As hovering - seen - through fog -

        And then - the size of this "small" life -
        The Sages - call it small -

Swelled - like Horizons - in my vest -
And I sneered - softly - "small"!

15

308 I breathed enough to take the Trick -
And now, removed from Air -
I simulate the Breath, so well -
That One, to be quite sure -

The Lungs are stirless - must descend   5
Among the cunning cells -
And touch the Pantomime - Himself,
How numb, the Bellows feels!

309 Kill your Balm - and it's Odors bless you -
Bare your Jessamine - to the storm -
And she will fling her maddest perfume -
Haply - your Summer night to Charm -

Stab the Bird - that built in your bosom - 5
Oh, could you catch her last Refrain -
Bubble! "forgive" - "Some better" - Bubble!
"Carol for Him - when I am gone"!

310 "Heaven" - is what I cannot reach!
The Apple on the Tree -
Provided it do hopeless - hang -
That - "Heaven" is - to Me!

The Color, on the cruising cloud -   5
The interdicted Land -
Behind the Hill - the House behind -
There - Paradise - is found!

Her teazing Purples - Afternoons -
The credulous - decoy -   10
Enamored - of the Conjuror -
That spurned us - Yesterday!

137 1862

311   I know some lonely Houses off the Road
A Robber'd like the look of -
Wooden barred,
And Windows hanging low,
Inviting to -
A Portico,   5
Where two could creep -
One - hand the Tools -
The other peep -
To make sure all's asleep -
Old fashioned eyes -   10
Not easy to surprise!

How orderly the Kitchen'd look, by night -
With just a Clock -
But they could gag the Tick -
And Mice wont bark -   15
And so the Walls - dont tell -
None - will -

A pair of Spectacles ajar just stir -
An Almanac's aware -
Was it the Mat - winked,   20
Or a nervous Star?
The Moon - slides down the stair -
To see who's there!

There's plunder - where -
Tankard, or Spoon -   25
Earring - or Stone -
A Watch - Some Ancient Brooch
To match the Grandmama -
Staid sleeping - there -
                  30
Day - rattles - too -
Stealth's - slow -
The Sun has got as far
As the third Sycamore -
Screams Chanticleer
"Who's there"?   35

And Echoes - Trains away,
Sneer - "Where"!

While the old Couple, just astir,
Fancy the Sunrise - left the door ajar!   40

312   I can wade Grief -
Whole Pools of it -
I'm used to that -
But the least push of Joy
Breaks up my feet -   5
And I tip - drunken -
Let no Pebble - smile -
'Twas the New Liquor -
That was all!

Power is only Pain -   10
Stranded - thro' Discipline,
Till Weights - will hang -
Give Balm - to Giants -
And they'll wilt, like Men -
Give Himmaleh -   15
They'll carry - Him!

313   You see I cannot see - your lifetime -
I must guess -
How many times it ache for me - today - Confess -
How many times for my far sake
The brave eyes film -   5
But I guess guessing hurts -
Mine - get so dim!

Too vague - the face -
My own - so patient - covets -
Too far - the strength -   10
My timidness enfolds -
Haunting the Heart -
Like her translated faces -
Teazing the want -
It - only - can suffice!   15

314   "Hope" is the thing with feathers -
       That perches in the soul -
       And sings the tune without the words -
       And never stops - at all -

       And sweetest - in the Gale - is heard -   5
       And sore must be the storm -
       That could abash the little Bird
       That kept so many warm -

       I've heard it in the chillest land -
       And on the strangest Sea -   10
       Yet - never - in Extremity,
       It asked a crumb - of me.

315   To die - takes just a little while -
       They say it does'nt hurt -
       It's only fainter - by degrees -
       And then - it's out of sight -

       A darker Ribbon - for a Day -   5
       A Crape opon the Hat -
       And then the pretty sunshine comes -
       And helps us to forget -

       The absent - mystic - creature -
       That but for love of us -   10
       Had gone to sleep - that soundest time -
       Without the weariness -

316   If I'm lost - now -
       That I was found -
       Shall still my transport be -
       That once - on me - those Jasper Gates
       Blazed open - suddenly -   5

       That in my awkward - gazing - face -
       The Angels - softly peered -
       And touched me with their fleeces,
       Almost as if they cared -

I'm banished - now - you know it -
How foreign that can be -
You'll know - Sir - when the Savior's face
Turns so - away from you -

317   Delight is as the flight -
Or in the Ratio of it,
As the Schools would say -
The Rainbow's way -
A Skein
Flung colored, after Rain,
Would suit as bright,
Except that flight
Were Aliment -

"If it would last"
I asked the East,
When that Bent Stripe
Struck up my childish
Firmament -
And I, for glee,
Took Rainbows, as the common way,
And empty skies
The Eccentricity -

And so with Lives -
And so with Butterflies -
Seen magic - through the fright
That they will cheat the sight -
And Dower latitudes far on -
Some sudden morn -
Our portion - in the fashion -
Done -

318   She sweeps with many-colored Brooms -
And leaves the shreds behind -
Oh Housewife in the Evening West -
Come back - and dust the Pond -

□

You dropped a Purple Ravelling in -
You dropped an Amber Thread -
And now you've littered all the East
With Duds of Emerald -

And still she plies Her spotted thrift
And still the scene prevails
Till Dusk obstructs the Diligence -
Or Contemplation fails.

319   Of Bronze - and Blaze -
        The North - tonight -
        So adequate - it forms -
        So preconcerted with itself -
        So distant - to alarms -
        An Unconcern so sovreign
        To Universe, or me -
        Infects my simple spirit
        With Taints of Majesty -
        Till I take vaster attitudes -
        And strut opon my stem -
        Disdaining Men, and Oxygen,
        For Arrogance of them -

        My Splendors, are Menagerie -
        But their Competeless Show
        Will entertain the Centuries
        When I, am long ago,
        An Island in dishonored Grass -
        Whom none but Daisies, know -

320   There's a certain Slant of light,
        Winter Afternoons -
        That oppresses, like the Heft
        Of Cathedral Tunes -

        Heavenly Hurt, it gives us -
        We can find no scar,

But internal difference -
Where the Meanings, are -

None may teach it - Any -
'Tis the Seal Despair -   10
An imperial affliction
Sent us of the Air -

When it comes, the Landscape listens -
Shadows - hold their breath -
When it goes, 'tis like the Distance   15
On the look of Death -

321   Blazing in Gold and quenching in Purple
Leaping like Leopards to the Sky
Then at the feet of the old Horizon
Laying her Spotted Face to die
Stooping as low as the Otter's Window   5
Touching the Roof and tinting the Barn
Kissing her Bonnet to the Meadow
And the Juggler of Day is gone

322   Good Night - Which put the Candle Out?
A jealous Zephyr - not a doubt -
Ah, friend, You little knew
How long at that celestial wick
The Angels - labored diligent -   5
Extinguished - now - for You -

It might have been the Light House Spark -
Some Sailor - rowing in the Dark -
Had importuned to see -
It might have been the waning Lamp   10
That lit the Drummer - from the Camp -
To purer Reveille -

323   Read - Sweet - how others - strove -
Till we - are stouter -

What they - renounced -
Till we - are less afraid -
How many times they - bore the faithful witness -   5
Till we - are helped -
As if a Kingdom - cared!

Read then - of faith -
That shone above the fagot -
Clear strains of Hymn   10
The River could not drown -
Brave names of Men -
And Celestial Women -
Passed out - of Record
Into - Renown!   15

324   Put up my lute!
       What of - my Music!
       Since the sole ear I cared to charm -
       Passive - as Granite - laps my music -
       Sobbing - will suit - as well as psalm!   5

       Would but the "Memnon" of the Desert -
       Teach me the strain
       That vanquished Him -
       When He - surrendered to the Sunrise -
       Maybe - that - would awaken - them!   10

325   There came a Day - at Summer's full -
       Entirely for me -
       I thought that such - were for the Saints -
       Where Resurrections - be -

       The Sun - as common - went abroad -   5
       The Flowers - accustomed - blew -
       As if no Soul the Solstice passed -
       That maketh all things new.

       The time was scarce profaned - by speech -
       The symbol of a word   10

Was needless - as at Sacrament -
The Wardrobe - of Our Lord -

Each was to each - the sealed church -
Permitted to commune - this time -
Lest we too awkward - show -   15
At "Supper of the Lamb."

The hours slid fast - as hours will -
Clutched tight - by greedy hands -
So - faces on two Decks - look back -
Bound to opposing Lands -   20

And so - when all the time had failed -
Without external sound -
Each - bound the other's Crucifix -
We gave no other bond -

Sufficient troth - that we shall rise -   25
Deposed - at length - the Grave -
To *that* New Marriage -
Justified - through Calvaries of Love!

326   The lonesome for they know not What -
       The Eastern Exiles - be -
       Who strayed beyond the Amber line
       Some madder Holiday -

       And ever since - the purple Moat   5
       They strive to climb - in vain -
       As Birds - that tumble from the clouds
       Do fumble at the strain -

       The Blessed Ether - taught them -
       Some Transatlantic Morn -   10
       When Heaven - was too common - to miss -
       Too sure - to dote opon!

327   How the old Mountains drip with Sunset
       How the Hemlocks burn -

How the Dun Brake is draped in Cinder
By the Wizard Sun -

How the old Steeples hand the Scarlet   5
Till the Ball is full -
Have I the lip of the Flamingo
That I dare to tell?

Then, how the Fire ebbs like Billows -
Touching all the Grass   10
With a departing - Sapphire - feature -
As a Duchess passed -

How a small Dusk crawls on the Village
Till the Houses blot
And the odd Flambeau, no men carry   15
Glimmer on the Street -

How it is Night - in Nest and Kennel -
And where was the Wood -
Just a Dome of Abyss is Bowing
Into Solitude -   20

These are the Visions flitted Guido -
Titian - never told -
Domenichino dropped his pencil -
Paralyzed, with Gold -

328   Of Tribulation - these are They,
Denoted by the White.
The Spangled Gowns, a lesser Rank
Of Victors, designate -

All these - did conquer -   5
But the Ones who overcame most times -
Wear nothing commoner than Snow -
No Ornament - but Palms -

"Surrender" - is a sort unknown
On this superior soil -   10
"Defeat", an Outgrown Anguish,
Remembered, as the Mile

□

Our panting Ancle barely passed,
When Night devoured the Road -
But we - stood - whispering in the House -   15
And all we said - was Saved!

329   If your Nerve, deny you -
Go above your Nerve -
He can lean against the Grave,
If he fear to swerve -

That's a steady posture -   5
Never any bend
Held of those Brass arms -
Best Giant made -

If your Soul seesaw -
Lift the Flesh door -   10
The Poltroon wants Oxygen -
Nothing more -

330   He put the Belt around my life -
I heard the Buckle snap -
And turned away, imperial,
My Lifetime folding up -
Deliberate, as a Duke would do   5
A Kingdom's Title Deed -
Henceforth - a Dedicated sort -
A Member of the Cloud -

Yet not too far to come at call -
And do the little Toils   10
That make the Circuit of the Rest -
And deal occasional smiles
To lives that stoop to notice mine -
And kindly ask it in -
Whose invitation, know you not   15
For Whom I must decline?

331   The only Ghost I ever saw
        Was dressed in Mechlin - so -
        He had no sandal on his foot -
        And stepped like flakes of snow -
        His Mien, was soundless, like the Bird -   5
        But rapid - like the Roe -
        His fashions, quaint, Mosaic -
        Or haply, Mistletoe -

        His conversation - seldom -
        His laughter, like the Breeze   10
        That dies away in Dimples
        Among the pensive Trees -

        Our interview - was transient -
        Of me, himself was shy -
        And God forbid I look behind -   15
        Since that appalling Day!

332   Doubt Me! My Dim Companion!
        Why, God, would be content
        With but a fraction of the Life -
        Poured thee, without a stint -
        The whole of me - forever -   5
        What more the Woman can,
        Say quick, that I may dower thee
        With last Delight I own!

        It cannot be my spirit -
        For that was thine, before -   10
        I ceded all of Dust I knew -
        What Opulence the more
        Had I - a freckled Maiden,
        Whose farthest of Degree,
        Was - that she might -   15
        Some distant Heaven,
        Dwell timidly - with thee!

        Sift her, from Brow to Barefoot!
        Strain till your last Surmise -
        Drop, like a Tapestry, away,   20

Before the Fire's Eyes -
Winnow her finest fondness -
But hallow just the snow
Intact, in Everlasting flake -
Oh, Caviler, for you!   25

333   Many a phrase has the English language -
        I have heard but one -
        Low as the laughter of the Cricket,
        Loud, as the Thunder's Tongue -

        Murmuring, like old Caspian Choirs,   5
        When the Tide's a'lull -
        Saying itself in new inflection -
        Like a Whippowil -

        Breaking in bright Orthography
        On my simple sleep -   10
        Thundering it's Prospective -
        Till I stir, and weep -

        Not for the Sorrow, done me -
        But the push of Joy -
        Say it again, Saxon!   15
        Hush - Only to me!

334   Of all the Sounds despatched abroad
        There's not a Charge to me
        Like that old measure in the Boughs -
        That Phraseless Melody -
        The Wind does - working like a Hand -   5
        Whose fingers comb the Sky -
        Then quiver down, with tufts of tune -
        Permitted Gods - and me -

        Inheritance it is to us
        Beyond the Art to Earn -   10
        Beyond the trait to take away
        By Robber - since the Gain
        Is gotten not of fingers -

And inner than the Bone
Hid golden, for the Whole of days -   15
And even in the Urn -
I cannot vouch the merry Dust
Do not arise and play,
In some odd Pattern of it's own -
Some quainter Holiday -   20
When Winds go round and round in Bands -
And thrum opon the Door -
And Birds take places - overhead -
To bear them Orchestra -

I crave Him Grace of Summer Boughs -   25
If such an Outcast be -
Who never heard that Fleshless Chant -
Rise solemn on the Tree -
As if some Caravan of Sound -
Off Deserts in the Sky -   30
Had parted Rank -
Then knit and swept
In Seamless Company -

335   Her smile was shaped like other smiles -
       The Dimples ran along -
       And still it hurt you, as some Bird
       Did hoist herself, to sing,
       Then recollect a Ball, she got -   5
       And hold opon the Twig, -
       Convulsive, while the Music broke -
       Like Beads - among the Bog -

       A happy lip - breaks sudden -
       It does'nt state you how   10
       It contemplated - smiling -
       Just consummated - now -
       But this one, wears it's merriment
       So patient - like a pain -
       Fresh gilded - to elude the eyes   15
       Unqualified, to scan -

336   Before I got my eye put out -
I liked as well to see
As other creatures, that have eyes -
And know no other way -

But were it told to me, Today,   5
That I might have the Sky
For mine, I tell you that my Heart
Would split, for size of me -

The Meadows - mine -
The Mountains - mine -   10
All Forests - Stintless stars -
As much of noon, as I could take -
Between my finite eyes -

The Motions of the Dipping Birds -
The Morning's Amber Road -   15
For mine - to look at when I liked,
The news would strike me dead -

So safer - guess - with just my soul
Opon the window pane
Where other creatures put their eyes -   20
Incautious - of the Sun -

337   Of nearness to her sundered Things
The Soul has special times -
When Dimness - looks the Oddity -
Distinctness - easy - seems -

The Shapes we buried, dwell about,   5
Familiar, in the Rooms -
Untarnished by the Sepulchre,
The Mouldering Playmate comes -

In just the Jacket that he wore -
Long buttoned in the Mold   10
Since we - old mornings, Children - played -
Divided - by a world -

The Grave yields back her Robberies -
The Years, our pilfered Things -

Bright Knots of Apparitions   15
Salute us, with their wings -

As we - it were - that perished -
Themself - had just remained till we rejoin them -
And 'twas they, and not ourself
That mourned -   20

338   Tie the strings to my Life, My Lord,
       Then, I am ready to go!
       Just a look at the Horses -
       Rapid! That will do!

       Put me in on the firmest side -   5
       So I shall never fall -
       For we must ride to the Judgment -
       And it's partly, down Hill -

       But never I mind the steepest -
       And never I mind the Sea -   10
       Held fast in Everlasting Race -
       By my own Choice, and Thee -

       Good bye to the Life I used to live -
       And the World I used to know -
       And kiss the Hills, for me, just once -   15
       Then - I am ready to go!

339   I like a look of Agony,
       Because I know it's true -
       Men do not sham Convulsion,
       Nor simulate, a Throe -

       The eyes glaze once - and that is Death -   5
       Impossible to feign
       The Beads opon the Forehead
       By homely Anguish strung.

340   I felt a Funeral, in my Brain,
      And Mourners to and fro
      Kept treading - treading - till it seemed
      That Sense was breaking through -

      And when they all were seated,   5
      A Service, like a Drum -
      Kept beating - beating - till I thought
      My mind was going numb -

      And then I heard them lift a Box
      And creak across my Soul   10
      With those same Boots of Lead, again,
      Then Space - began to toll,

      As all the Heavens were a Bell,
      And Being, but an Ear,
      And I, and Silence, some strange Race   15
      Wrecked, solitary, here -

      And then a Plank in Reason, broke,
      And I dropped down, and down -
      And hit a World, at every plunge,
      And Finished knowing - then -   20

341   'Tis so appalling - it exhilirates -
      So over Horror, it half captivates -
      The Soul stares after it, secure -
      To know the worst, leaves no dread more -

      To scan a Ghost, is faint -   5
      But grappling, conquers it -
      How easy, Torment, now -
      Suspense kept sawing so -

      The Truth, is Bald - and Cold -
      But that will hold -   10
      If any are not sure -
      We show them - prayer -
      But we, who know,
      Stop hoping, now -

                                                        □

Looking at Death, is Dying -   15
Just let go the Breath -
And not the pillow at your cheek
So slumbereth -

Others, can wrestle -
Your's, is done -   20
And so of Wo, bleak dreaded - come,
It sets the Fright at liberty -
And Terror's free -
Gay, Ghastly, Holiday!

342   How noteless Men, and Pleiads, stand,
       Until a sudden sky
       Reveals the fact that One is rapt
       Forever from the eye -

       Members of the Invisible,   5
       Existing, while we stare,
       In Leagueless Opportunity,
       O'ertakeless, as the Air -

       Why did'nt we detain Them?
       The Heavens with a smile,   10
       Sweep by our disappointed Heads,
       Without a syllable -

343   When we stand on the tops of Things -
       And like the Trees, look down,
       The smoke all cleared away from it -
       And mirrorrs on the scene -

       Just laying light - no soul will wink   5
       Except it have the flaw -
       The Sound ones, like the Hills - shall stand -
       No lightning, scares away -

       The Perfect, nowhere be afraid -
       They bear their dauntless Heads,   10

Where others, dare not go at noon,
Protected by their deeds -

The Stars dare shine occasionally
Opon a spotted World -
And Suns, go surer, for their Proof,   15
As if an axle, held -

344   'Twas just this time, last year, I died.
        I know I heard the Corn,
        When I was carried by the Farms -
        It had the Tassels on -

        I thought how yellow it would look -   5
        When Richard went to mill -
        And then, I wanted to get out,
        But something held my will.

        I thought just how Red - Apples wedged
        The Stubble's joints between -   10
        And Carts went stooping round the fields
        To take the Pumpkins in -

        I wondered which would miss me, least,
        And when Thanksgiving, came,
        If Father'd multiply the plates -   15
        To make an even Sum -

        And would it blur the Christmas glee
        My stocking hang too high
        For any Santa Claus to reach
        The altitude of me -   20

        But this sort, grieved myself,
        And so, I thought the other way,
        How just this time, some perfect year -
        Themself, should come to me -

345   Afraid! Of whom am I afraid?
        Not Death - for who is He?

The Porter of my Father's Lodge
As much abasheth me!

Of Life? 'Twere odd I fear a thing   5
That comprehendeth me
In one or two existences -
Just as the case may be -

Of Resurrection? Is the East
Afraid to trust the Morn   10
With her fastidious forehead?
As soon impeach my Crown!

346   He showed me Hights I never saw -
       "Would'st Climb" - He said?
       I said, "Not so" -
       "With me -" He said - "With me"?

       He showed me secrets - Morning's Nest -   5
       The Rope the Nights were put across -
       "And now, Would'st have me for a Guest"?
       I could not find my "Yes" -

       And then - He brake His Life - And lo,
       A light for me, did solemn glow -   10
       The larger, as my face withdrew -
       And could I further "No"?

347   I dreaded that first Robin, so,
       But He is mastered, now,
       I'm some accustomed to Him grown,
       He hurts a little, though -

       I thought if I could only live   5
       Till that first Shout got by -
       Not all Pianos in the Woods
       Had power to mangle me -

       I dared not meet the Daffodils -
       For fear their Yellow Gown   10

Would pierce me with a fashion
So foreign to my own -

I wished the Grass would hurry -
So when 'twas time to see -
He'd be too tall, the tallest one   15
Could stretch to look at me -

I could not bear the Bees should come,
I wished they'd stay away
In those dim countries where they go,
What word had they, for me?   20

They're here, though; not a creature failed -
No Blossom stayed away
In gentle deference to me -
The Queen of Calvary -

Each one salutes me, as he goes,   25
And I, my childish Plumes,
Lift, in bereaved acknowledgement
Of their unthinking Drums -

348   I would not paint - a picture -
       I'd rather be the One
       It's bright impossibility
       To dwell - delicious - on -
       And wonder how the fingers feel   5
       Whose rare - celestial - stir -
       Evokes so sweet a torment -
       Such sumptuous - Despair -

       I would not talk, like Cornets -
       I'd rather be the One   10
       Raised softly to the Ceilings -
       And out, and easy on -
       Through Villages of Ether -
       Myself endued Balloon
       By but a lip of Metal -   15
       The pier to my Pontoon -

                                                      □

Nor would I be a Poet -
It's finer - Own the Ear -
Enamored - impotent - content -
The License to revere,   20
A privilege so awful
What would the Dower be,
Had I the Art to stun myself
With Bolts - of Melody!

349   He touched me, so I live to know
That such a day, permitted so,
I groped opon his breast -

It was a boundless place to me
And silenced, as the awful Sea   5
Puts minor streams to rest.

And now, I'm different from before,
As if I breathed superior air -
Or brushed a Royal Gown -
My feet, too, that had wandered so -   10
My Gypsy face - transfigured now -
To tenderer Renown -

Into this Port, if I might come,
Rebecca, to Jerusalem,
Would not so ravished turn -   15
Nor Persian, baffled at her shrine
Lift such a Crucifixal sign
To her imperial Sun.

350   I had the Glory - that will do -
An Honor, Thought can turn her to
When lesser Fames invite -
With one long "Nay" -
Bliss' early shape   5
Deforming - Dwindling - Gulphing up -
Time's possibility -

351   She sights a Bird - she chuckles -
She flattens - then she crawls -
She runs without the look of feet -
Her eyes increase to Balls -

Her Jaws stir - twitching - hungry -   5
Her Teeth can hardly stand -
She leaps, but Robin leaped the first -
Ah, Pussy, of the Sand,

The Hopes so juicy ripening -
You almost bathed your Tongue -   10
When Bliss disclosed a hundred Toes -
And fled with every one -

352   They leave us with the Infinite.
But He - is not a man -
His fingers are the size of fists -
His fists, the size of men -

And whom he foundeth, with his Arm   5
As Himmaleh, shall stand -
Gibraltar's everlasting Shoe
Poised lightly on his Hand,

So trust him, Comrade -
You for you, and I, for you and - me   10
Eternity is ample,
And quick enough, if true.

353   I'm ceded - I've stopped being Their's -
The name They dropped opon my face
With water, in the country church
Is finished using, now,
And They can put it with my Dolls,   5
My childhood, and the string of spools,
I've finished threading - too -

Baptized, before, without the choice,
But this time, consciously, Of Grace -

Unto supremest name -
Called to my Full - The Crescent dropped -
Existence's whole Arc, filled up,
With one - small Diadem -

My second Rank - too small the first -
Crowned - Crowing - on my Father's breast -
A half unconscious Queen -
But this time - Adequate - Erect,
With Will to choose,
Or to reject,
And I choose, just a Crown -

354   If Anybody's friend be dead
It's sharpest of the theme
The thinking how they walked alive -
At such and such a time -

Their costume, of a Sunday,
Some manner of the Hair -
A prank nobody knew but them
Lost, in the Sepulchre -

How warm, they were, on such a day,
You almost feel the date -
So short way off it seems -
And now - they're Centuries from that -

How pleased they were, at what you said!
You try to touch the smile
And dip your fingers in the frost -
When was it - Can you tell -

You asked the Company to tea -
Acquaintance - just a few -
And chatted close with this Grand Thing
That dont remember you -

Past Bows, and Invitations -
Past Interview, and Vow -
Past what Ourself can estimate -
That - makes the Quick of Wo!

10

15

20

5

10

15

20

355   It was not Death, for I stood up,
And all the Dead, lie down -
It was not Night, for all the Bells
Put out their Tongues, for Noon.

It was not Frost, for on my Flesh   5
I felt Siroccos - crawl -
Nor Fire - for just my marble feet
Could keep a Chancel, cool -

And yet, it tasted, like them all,
The Figures I have seen   10
Set orderly, for Burial,
Reminded me, of mine -

As if my life were shaven,
And fitted to a frame,
And could not breathe without a key,   15
And 'twas like Midnight, some -

When everything that ticked - has stopped -
And space stares - all around -
Or Grisly frosts - first Autumn morns,
Repeal the Beating Ground -   20

But, most, like Chaos - Stopless - cool -
Without a Chance, or spar -
Or even a Report of Land -
To justify - Despair.

356   If you were coming in the Fall,
I'd brush the Summer by
With half a smile, and half a spurn,
As Housewives do, a Fly.

If I could see you in a year,   5
I'd wind the months in balls -
And put them each in separate Drawers,
For fear the numbers fuse -

If only Centuries, delayed,
I'd count them on my Hand,   10

Subtracting, till my fingers dropped
Into Van Dieman's Land.

If certain, when this life was out -
That your's and mine, should be -
I'd toss it yonder, like a Rind,   15
And take Eternity -

But, now, uncertain of the length
Of this, that is between,
It goads me, like the Goblin Bee -
That will not state - it's sting.   20

357   I felt my life with both my hands
       To see if it was there -
       I held my spirit to the Glass,
       To prove it possibler -

       I turned my Being round and round   5
       And paused at every pound
       To ask the Owner's name -
       For doubt, that I should know the sound -

       I judged my features - jarred my hair -
       I pushed my dimples by, and waited -   10
       If they - twinkled back -
       Conviction might, of me -

       I told myself, "Take Courage, Friend -
       That - was a former time -
       But we might learn to like the Heaven,   15
       As well as our Old Home"!

358   Perhaps I asked too large -
       I take - no less than skies -
       For Earths, grow thick as
       Berries, in my native Town -

       My Basket holds - just - Firmaments -   5
       Those - dangle easy - on my arm,
       But smaller bundles - Cram.

359   A Bird, came down the Walk -
He did not know I saw -
He bit an Angle Worm in halves
And ate the fellow, raw,

And then, he drank a Dew   5
From a convenient Grass -
And then hopped sidewise to the Wall
To let a Beetle pass -

He glanced with rapid eyes,
That hurried all abroad -   10
They looked like frightened Beads, I thought,
He stirred his Velvet Head. -

Like one in danger, Cautious,
I offered him a Crumb,
And he unrolled his feathers,   15
And rowed him softer Home -

Than Oars divide the Ocean,
Too silver for a seam,
Or Butterflies, off Banks of Noon,
Leap, plashless as they swim.   20

360   The Soul has Bandaged moments -
When too appalled to stir -
She feels some ghastly Fright come up
And stop to look at her -

Salute her, with long fingers -   5
Caress her freezing hair -
Sip, Goblin, from the very lips
The Lover - hovered - o'er -
Unworthy, that a thought so mean
Accost a Theme - so - fair -   10

The soul has moments of escape -
When bursting all the doors -
She dances like a Bomb, abroad,
And swings opon the Hours,

□

As do the Bee - delirious borne -   15
Long Dungeoned from his Rose -
Touch Liberty - then know no more -
But Noon, and Paradise -

The Soul's retaken moments -
When, Felon led along,   20
With shackles on the plumed feet,
And staples, in the song,

The Horror welcomes her, again,
These, are not brayed of Tongue -

361   Like Flowers, that heard the news of Dews,
        But never deemed the dripping prize
        Awaited their - low Brows -

        Or Bees - that thought the Summer's name
        Some rumor of Delirium,   5
        No Summer - could - for Them -

        Or Arctic Creatures, dimly stirred -
        By Tropic Hint - some Travelled Bird
        Imported to the Wood -

        Or Wind's bright signal to the Ear -   10
        Making that homely, and severe,
        Contented, known, before -

        The Heaven - unexpected come,
        To Lives that thought the Worshipping
        A too presumptuous Psalm -   15

362   It's thoughts - and just One Heart -
        And Old Sunshine - about -
        Make frugal - Ones - Content -
        And two or three - for Company -
        Opon a Holiday -
        Crowded - as Sacrament -   5

                                                                         □

Books - when the Unit -
Spare the Tenant - long eno' -
A Picture - if it Care -
Itself - a Gallery too rare -   10
For needing more -

Flowers - to keep the eyes - from going awkward -
When it snows -
A Bird - if they - prefer -
Though winter fire - sing clear as Plover -   15
To our - ear -

A Landscape - not so great
To suffocate the eye -
A Hill - perhaps -
Perhaps - the profile of a Mill   20
Turned by the wind -
Tho' *such* - are *luxuries* -

It's thoughts - and just two Heart -
And Heaven - about -
At least - a Counterfeit -   25
We would not have Correct -
And Immortality - can be almost -
Not quite - Content -

363   I know a place where Summer strives
        With such a practised Frost -
        She - each year - leads her Daisies back -
        Recording briefly - "Lost" -

        But when the South Wind stirs the Pools   5
        And struggles in the lanes -
        Her Heart misgives Her, for Her Vow -
        And she pours soft Refrains

        Into the lap of Adamant -
        And spices - and the Dew -   10
        That stiffens quietly to Quartz -
        Opon her Amber Shoe -

364   As far from pity, as complaint -
       As cool to speech - as stone -
       As numb to Revelation
       As if my Trade were Bone -

       As far from Time - as History -   5
       As near yourself - Today -
       As Children, to the Rainbow's scarf -
       Or Sunset's Yellow play

       To eyelids in the Sepulchre -
       How dumb the Dancer lies -   10
       While Color's Revelations break -
       And blaze - the Butterflies!

365   I know that He exists.
       Somewhere - in silence -
       He has hid his rare life
       From our gross eyes.

       'Tis an instant's play -   5
       'Tis a fond Ambush -
       Just to make Bliss
       Earn her own surprise!

       But - should the play
       Prove piercing earnest -   10
       Should the glee - glaze -
       In Death's - stiff - stare -

       Would not the fun
       Look too expensive!
       Would not the jest -   15
       Have crawled too far!

366   He strained my faith -
       Did he find it supple?
       Shook my strong trust -
       Did it then - yield?

                                                            □

Hurled my belief -   5
But - did he shatter - it?
Racked - with suspense -
Not a nerve failed!

Wrung me - with Anguish -
But I never doubted him -   10
Tho' for what wrong
He did never say -

Stabbed - while I sued
His sweet forgiveness -
Jesus - it's your little "John"!   15
Dont you know - me?

367   I tend my flowers for thee -
        Bright Absentee!
        My Fuschzia's Coral Seams
        Rip - while the Sower - dreams -

        Geraniums - tint - and spot -   5
        Low Daisies - dot -
        My Cactus - splits her Beard
        To show her throat -

        Carnations - tip their spice -
        And Bees - pick up -   10
        A Hyacinth - I hid -
        Puts out a Ruffled Head -
        And odors fall
        From flasks - so small -
        You marvel how they held -   15

        Globe Roses - break their satin flake -
        Opon my Garden floor -
        Yet - thou - not there -
        I had as lief they bore
        No crimson - more -   20

        Thy flower - be gay -
        Her Lord - away!
        It ill becometh me -

I'll dwell in Calyx - Gray -
How modestly - alway -
Thy Daisy -
Draped for thee!

25

368 I envy Seas, whereon He rides -
I envy Spokes of Wheels
Of Chariots, that Him convey -
I envy Crooked Hills

That gaze opon His journey -
How easy all can see
What is forbidden utterly
As Heaven - unto me!

5

I envy Nests of Sparrows -
That dot His distant Eaves;
The wealthy Fly, opon His Pane -
The happy - happy Leaves -

10

That just abroad His Window
Have Summer's leave to play -
The Ear Rings of Pizarro
Could not obtain for me -

15

I envy Light - that wakes Him -
And Bells - that boldly ring
To tell Him it is Noon, abroad -
Myself - be Noon to Him -

20

Yet interdict - my Blossom -
And abrogate - my Bee -
Lest Noon in everlasting night -
Drop Gabriel - and me -

369 Those fair - fictitious People -
The Women - plucked away
From our familiar Lifetime -
The Men of Ivory -

□

Those Boys and Girls, in Canvas -   5
Who stay opon the Wall
In everlasting Keepsake -
Can anybody tell?

We trust - in places perfecter -
Inheriting Delight   10
Beyond our faint Conjecture -
Our dizzy Estimate -

Remembering ourselves, we trust -
Yet Blesseder - than we -
Through Knowing - where we only hope -   15
Receiving - where we - pray -

Of Expectation - also -
Anticipating us
With transport, that would be a pain
Except for Holiness -   20

Esteeming us - as Exile -
Themself - admitted Home -
Through easy Miracle of Death -
The Way ourself, must come -

370   Within my Garden, rides a Bird
        Opon a single Wheel -
        Whose spokes a dizzy music make
        As 'twere a travelling Mill -

        He never stops, but slackens   5
        Above the Ripest Rose -
        Partakes without alighting
        And praises as he goes,

        Till every spice is tasted -
        And then his Fairy Gig   10
        Reels in remoter atmospheres -
        And I rejoin my Dog,

        And He and I, perplex us
        If positive, 'twere we -

Or bore the Garden in the Brain   15
This Curiosity -

But He, the best Logician,
Refers my clumsy eye -
To just vibrating Blossoms!
An exquisite Reply!   20

371   Is Bliss then, such Abyss -
        I must not put my foot amiss
        For fear I spoil my shoe?

        I'd rather suit my foot
        Than save my Boot -   5
        For yet to buy another Pair
        Is possible,
        At any store -

        But Bliss, is sold just once.
        The Patent lost   10
        None buy it any more -
        Say, Foot, decide the point!
        The Lady cross, or not?
        Verdict for Boot!

372   After great pain, a formal feeling comes -
        The Nerves sit ceremonious, like Tombs -
        The stiff Heart questions 'was it He, that bore,'
        And 'Yesterday, or Centuries before'?

        The Feet, mechanical, go round -   5
        A Wooden way
        Of Ground, or Air, or Ought -
        Regardless grown,
        A Quartz contentment, like a stone -

        This is the Hour of Lead -   10
        Remembered, if outlived,
        As Freezing persons, recollect the Snow -
        First - Chill - then Stupor - then the letting go -

373   This World is not conclusion.
A Species stands beyond -
Invisible, as Music -
But positive, as Sound -
It beckons, and it baffles -   5
Philosophy, dont know -
And through a Riddle, at the last -
Sagacity, must go -
To guess it, puzzles scholars -
To gain it, Men have borne   10
Contempt of Generations
And Crucifixion, shown -
Faith slips - and laughs, and rallies -
Blushes, if any see -
Plucks at a twig of Evidence -   15
And asks a Vane, the way -
Much Gesture, from the Pulpit -
Strong Hallelujahs roll -
Narcotics cannot still the Tooth
That nibbles at the soul -   20

374   It will be Summer - eventually.
Ladies - with parasols -
Sauntering Gentlemen - with Canes -
And little Girls - with Dolls -

Will tint the pallid landscape -   5
As 'twere a bright Boquet -
Tho' drifted deep, in Parian -
The Village lies - today -

The Lilacs - bending many a year -
Will sway with purple load -   10
The Bees - will not despise the tune -
Their Forefathers - have hummed -

The Wild Rose - redden in the Bog -
The Aster - on the Hill
Her everlasting fashion - set -   15
And Covenant Gentians - frill -

                                  □

Till Summer folds her miracle -
As Women - do - their Gown -
Or Priests - adjust the Symbols -
When Sacrament - is done -   20

375   My Reward for Being - was this -
        My Premium - My Bliss -
        An Admiralty, less -
        A Sceptre - penniless -
        And Realms - just Dross -   5

        When Thrones - accost my Hands -
        With "Me - Miss - Me" -
        I'll unroll - Thee -
        Sufficient Dynasty -
        Creation - powerless -   10
        To Peer this Grace -
        Empire - State -
        Too little - Dust -
        To Dower - so Great -

376   'Twas the old - road - through pain -
        That unfrequented - One -
        With many a turn - and thorn -
        That stops - at Heaven -

        This - was the Town - she passed -   5
        There - where she - rested - last -
        Then - stepped more fast -
        The little tracks - close prest -
        Then - not so swift -
        Slow - slow - as feet did weary - grow -   10
        Then - stopped - no other track!

        Wait! Look! Her little Book -
        The leaf - at love - turned back -
        Her very Hat -
        And this worn shoe just fits the track -   15
        Herself - though - fled!

                                                     □

Another bed - a short one -
Women make - tonight -
In Chambers bright -
Too out of sight - though -   20
For our hoarse Good Night -
To touch her Head!

377   At least - to pray - is left - is left -
      Oh Jesus - in the Air -
      I know not which thy chamber is -
      I'm knocking - everywhere -

      Thou settest Earthquake in the South -   5
      And Maelstrom, in the Sea -
      Say, Jesus Christ of Nazareth -
      Hast thou no arm for Me?

378   Better - than Music!
      For I - who heard it -
      I was used - to the Birds - before -
      This - was different - 'Twas Translation -
      Of all tunes I knew - and more -   5

      'Twas'nt contained - like other stanza -
      No one could play it - the second time -
      But the Composer - perfect Mozart -
      Perish with him - that keyless Rhyme!

      Children - so - told how Brooks in Eden -   10
      Bubbled a better - melody -
      Quaintly infer - Eve's great surrender -
      Urging the feet - that would - not - fly -

      Children - matured - are wiser - mostly -
      Eden - a legend - dimly told -   15
      Eve - and the Anguish - Grandame's story -
      But - I was telling a tune - I heard -

      Not such a strain - the Church - baptizes -
      When the last Saint - goes up the Aisles -

Not such a stanza splits the silence -
When the Redemption strikes her Bells -

Let me not spill - it's smallest cadence -
Humming - for promise - when alone -
Humming - until my faint Rehearsal -
Drop into tune - around the Throne -   25

379   The Grass so little has to do,
        A Sphere of simple Green -
        With only Butterflies, to brood,
        And Bees, to entertain -

        And stir all day to pretty tunes   5
        The Breezes fetch along,
        And hold the Sunshine, in it's lap
        And bow to everything,

        And thread the Dews, all night, like Pearl,
        And make itself so fine   10
        A Duchess, were too common
        For such a noticing,

        And even when it die, to pass
        In odors so divine -
        As lowly spices, laid to sleep -   15
        Or Spikenards perishing -

        And then to dwell in Sovreign Barns,
        And dream the Days away,
        The Grass so little has to do,
        I wish I were a Hay -   20

380   All the letters I can write
        Are not fair as this -
        Syllables of Velvet -
        Sentences of Plush,
        Depths of Ruby, undrained,   5
        Hid, Lip, for Thee -

Play it were a Humming Bird -
And just sipped - me -

381   I cannot dance opon my Toes -
        No Man instructed me -
        But oftentimes, among my mind,
        A Glee possesseth me,

        That had I Ballet Knowledge -   5
        Would put itself abroad
        In Pirouette to blanch a Troupe -
        Or lay a Prima, mad,

        And though I had no Gown of Gauze -
        No Ringlet, to my Hair,   10
        Nor hopped for Audiences - like Birds -
        One Claw opon the air -

        Nor tossed my shape in Eider Balls,
        Nor rolled on wheels of snow
        Till I was out of sight, in sound,   15
        The House encore me so -

        Nor any know I know the Art
        I mention - easy - Here -
        Nor any Placard boast me -
        It's full as Opera -   20

382   Good Morning - Midnight -
        I'm coming Home -
        Day - got tired of Me -
        How could I - of Him?

        Sunshine was a sweet place -   5
        I liked to stay -
        But Morn - did'nt want me - now -
        So - Good night - Day!

        I can look - cant I -
        When the East is Red?   10

The Hills - have a way - then -
That puts the Heart - abroad -

You - are not so fair - Midnight -
I chose - Day -
But - please take a little Girl -   15
He turned away!

383   I like to see it lap the Miles -
       And lick the Valleys up -
       And stop to feed itself at Tanks -
       And then - prodigious step

       Around a Pile of Mountains -   5
       And supercilious peer
       In Shanties - by the sides of Roads -
       And then a Quarry pare

       To fit it's sides
       And crawl between   10
       Complaining all the while
       In horrid - hooting stanza -
       Then chase itself down Hill -

       And neigh like Boanerges -
       Then - prompter than a Star   15
       Stop - docile and omnipotent
       At it's own stable door -

384   It dont sound so terrible - quite - as it did -
       I run it over - "Dead", Brain - "Dead".
       Put it in Latin - left of my school -
       Seems it dont shriek so - under rule.

       Turn it, a little - full in the face   5
       A Trouble looks bitterest -
       Shift it - just -
       Say "When Tomorrow comes this way -
       I shall have waded down one Day".

                                                       □

I suppose it will interrupt me some   10
Till I get accustomed - but then the Tomb
Like other new Things - shows largest - then -
And smaller, by Habit -

It's shrewder then
Put the Thought in advance - a Year -   15
How like "a fit" - then -
Murder - wear!

385 I'll clutch - and clutch -
Next - One - Might be the golden touch -
Could take it -
Diamonds - Wait -
I'm diving - just a little late -   5
But stars - go slow - for night -

I'll string you - in fine necklace -
Tiaras - make - of some -
Wear you on Hem -
Loop up a Countess - with you -   10
Make - a Diadem - and mend my old One -
Count - Hoard - then lose -
And doubt that you are mine -
To have the joy of feeling it - again -

I'll show you at the Court -   15
Bear you - for Ornament
Where Women breathe -
That every sigh - may lift you
Just as high - as I -

And - when I die -   20
In meek array - display you -
Still to show - how rich I go -
Lest Skies impeach a wealth so wonderful -
And banish me -

386 Taking up the fair Ideal,
Just to cast her down

When a fracture - we discover -
Or a splintered Crown -
Makes the Heavens portable - 5
And the Gods - a lie -
Doubtless - "Adam" - scowled at Eden -
For *his* perjury!

Cherishing - our poor Ideal -
Till in purer dress - 10
We behold her - glorified -
Comforts - search - like this -
Till the broken creatures -
We adored - for whole -
Stains - all washed - 15
Transfigured - mended -
Meet us - with a smile -

387   The Moon is distant from the Sea -
And yet, with Amber Hands -
She leads Him - docile as a Boy -
Along appointed Sands -

He never misses a Degree - 5
Obedient to Her eye -
He comes just so far - toward the Town -
Just so far - goes away -

Oh, Signor, Thine, the Amber Hand -
And mine - the distant Sea - 10
Obedient to the least command
Thine eye impose on me -

388   It would never be Common - more - I said -
Difference - had begun -
Many a bitterness - had been -
But that old sort - was done -

Or - if it sometime - showed - as 'twill - 5
Opon the Downiest - morn -

Such bliss - had I - for all the years -
'Twould give an easier - pain -

I'd so much joy - I told it - Red -
Opon my simple Cheek -
I felt it publish - in my eye -
'Twas needless - any speak -

I walked - as wings - my body bore -
The feet - I former used -
Unnescessary - now to me -
As boots - would be - to Birds -

I put my pleasure all abroad -
I dealt a word of Gold
To every Creature - that I met -
And Dowered - all the World -

When - suddenly - my Riches shrank -
A Goblin - drank my Dew -
My Palaces - dropped tenantless -
Myself - was beggared - too -

I clutched at sounds -
I groped at shapes -
I touched the tops of Films -
I felt the Wilderness roll back
Along my Golden lines -

The Sackcloth - hangs opon the nail -
The Frock I used to wear -
But where my moment of Brocade -
My - drop - of India?

389   Me - Come! My dazzled face
In such a shining place!
Me - hear! My foreign Ear
The sounds of Welcome - there!

The Saints forget
Our bashful feet -

□

179   ⌒   1862

My Holiday, shall be
That They - remember me -
My Paradise - the fame
That They - pronounce my name -   10

390   Do People moulder equally,
           They bury, in the Grave?
           I do believe a species
           As positively live

           As I, who testify it   5
           Deny that I - am dead -
           And fill my Lungs, for Witness -
           From Tanks - above my Head -

           I say to you, said Jesus,
           That there be standing here -   10
           A sort, that shall not taste of Death -
           If Jesus was sincere -

           I need no further Argue -
           The statement of the Lord
           Is not a controvertible -   15
           He told me, Death was dead -

391   Knows how to forget!
           But could It teach it?
           Easiest of Arts, they say
           When one learn how

           Dull Hearts have died   5
           In the Acquisition
           Sacrifice for Science
           Is common, though, now -

           I - went to School
           But was not wiser   10
           Globe did not teach it
           Nor Logarithm Show

                                                       □

"How to forget"!
Say some Philosopher!
Ah, to be erudite   15
Enough to know!

Is it in a Book?
So, I could buy it -
Is it like a Planet?
Telescopes would know -   20

If it be invention
It must have a Patent -
Rabbi of the Wise Book
Dont you know?

392   We talked as Girls do -
       Fond, and late -
       We speculated fair, on every subject, but the Grave -
       Of our's, none affair -

       We handled Destinies, as cool -   5
       As we - Disposers - be -
       And God, a Quiet Party
       To our authority -

       But fondest, dwelt opon Ourself
       As we eventual - be -   10
       When Girls, to Women, softly raised
       We - occupy - Degree -

       We parted with a contract
       To cherish, and to write
       But Heaven made both, impossible   15
       Before another night.

393   Empty my Heart, of Thee -
       It's single Artery -
       Begin, and leave Thee out -
       Simply Extinction's Date -

                                                 □

Much Billow hath the Sea -
One Baltic - They -
Subtract Thyself, in play,
And not enough of me
Is left - to put away -
"Myself" meant Thee -

Erase the Root - no Tree -
Thee - then - no me -
The Heavens stripped -
Eternity's vast pocket, picked.

5

10

394   I cried at Pity - not at Pain -
           I heard a Woman say
           "Poor Child" - and something in her voice
           Convinced me - of me -

           So long I fainted, to myself
           It seemed the common way,
           And Health, and Laughter, curious things -
           To look at, like a Toy -

           To sometimes hear "Rich people" buy -
           And see the Parcel rolled -
           And carried, we supposed - to Heaven,
           For children, made of Gold -

           But not to touch, or wish for,
           Or think of, with a sigh -
           As so and so - had been to us,
           Had God willed differently.

           I wish I knew that Woman's name -
           So when she comes this way,
           To hold my life, and hold my ears
           For fear I hear her say

           She's "sorry I am dead" - again -
           Just when the Grave and I -
           Have sobbed ourselves almost to sleep,
           Our only Lullaby -

5

10

15

20

395   The face I carry with me - last -
       When I go out of Time -
       To take my Rank - by - in the West -
       That face - will just be thine -

       I'll hand it to the Angel -   5
       That - Sir - was my Degree -
       In Kingdoms - you have heard the Raised -
       Refer to - possibly.

       He'll take it - scan it - step aside -
       Return - with such a crown   10
       As Gabriel - never capered at -
       And beg me put it on -

       And then - he'll turn me round and round -
       To an admiring sky -
       As One that bore her Master's name -   15
       Sufficient Royalty!

396   I took one Draught of Life -
       I'll tell you what I paid -
       Precisely an existence -
       The market price, they said.

       They weighed me, Dust by Dust -   5
       They balanced Film with Film,
       Then handed me my Being's worth -
       A single Dram of Heaven!

397   A train went through a burial gate,
       A bird broke forth and sang,
       And trilled, and quivered, and shook his throat
       Till all the churchyard rang;

       And then adjusted his little notes,   5
       And bowed and sang again.
       Doubtless, he thought it meet of him
       To say good bye to men.

398   The Morning after Wo -
'Tis frequently the Way -
Surpasses all that rose before -
For utter Jubilee -

As Nature did not Care -   5
And piled her Blossoms on -
The further to parade a Joy
Her Victim stared opon -

The Birds declaim their Tunes -
Pronouncing every word   10
Like Hammers - Did they know they fell
Like Litanies of Lead -

On here and there - a creature -
They'd modify the Glee
To fit some Crucifixal Clef -   15
Some key of Calvary -

399   Departed - to the Judgment -
A Mighty - Afternoon -
Great Clouds - like Ushers - leaning -
Creation - looking on -

The Flesh - Surrendered - Cancelled -   5
The Bodiless - begun -
Two Worlds - like Audiences - disperse -
And leave the Soul - alone -

400   I think the Hemlock likes to stand
Opon a Marge of Snow -
It suits his own Austerity -
And satisfies an awe

That men, must slake in Wilderness -   5
And in the Desert - cloy -
An instinct for the Hoar, the Bald -
Lapland's - nescessity -

☐

The Hemlock's nature thrives - on cold -
The Gnash of Northern winds 10
Is sweetest nutriment - to him -
His best Norwegian Wines -

To satin Races - he is nought -
But children on the Don,
Beneath his Tabernacles, play, 15
And Dnieper Wrestlers, run.

401   Dare you see a Soul at the "White Heat"?
        Then crouch within the door -
        Red - is the Fire's common tint -
        But when the vivid Ore

        Has vanquished Flame's conditions - 5
        It quivers from the Forge
        Without a color, but the Light
        Of unannointed Blaze -

        Least Village, boasts it's Blacksmith -
        Whose Anvil's even ring 10
        Stands symbol for the finer Forge
        That soundless tugs - within -

        Refining these impatient Ores
        With Hammer, and with Blaze
        Until the designated Light 15
        Repudiate the Forge -

402   To hear an Oriole sing
        May be a common thing -
        Or only a divine.

        It is not of the Bird
        Who sings the same, unheard, 5
        As unto Crowd -

        The Fashion of the Ear
        Attireth that it hear
        In Dun, or fair -

        □

So whether it be Rune -
Or whether it be none
Is of within.

The "Tune is in the Tree -"
The Skeptic - showeth me -
"No Sir! In Thee!"

403   I reason, Earth is short -
And Anguish - absolute -
And many hurt,
But, what of that?

I reason, we could die -
The best Vitality
Cannot excel Decay,
But, what of that?

I reason, that in Heaven -
Somehow, it will be even -
Some new Equation, given -
But, what of that?

404   To put this World down, like a Bundle -
And walk steady, away,
Requires Energy - possibly Agony -
'Tis the Scarlet way

Trodden with straight renunciation
By the Son of God -
Later, his faint Confederates
Justify the Road -

Flavors of that old Crucifixion -
Filaments of Bloom, Pontius Pilate sowed -
Strong Clusters, from Barabbas' Tomb -

Sacrament, Saints partook before us -
Patent, every drop,
With the Brand of the Gentile Drinker
Who indorsed the Cup -

405   Although I put away his life -
An Ornament too grand
For Forehead low as mine, to wear,
This might have been the Hand

That sowed the flower, he preferred -   5
Or smoothed a homely pain,
Or pushed the pebble from his path -
Or played his chosen tune -

On Lute the least - the latest -
But just his ear could know   10
That whatsoe'er delighted it,
I never would let go -

The foot to bear his errand -
A little Boot I know -
Would leap abroad like Antelope -   15
With just the grant to do -

His weariest Commandment -
A sweeter to obey,
Than "Hide and Seek" -
Or skip to Flutes -   20
Or all Day, chase the Bee -

Your Servant, Sir, will weary -
The Surgeon, will not come -
The World, will have it's own - to do -
The Dust, will vex your Fame -   25

The Cold will force your tightest door
Some Febuary Day,
But say my Apron bring the sticks
To make your Cottage gay -

That I may take that promise   30
To Paradise, with me -
To teach the Angels, avarice,
You, Sir, taught first - to me.

406   Over and over, like a Tune -
The Recollection plays -

Drums off the Phantom Battlements
Cornets of Paradise -

Snatches, from Baptized Generations -   5
Cadences too grand
But for the Justified Processions
At the Lord's Right hand.

407   One need not be a Chamber - to be Haunted -
       One need not be a House -
       The Brain has Corridors - surpassing
       Material Place -

       Far safer, of a midnight meeting   5
       External Ghost
       Than it's interior confronting -
       That cooler Host -

       Far safer, through an Abbey gallop,
       The Stones a'chase -   10
       Than unarmed, one's a'self encounter -
       In lonesome Place -

       Ourself behind ourself, concealed -
       Should startle most -
       Assassin hid in our Apartment   15
       Be Horror's least -

       The Body - borrows a Revolver -
       He bolts the Door -
       O'erlooking a superior spectre -
       Or More -   20

408   Like some Old fashioned Miracle
       When Summertime is done -
       Seems Summer's Recollection
       And the Affairs of June

       As infinite Tradition   5
       As Cinderella's Bays -

Or Little John - of Lincoln Green -
Or Blue Beard's Galleries -

Her Bees have a fictitious Hum -
Her Blossoms, like a Dream -   10
Elate us - till we almost weep -
So plausible - they seem -

Her Memories like Strains - Review -
When Orchestra is dumb -
The Violin in Baize replaced -   15
And Ear - and Heaven - numb -

409   The Soul selects her own Society -
Then - shuts the Door -
To her divine Majority -
Present no more -

Unmoved - she notes the Chariots - pausing -   5
At her low Gate -
Unmoved - an Emperor be kneeling
Opon her Mat -

I've known her - from an ample nation -
Choose One -   10
Then - close the Valves of her attention -
Like Stone -

410   How sick - to wait - in any place - but thine -
I knew last night - when some one tried to twine -
Thinking - perhaps - that I looked tired - or alone -
Or breaking - almost - with unspoken pain -

And I turned - ducal -   5
That right - was thine -
One port - suffices - for a Brig like *mine* -

Our's be the tossing - wild though the sea -
Rather than a mooring - unshared by thee.
Our's be the Cargo - *unladen - here* -   10

Rather than the *"spicy isles -"*
And thou - not there -

411 Mine - by the Right of the White Election!
Mine - by the Royal Seal!
Mine - by the sign in the Scarlet prison -
Bars - cannot conceal!

Mine - here - in Vision - and in Veto!   5
Mine - by the Grave's Repeal -
Titled - Confirmed -
Delirious Charter!
Mine - long as Ages steal!

412 She lay as if at play
Her life had leaped away -
Intending to return -
But not so soon -

Her merry Arms, half dropt -   5
As if for lull of sport -
An instant had forgot
The Trick to start -

Her dancing Eyes - ajar -
As if their Owner were   10
Still sparkling through
For fun - at you -

Her Morning at the door -
Devising, I am sure -
To force her sleep -   15
So light - so deep -

413 Heaven is so far of the Mind
That were the Mind dissolved -
The Site - of it - by Architect
Could not again be proved -

□

'Tis Vast - as our Capacity -   5
As fair - as our idea -
To Him of adequate desire
No further 'tis, than Here -

414   Inconceivably solemn!
      Things so gay
      Pierce - by the very Press
      Of Imagery -

      Their far Parades - order on the eye   5
      With a mute Pomp -
      A pleading Pageantry -

      Flags, are a brave sight -
      But no true Eye
      Ever went by One -   10
      Steadily -

      Music's triumphant -
      But the fine Ear
      Winces with delight
      Are Drums too near -   15

415   More Life - went out - when He went
      Than Ordinary Breath -
      Lit with a finer Phosphor -
      Requiring in the Quench -

      A Power of Renowned Cold,   5
      The Climate of the Grave
      A Temperature just adequate
      So Anthracite, to live -

      For some - an Ampler Zero -
      A Frost more needle keen   10
      Is nescessary, to reduce
      The Ethiop within.

      Others - extinguish easier -
      A Gnat's minutest Fan

Sufficient to obliterate   15
A Tract of Citizen -

Whose Peat life - amply vivid -
Ignores the solemn News
That Popocatapel exists -
Or Etna's Scarlets, Choose -   20

416   The Months have ends - the Years - a knot -
        No Power can untie
        To stretch a little further
        A Skein of Misery -

        The Earth lays back these tired lives   5
        In her mysterious Drawers -
        Too tenderly, that any doubt
        An ultimate Repose -

        The manner of the Children -
        Who weary of the Day -   10
        Themself - the noisy Plaything
        They cannot put away -

417   Removed from Accident of Loss
        By Accident of Gain
        Befalling not my simple Days -
        Myself had just to earn -

        Of Riches - as unconscious   5
        As is the Brown Malay
        Of Pearls in Eastern Waters -
        Marked His - What Holiday

        Would stir his slow conception -
        Had he the power to dream   10
        That but the Dower's fraction -
        Awaited even - Him -

418   Your Riches - taught me - Poverty.
       Myself - a Millionaire
       In little Wealths, as Girls could boast
       Till broad as Buenos Ayre -

       You drifted your Dominions -   5
       A Different Peru -
       And I esteemed all Poverty
       For Life's Estate with you -

       Of Mines, I little know, myself -
       But just the names, of Gems -   10
       The Colors of the Commonest -
       And scarce of Diadems -

       So much, that did I meet the Queen -
       Her Glory I should know -
       But this, must be a different Wealth -   15
       To miss it - beggars so -

       I'm sure 'tis India - all Day -
       To those who look on You -
       Without a stint - without a blame,
       Might I - but be the Jew -   20

       I'm sure it is Golconda -
       Beyond my power to deem -
       To have a smile for mine - each Day,
       How better, than a Gem!

       At least, it solaces to know   25
       That there exists - a Gold -
       Altho' I prove it, just in time
       It's distance - to behold -

       It's far - far Treasure to surmise -
       And estimate the Pearl -   30
       That slipped my simple fingers through -
       While just a Girl at school.

419   A Toad, can die of Light -
       Death is the Common Right

Of Toads and Men -
Of Earl and Midge
The privilege -   5
Why swagger, then?
The Gnat's supremacy is large as Thine -

Life - is a different Thing -
So measure Wine -
Naked of Flask - Naked of Cask -   10
Bare Rhine -
Which Ruby's mine?

420   There are two Ripenings -
       One - of Sight - whose Forces spheric wind
       Until the Velvet Product
       Drop, spicy, to the Ground -

       A Homelier - maturing -   5
       A Process in the Bur -
       That Teeth of Frosts, alone disclose -
       On far October Air -

421   It ceased to hurt me, though so slow
       I could not see the trouble go -
       But only knew by looking back -
       That something - had benumbed the Track -

       Nor when it altered, I could say,   5
       For I had worn it, every day,
       As constant as the Childish frock -
       I hung opon the Peg, at night.

       But not the Grief - that nestled Close
       As Needles - ladies softly press   10
       To Cushions Cheeks -
       To keep their place -

       Nor what consoled it, I could trace -
       Except, whereas 'twas Wilderness -
       It's better - almost Peace -   15

422   Give little Anguish -
Lives will fret -
Give Avalanches -
And they'll slant -
Straighten - look cautious for their Breath -   5
But make no syllable - like Death -
Who only shows his Marble Disc -
Sublimer sort - than Speech -

423   The first Day's Night had come -
And grateful that a thing
So terrible - had been endured -
I told my Soul to sing -

She said her strings were snapt -   5
Her Bow - to atoms blown -
And so to mend her - gave me work
Until another Morn -

And then - a Day as huge
As Yesterdays in pairs,   10
Unrolled it's horror in my face -
Until it blocked my eyes -

My Brain - begun to laugh -
I mumbled - like a fool -
And tho' 'tis Years ago - that Day -   15
My Brain keeps giggling - still.

And Something's odd - within -
That person that I was -
And this One - do not feel the same -
Could it be Madness - this?   20

424   The Color of the Grave is Green -
The Outer Grave - I mean -
You would not know it from the Field -
Except it own a Stone -

□

To help the fond - to find it -   5
Too infinite asleep
To stop and tell them where it is -
But just a Daisy - deep -

The Color of the Grave is white -
The outer Grave - I mean -   10
You would not know it from the Drifts -
In Winter - till the Sun -

Has furrowed out the Aisles -
Then - higher than the Land
The little Dwelling Houses rise   15
Where Each - has left a friend -

The Color of the Grave within -
The Duplicate - I mean -
Not all the snows c'd make it white -
Not all the Summers - Green -   20

You've seen the Color - maybe -
Opon a Bonnet bound -
When that you met it with before -
The Ferret - Cannot find -

425   'Twas like a Maelstrom, with a notch,
        That nearer, every Day,
        Kept narrowing it's boiling Wheel
        Until the Agony

        Toyed coolly with the final inch   5
        Of your delirious Hem -
        And you dropt, lost,
        When something broke -
        And let you from a Dream -

        As if a Goblin with a Guage -   10
        Kept measuring the Hours -
        Until you felt your Second
        Weigh, helpless, in his Paws -

        And not a Sinew - stirred - could help,
        And Sense was setting numb -   15

When God - remembered - and the Fiend
Let go, then, Overcome -

As if your Sentence stood - pronounced -
And you were frozen led
From Dungeon's luxury of Doubt   20
To Gibbets, and the Dead -

And when the Film had stitched your eyes
A Creature gasped "Reprieve"!
Which Anguish was the utterest - then -
To perish, or to live?   25

426   I gave Myself to Him -
       And took Himself, for Pay -
       The solemn contract of a Life
       Was ratified, this way -

       The Wealth might disappoint -   5
       Myself a poorer prove
       Than this great Purchaser suspect,
       The Daily Own - of Love

       Depreciate the Vision -
       But till the Merchant buy -   10
       Still Fable - in the Isles of spice -
       The subtle Cargoes - lie -

       At least - 'tis Mutual - Risk -
       Some - found it - Mutual Gain -
       Sweet Debt of Life - Each Night to owe -   15
       Insolvent - every Noon -

427   Sunset at Night - is natural -
       But Sunset on the Dawn
       Reverses Nature - Master -
       So Midnight's - due - at Noon -

       Eclipses be - predicted -   5
       And Science bows them in -

But do One face us suddenly -
Jehovah's Watch - is wrong -

428   We grow accustomed to the Dark -
        When Light is put away -
        As when the Neighbor holds the Lamp
        To witness her Good bye -

        A Moment - We uncertain step   5
        For newness of the night -
        Then - fit our Vision to the Dark -
        And meet the Road - erect -

        And so of larger - Darknesses -
        Those Evenings of the Brain -   10
        When not a Moon disclose a sign -
        Or Star - come out - within -

        The Bravest - grope a little -
        And sometimes hit a Tree
        Directly in the Forehead -   15
        But as they learn to see -

        Either the Darkness alters -
        Or something in the sight
        Adjusts itself to Midnight -
        And Life steps almost straight.   20

429   You'll know it - as you know 'tis Noon -
        By Glory -
        As you do the Sun -
        By Glory -
        As you will in Heaven -   5
        Know God the Father - and the Son.

        By intuition, Mightiest Things
        Assert themselves - and not by terms -
        "I'm Midnight" - need the Midnight say -
        "I'm Sunrise" - Need the Majesty?   10

                                                         □

Omnipotence - had not a Tongue -
His lisp - is Lightning - and the Sun -
His Conversation - with the Sea -
"How shall you know"?
Consult your Eye! 15

430 A Charm invests a face
Imperfectly beheld -
The Lady dare not lift her Vail
For fear it be dispelled -

But peers beyond her mesh - 5
And wishes - and denies -
Lest Interview - annul a want
That Image - satisfies -

431 If I may have it, when it's dead,
I'll be contented - so -
If just as soon as Breath is out
It shall belong to me -

Until they lock it in the Grave, 5
'Tis Bliss I cannot weigh -
For tho' they lock Thee in the Grave,
Myself - can own the key -

Think of it Lover! I and Thee
Permitted - face to face to be - 10
After a Life - a Death - we'll say -
For Death was That -
And This - is Thee -

I'll tell Thee All - how Bald it grew -
How Midnight felt, at first - to me - 15
How all the Clocks stopped in the World -
And Sunshine pinched me - 'Twas so cold -

Then how the Grief got sleepy - some -
As if my soul were deaf and dumb -

Just making signs - across - to Thee -   20
That this way - thou could'st notice me -

I'll tell you how I tried to keep
A smile, to show you, when this Deep
All Waded - We look back for Play,
At those Old Times - in Calvary.   25

Forgive me, if the Grave come slow -
For Coveting to look at Thee -
Forgive me, if to stroke thy frost
Outvisions Paradise!

432   I read my sentence - steadily -
        Reviewed it with my eyes,
        To see that I made no mistake
        In it's extremest clause -
        The Date, and manner, of the shame -   5
        And then the Pious Form
        That "God have mercy" on the Soul
        The Jury voted Him -
        I made my soul familiar - with her extremity -
        That at the last, it should not be a novel Agony -   10
        But she, and Death, acquainted -
        Meet tranquilly, as friends -
        Salute, and pass, without a Hint -
        And there, the Matter Ends -

433   A Murmur in the Trees - to note -
        Not loud enough - for Wind -
        A star - not far enough to seek -
        Nor near enough - to find -

        A long - long Yellow - on the Lawn -   5
        A Hubbub - as of feet -
        Not audible - as Our's - to us -
        But dapperer - more sweet -

        A Hurrying Home of little Men
        To Houses unperceived -   10

All this - and more - if I should tell -
Would never be believed -

Of Robins in the Trundle bed
How many I espy
Whose Nightgowns could not hide the Wings -   15
Although I heard them try -

But then I promised ne'er to tell -
How could I break My word?
So go your way - and I'll go Mine -
No fear you'll miss the Road.   20

434   It is dead - Find it -
Out of sound - Out of Sight -
"Happy"? Which is wiser -
You, or the Wind?
"Conscious"? Wont you ask that -   5
Of the low Ground?

"Homesick"? Many met it -
Even through them - This cannot testify -
Themself - as dumb -

435   Not in this World to see his face -
Sounds long - until I read the place
Where this - is said to be
But just the Primer - to a life -
Unopened - rare - Opon the Shelf -   5
Clasped yet - to Him - and me -

And yet - My Primer suits me so
I would not choose - a Book to know
Than that - be sweeter wise -
Might some one else - so learned - be -   10
And leave me - just my A - B - C -
Himself - could have the Skies -

436   I found the words to every thought
I ever had - but One -
And that - defies Me -
As a Hand did try to chalk the Sun

To Races - nurtured in the Dark -   5
How would your Own - begin?
Can Blaze be shown in Cochineal -
Or Noon - in Mazarin?

437   I never felt at Home - Below -
And in the Handsome skies
I shall not feel at Home - I know -
I dont like Paradise -

Because it's Sunday - all the time -   5
And Recess - never comes -
And Eden'll be so lonesome
Bright Wednesday Afternoons -

If God could make a visit -
Or ever took a Nap -   10
So not to see us - but they say
Himself - a Telescope

Perennial beholds us -
Myself would run away
From Him - and Holy Ghost - and all -   15
But there's the "Judgment Day"!

438   The Body grows without -
The more convenient way -
That if the Spirit - like to hide
It's Temple stands, alway,

Ajar - secure - inviting -   5
It never did betray
The Soul that asked it's shelter
In solemn honesty

439 I had been hungry, all the Years -
   My Noon had Come - to dine -
   I trembling drew the Table near -
   And touched the Curious Wine -

   'Twas this on Tables I had seen -   5
   When turning, hungry, Home
   I looked in Windows, for the Wealth
   I could not hope - for Mine -

   I did not know the ample Bread -
   'Twas so unlike the Crumb   10
   The Birds and I, had often shared
   In Nature's - Dining Room -

   The Plenty hurt me - 'twas so new -
   Myself felt ill - and odd -
   As Berry - of a Mountain Bush -   15
   Transplanted - to the Road -

   Nor was I hungry - so I found
   That Hunger - was a way
   Of persons Outside Windows -
   The entering - takes away -   20

440 I Years had been from Home
   And now before the Door
   I dared not enter, lest a Face
   I never saw before

   Stare stolid into mine   5
   And ask my Business there -
   "My Business but a Life I left
   Was such remaining there?"

   I leaned opon the Awe -
   I lingered with Before -   10
   The Second like an Ocean rolled
   And broke against my ear -

   I laughed a crumbling Laugh
   That I could fear a Door

Who Consternation compassed   15
And never winced before.

I fitted to the Latch
My Hand, with trembling care
Lest back the awful Door should spring
And leave me in the Floor -   20

Then moved my Fingers off
As cautiously as Glass
And held my ears, and like a Thief
Fled gasping from the House -

441   You'll find - it when you try to die -
The easier to let go -
For recollecting such as went -
You could not spare - you know.

And though their places somewhat filled -   5
As did their Marble names
With Moss - they never grew so full -
You chose the newer names -

And when this World - sets further back -
As Dying - say it does -   10
The former love - distincter grows -
And supersedes the fresh -

And Thought of them - so fair invites -
It looks too tawdry Grace
To stay behind - with just the Toys   15
We bought - to ease their place -

442   I see thee better - in the Dark -
I do not need a Light -
The Love of Thee - a Prism be -
Excelling Violet -

I see thee better for the Years   5
That hunch themselves between -

The Miner's Lamp - sufficient be -
To nullify the Mine -

And in the Grave - I see Thee best -
It's little Panels be   10
A'glow - All ruddy - with the Light
I held so high, for Thee -

What need of Day -
To Those whose Dark - hath so - surpassing Sun -
It deem it be - Continually -   15
At the Meridian?

443   Could - I do more - for Thee -
        Wert Thou a Bumble Bee -
        Since for the Queen, have I -
        Nought but Boquet?

444   It would have starved a Gnat -
        To live so small as I -
        And yet, I was a living child -
        With Food's nescessity

        Opon me - like a Claw -   5
        I could no more remove
        Than I could coax a Leech away -
        Or make a Dragon - move -

        Nor like the Gnat - had I -
        The privilege to fly   10
        And seek a Dinner for myself -
        How mightier He - than I!

        Nor like Himself - the Art
        Opon the Window Pane
        To gad my little Being out -   15
        And not begin - again -

445   They shut me up in Prose -
       As when a little Girl
       They put me in the Closet -
       Because they liked me "still" -

       Still! Could themself have peeped -   5
       And seen my Brain - go round -
       They might as wise have lodged a Bird
       For Treason - in the Pound -

       Himself has but to will
       And easy as a Star   10
       Look down opon Captivity -
       And laugh - No more have I -

446   This was a Poet -
       It is That
       Distills amazing sense
       From Ordinary Meanings -
       And Attar so immense   5

       From the familiar species
       That perished by the Door -
       We wonder it was not Ourselves
       Arrested it - before -

       Of Pictures, the Discloser -   10
       The Poet - it is He -
       Entitles Us - by Contrast -
       To ceaseless Poverty -

       Of Portion - so unconscious -
       The Robbing - could not harm -   15
       Himself - to Him - a Fortune -
       Exterior - to Time -

447   In falling Timbers buried -
       There breathed a Man -
       Outside - the spades - were plying -
       The Lungs - within -

                                                          □

Could He - know - they sought Him -   5
Could They - know - He breathed -
Horrid Sand Partition -
Neither - could be heard -

Never slacked the Diggers -
But when spades had done -   10
Oh, Reward of Anguish,
It was dying - Then -

Many Things - are fruitless -
'Tis a Baffling Earth -
But there is no Gratitude   15
Like the Grace - of Death -

448   I died for Beauty - but was scarce
        Adjusted in the Tomb
        When One who died for Truth, was lain
        In an adjoining Room -

        He questioned softly "Why I failed"?   5
        "For Beauty", I replied -
        "And I - for Truth - Themself are One -
        We Bretheren, are", He said -

        And so, as Kinsmen, met a Night -
        We talked between the Rooms -   10
        Until the Moss had reached our lips -
        And covered up - Our names -

449   Dreams - are well - but Waking's better -
        If One wake at Morn -
        If One wake at Midnight - better -
        Dreaming - of the Dawn -

        Sweeter - the Surmising Robins -   5
        Never gladdened Tree -
        Than a Solid Dawn - confronting -
        Leading to no Day -

450   The Outer - from the Inner
       Derives it's magnitude -
       'Tis Duke, or Dwarf, according
       As is the central mood -

       The fine - unvarying Axis   5
       That regulates the Wheel -
       Though Spokes - spin - more conspicuous
       And fling a dust - the while.

       The Inner - paints the Outer -
       The Brush without the Hand -   10
       It's Picture publishes - precise -
       As is the inner Brand -

       On fine - Arterial Canvas -
       A Cheek - perchance a Brow -
       The Star's whole secret - in the Lake -   15
       Eyes were not meant to know.

451   The Malay - took the Pearl -
       Not - I - the Earl -
       I - feared the Sea - too much
       Unsanctified - to touch -

       Praying that I might be   5
       Worthy - the Destiny -
       The Swarthy fellow swam -
       And bore my Jewel - Home -

       Home to the Hut! What lot
       Had I - the Jewel - got -   10
       Borne on a Dusky Breast -
       I had not deemed a Vest
       Of Amber - fit -

       The Negro never knew
       I - wooed it - too -   15
       To gain, or be undone -
       Alike to Him - One -

452   Love - thou art high -
I cannot climb thee -
But, were it Two -
Who knows but we -
Taking turns - at the Chimborazo -
Ducal - at last - stand up by thee -

Love - thou art deep -
I cannot cross thee -
But, were there Two
Instead of One -   10
Rower, and Yacht - some sovreign Summer -
Who knows - but we'd reach the Sun?

Love - thou art Vailed -
A few - behold thee -
Smile - and alter - and prattle - and die -   15
Bliss - were an Oddity - without thee -
Nicknamed by God -
Eternity -

453   Our journey had advanced -
Our feet were almost come
To that odd Fork in Being's Road -
Eternity - by Term -

Our pace took sudden awe -   5
Our feet - reluctant - led -
Before - were Cities - but Between -
The Forest of the Dead -

Retreat - was out of Hope -
Behind - a Sealed Route -   10
Eternity's White Flag - Before -
And God - at every Gate -

454   I rose - because He sank -
I thought it would be opposite -
But when his power dropped -
My Soul grew straight.

□

.ed my fainting Prince -
ьang firm - even - Chants -
I helped his Film - with Hymn -

And when the Dews drew off
That held his Forehead stiff -
I met him -   10
Balm to Balm -

I told him Best - must pass
Through this low Arch of Flesh -
No Casque so brave
It spurn the Grave -   15

I told him Worlds I knew
Where Emperors grew -
Who recollected us
If we were true -

And so with Thews of Hymn -   20
And Sinew from within -
And ways I knew not that I knew - till then -
I lifted Him -

455   It was given to me by the Gods -
       When I was a little Girl -
       They give us Presents most - you know -
       When we are new - and small.
       I kept it in my Hand -   5
       I never put it down -
       I did not dare to eat - or sleep -
       For fear it would be gone -
       I heard such words as "Rich" -
       When hurrying to school -   10
       From lips at Corners of the Streets -
       And wrestled with a smile.
       Rich! 'Twas Myself - was rich -
       To take the name of Gold -
       And Gold to own - in solid Bars -   15
       The Difference - made me bold -

456   A Prison gets to be a friend -
Between it's Ponderous face
And Our's - a Kinsmanship express -
And in it's narrow Eyes -

We come to look with gratitude   5
For the appointed Beam
It deal us - stated as Our food -
And hungered for - the same -

We learn to know the Planks -
That answer to Our feet -   10
So miserable a sound - at first -
Nor even now - so sweet -

As plashing in the Pools -
When Memory was a Boy -
But a Demurer Circuit -   15
A Geometric Joy -

The Posture of the Key
That interrupt the Day
To Our Endeavor - Not so real
The Cheek of Liberty -   20

As this Phantasm steel -
Whose features - Day and Night -
Are present to us - as Our Own -
And as escapeless - quite -

The narrow Round - the stint -   25
The slow exchange of Hope -
For something passiver - Content
Too steep for looking up -

The Liberty we knew
Avoided - like a Dream -   30
Too wide for any night but Heaven -
If That - indeed - redeem -

457   Nature - sometimes sears a Sapling -
Sometimes - scalps a Tree -

Her Green People recollect it
When they do not die -

Fainter Leaves - to Further Seasons -   5
Dumbly testify -
We - who have the Souls -
Die oftener - Not so vitally -

458   She dealt her pretty words like Blades -
How glittering they shone -
And every One unbared a Nerve
Or wantoned with a Bone -

She never deemed - she hurt -   5
That - is not Steel's Affair -
A vulgar grimace in the Flesh -
How ill the Creatures bear -

To Ache is human - not polite -
The Film opon the eye   10
Mortality's old Custom -
Just locking up - to Die -

459   "Why do I love" You, Sir?
Because -
The Wind does not require the Grass
To answer - Wherefore when He pass
She cannot keep Her place.   5

Because He knows - and
Do not You -
And We know not -
Enough for Us
The Wisdom it be so -   10

The Lightning - never asked an Eye
Wherefore it shut - when He was by -
Because He knows it cannot speak -
And reasons not contained - Of Talk -
There be - preferred by Daintier Folk -   15

The Sunrise - Sir - compelleth Me -
Because He's Sunrise - and I see -
Therefore - Then -
I love Thee -

460   The Himmaleh was known to stoop
       Unto the Daisy low -
       Transported with Compassion
       That such a Doll should grow
       Where Tent by Tent - Her Universe   5
       Hung Out it's Flags of Snow -

461   We Cover Thee - Sweet Face -
       Not that We tire of Thee -
       But that Thyself fatigue of Us -
       Remember - as Thou go -
       We follow Thee until   5
       Thou notice Us - no more -
       And then - reluctant - turn away
       To Con Thee o'er and o'er -

       And blame the scanty love
       We were Content to show -   10
       Augmented - Sweet - a Hundred fold -
       If Thou would'st take it - now -

462   Of Being is a Bird
       The likest to the Down
       An Easy Breeze do put afloat
       The General Heavens - opon -

       It soars - and shifts - and whirls -   5
       And measures with the Clouds
       In easy - even - dazzling pace -
       No different the Birds -

       Except a Wake of Music
       Accompany their feet -   10

As did the Down emit a Tune -
For Extasy - of it

463   A long - long Sleep -
A famous - Sleep -
That makes no show for Morn -
By Stretch of Limb - or stir of Lid -
An independent One -   5

Was ever idleness like This?
Opon a Bank of Stone
To bask the Centuries away -
Nor once look up - for Noon?

464   Without this - there is nought -
All other Riches be
As is the Twitter of a Bird -
Heard opposite the Sea -

I could not care - to gain   5
A lesser than the Whole -
For did not this include themself -
As Seams - include the Ball?

Or wished a way might be
My Heart to subdivide -   10
'Twould magnify - the Gratitude -
And not reduce - the Gold -

465   The name - of it - is "Autumn" -
The hue - of it - is Blood -
An Artery - opon the Hill -
A Vein - along the Road -

Great Globules - in the Alleys -   5
And Oh, the Shower of Stain -
When Winds - upset the Basin -
And spill the Scarlet Rain -

□

It sprinkles Bonnets - far below -
It gathers ruddy Pools -
Then - eddies like a Rose - away -
Opon Vermillion Wheels -

10

466   I dwell in Possibility -
A fairer House than Prose -
More numerous of Windows -
Superior - for Doors -

Of Chambers as the Cedars -
Impregnable of eye -
And for an everlasting Roof
The Gambrels of the Sky -

5

Of Visitors - the fairest -
For Occupation - This -
The spreading wide my narrow Hands
To gather Paradise -

10

467   A Solemn thing within the Soul
To feel itself get ripe -
And golden hang - while farther up -
The Maker's Ladders stop -
And in the Orchard far below -
You hear a Being - drop -

5

A wonderful - to feel the sun
Still toiling at the cheek
You thought was finished -
Cool of eye, and critical of Work -
He shifts the stem - a little -
To give your Core - a look -

10

But solemnest - to know
Your chance in Harvest moves
A little nearer - Every sun
The single - to some lives.

15

468   Whole Gulfs - of Red, and Fleets - of Red -
       And Crews - of solid Blood -
       Did place about the West - Tonight -
       As 'twere specific Ground -

       And They - appointed Creatures -   5
       In Authorized Arrays -
       Due - promptly - as a Drama -
       That bows - and disappears -

469   My Garden - like the Beach -
       Denotes there be - a Sea -
       That's Summer -
       Such as These - the Pearls
       She fetches - such as Me   5

470   That first Day, when you praised Me, Sweet,
       And said that I was strong -
       And could be mighty, if I liked -
       That Day - the Days among -

       Glows central - like a Jewel   5
       Between Diverging Golds -
       The Minor One - that gleamed behind -
       And Vaster - of the World's.

471   To make One's Toilette - after Death
       Has made the Toilette cool
       Of only Taste we cared to please
       Is difficult, and still -

       That's easier - than Braid the Hair -   5
       And make the Boddice gay -
       When Eyes that fondled it are wrenched
       By Decalogues - away -

472 'Tis good - the looking back on Grief -
   To re-endure a Day -
   We thought the mighty Funeral -
   Of all conceived Joy -

   To recollect how Busy Grass   5
   Did meddle - one by one -
   Till all the Grief with Summer - waved
   And none could see the stone.

   And though the Wo you have Today
   Be larger - As the Sea   10
   Exceeds it's unremembered Drop -
   They're Water - equally -

473 I was the slightest in the House -
   I took the smallest Room -
   At night, my little Lamp, and Book -
   And one Geranium -

   So stationed I could catch the mint   5
   That never ceased to fall -
   And just my Basket -
   Let me think - I'm sure
   That this was all -

   I never spoke - unless addressed -   10
   And then, 'twas brief and low -
   I could not bear to live - aloud -
   The Racket shamed me so -

   And if it had not been so far -
   And any one I knew   15
   Were going - I had often thought
   How noteless - I could die -

474 You love the Lord - you cannot see -
   You write Him - every day -
   A little note - when you awake -
   And further in the Day,

                □

An Ample Letter - How you miss -   5
And would delight to see -
But then His House - is but a step -
And mine's - in Heaven - You see -

475   Myself was formed - a Carpenter -
       An unpretending time
       My Plane, and I, together wrought
       Before a Builder came -

       To measure our attainments -   5
       Had we the Art of Boards
       Sufficiently developed - He'd hire us
       At Halves -

       My Tools took Human - Faces -
       The Bench, where we had toiled -   10
       Against the Man, persuaded -
       We - Temples build - I said -

476   We pray - to Heaven -
       We prate - of Heaven -
       Relate - when Neighbors die -
       At what o'clock to Heaven - they fled -
       Who saw them - Wherefore fly?   5

       Is Heaven a Place - a Sky - a Tree?
       Location's narrow way is for Ourselves -
       Unto the Dead
       There's no Geography -

       But State - Endowal - Focus -   10
       Where - Omnipresence - fly?

477   He fumbles at your Soul
       As Players at the Keys -
       Before they drop full Music on -
       He stuns you by Degrees -

                                                                    □

Prepares your brittle nature
For the etherial Blow
By fainter Hammers - further heard -
Then nearer - Then so - slow -

Your Breath - has time to straighten -
Your Brain - to bubble cool -
Deals One - imperial Thunderbolt -
That scalps your naked soul -

When Winds hold Forests in their Paws -
The Universe - is still -

478   Just Once! Oh least Request!
Could Adamant refuse
So small a Grace
So scanty put,
Such agonizing terms?
Would not a God of Flint
Be conscious of a sigh
As down His Heaven dropt remote
"Just Once" Sweet Deity?

479   Because I could not stop for Death -
He kindly stopped for me -
The Carriage held but just Ourselves -
And Immortality.

We slowly drove - He knew no haste
And I had put away
My labor and my leisure too,
For His Civility -

We passed the School, where Children strove
At Recess - in the Ring -
We passed the Fields of Gazing Grain -
We passed the Setting Sun -

Or rather - He passed Us -
The Dews drew quivering and Chill -

For only Gossamer, my Gown -
My Tippet - only Tulle -

We paused before a House that seemed
A Swelling of the Ground -
The Roof was scarcely visible -
The Cornice - in the Ground -

Since then - 'tis Centuries - and yet
Feels shorter than the Day
I first surmised the Horses' Heads
Were toward Eternity -

15

20

480   He fought like those Who've nought to lose -
Bestowed Himself to Balls
As One who for a further Life
Had not a further Use -

Invited Death - with bold attempt -
But Death was Coy of Him
As Other Men, were Coy of Death.
To Him - to live - was Doom -

His Comrades, shifted like the Flakes
When Gusts reverse the Snow -
But He - was left alive Because
Of Greediness to die -

5

10

481   Fame of Myself, to justify,
All other Plaudit be
Superfluous - An Incense
Beyond Nescessity -

Fame of Myself to lack - Although
My Name be else supreme -
This were an Honor honorless -
A futile Diadem -

5

482 Wolfe demanded during dying
  "Which obtain the Day"?
  "General, the British" - "Easy"
  Answered Wolfe "to die"

  Montcalm, his opposing Spirit   5
  Rendered with a smile
  "Sweet" said he "my own Surrender
  Liberty's beguile"

483 Most she touched me by her muteness -
  Most she won me by the way
  She presented her small figure -
  Plea itself - for Charity -

  Were a Crumb my whole possession -   5
  Were there famine in the land -
  Were it my resource from starving -
  Could I such a plea withstand -

  Not opon her knee to thank me
  Sank this Beggar from the Sky -   10
  But the Crumb partook - departed -
  And returned on High -

  I supposed - when sudden
  Such a Praise began
  'Twas as Space sat singing   15
  To herself - and men -

  'Twas the Winged Beggar -
  Afterward I learned
  To her Benefactor
  Making Gratitude   20

484 From Blank to Blank -
  A Threadless Way
  I pushed Mechanic feet -
  To stop - or perish - or advance -
  Alike indifferent -   5

            ☐

If end I gained
It ends beyond
Indefinite disclosed -
I shut my eyes - and groped as well
'Twas lighter - to be Blind -   10

485   The Whole of it came not at once -
        'Twas Murder by degrees -
        A Thrust - and then for Life a chance -
        The Bliss to cauterize -

        The Cat reprieves the mouse   5
        She eases from her teeth
        Just long enough for Hope to teaze -
        Then mashes it to death -

        'Tis Life's award - to die -
        Contenteder if once -   10
        Than dying half - then rallying
        For consciouser Eclipse -

486   He told a homely tale
        And spotted it with tears -
        Opon his infant face was set
        The Cicatrice of years -

        All crumpled was the cheek   5
        No other kiss had known
        Than flake of snow, divided with
        The Redbreast of the Barn -

        If Mother - in the Grave -
        Or Father - on the Sea -   10
        Or Father in the Firmament -
        Or Bretheren, had he -

        If Commonwealth below,
        Or Commonwealth above
        Have missed a Barefoot Citizen -   15
        I've ransomed it - alive -

487   Presentiment - is that long shadow - on the Lawn -
        Indicative that Suns go down -

        The notice to the startled Grass
        That Darkness - is about to pass -

488   You constituted Time -
        I deemed Eternity
        A Revelation of Yourself -
        'Twas therefore Deity

        The Absolute - removed   5
        The Relative away -
        That I unto Himself adjust
        My slow idolatry -

489   My Faith is larger than the Hills -
        So when the Hills decay -
        My Faith must take the Purple Wheel
        To show the Sun the way -

        'Tis first He steps opon the Vane -   5
        And then - opon the Hill -
        And then abroad the World He go
        To do His Golden Will -

        And if His Yellow feet should miss -
        The Bird would not arise -   10
        The Flowers would slumber on their Stems -
        No Bells have Paradise -

        How dare I, therefore, stint a faith
        On which so vast depends -
        Lest Firmament should fail for me -   15
        The Rivet in the Bands

490   Rests at Night
        The Sun from shining,
        Nature - and some Men -

Rest at Noon - some Men -
While Nature
And the Sun - go on -   5

491   The World - feels Dusty
        When We stop to Die -
        We want the Dew - then -
        Honors - taste dry -

        Flags - vex a Dying face -   5
        But the least Fan
        Stirred by a friend's Hand -
        Cools - like the Rain -

        Mine be the Ministry
        When thy Thirst comes -   10
        Dews of Thessaly, to fetch -
        And Hybla Balms -

492   To offer brave assistance
        To Lives that stand alone -
        When One has failed to stop them -
        Is Human - but Divine

        To lend an ample Sinew   5
        Unto a Nameless Man -
        Whose Homely Benediction
        No other - stopped to earn -

493   When I hoped, I recollect
        Just the place I stood -
        At a Window facing West -
        Roughest Air - was good -

        Not a Sleet could bite me -   5
        Not a frost could cool -
        Hope it was that kept me warm -
        Not Merino shawl -

                                                         □

When I feared - I recollect
Just the Day it was -   10
Worlds were lying out to Sun -
Yet how Nature froze -

Icicles opon my soul
Prickled Blue and cool -
Bird went praising everywhere -   15
Only Me - was still -

And the Day that I despaired -
This - if I forget
Nature will - that it be Night
After Sun has set -   20
Darkness intersect her face -
And put out her eye -
Nature hesitate - before
Memory and I -

494   The Wind did'nt come from the Orchard - today -
         Further than that -
         Nor stop to play with the Hay -
         Nor threaten a Hat -
         He's a transitive fellow - very -   5
         Rely on that -

         If He leave a Bur at the door
         We know He has climbed a Fir -
         But the Fir is Where - Declare -
         Were you ever there?   10

         If He bring Odors of Clovers -
         And that is His business - not Our's -
         Then He has been with the Mowers -
         Whetting away the Hours
         To sweet pauses of Hay -   15
         His Way - of a June Day -

         If He fling Sand, and Pebble -
         Little Boy's Hats - and stubble -
         With an occasional steeple -
         And a hoarse "Get out of the Way, I say",   20

Who'd be the fool to stay?
Would you - Say -
Would you be the fool to stay?

495   The Day undressed - Herself -
       Her Garter - was of Gold -
       Her Petticoat of Purple - plain -
       Her Dimities as old

       Exactly - as the World   5
       And yet the newest Star
       Enrolled opon the Hemisphere -
       Be wrinkled - much as Her -

       Too near to God - to pray -
       Too near to Heaven - to fear -   10
       The Lady of the Occident
       Retired without a Care -

       Her Candle so expire
       The Flickering be seen
       On Ball of Mast - in Bosporus -   15
       And Dome - and Window Pane.

496   The Beggar Lad - dies early -
       It's Somewhat in the Cold -
       And somewhat in the Trudging feet -
       And haply, in the World -

       The Cruel - smiling - bowing World -   5
       That took it's Cambric Way -
       Nor heard the timid cry for "Bread -"
       "Sweet Lady - Charity" -

       Among Redeemed Children
       If Trudging feet may stand -   10
       The Barefoot time forgotten - so -
       The Sleet - the bitter Wind -

       The Childish Hands that teazed for Pence
       Lifted adoring - then -

To Him whom never Ragged - Coat
Did supplicate in vain -

497   One and One - are One -
Two - be finished using -
Well enough for schools -
But for minor Choosing -

Life - just - Or Death -
Or the Everlasting -
More - would be too vast
For the Soul's Comprising -

498   I lived on Dread -
To Those who know
The stimulus there is
In Danger - Other impetus
Is numb - and vitalless -

As 'twere a Spur - opon the Soul -
A Fear will urge it where
To go without the spectre's aid
Were challenging Despair.

499 Best Gains - must have the Losses' test -
   To constitute them - Gains.

500 Not "Revelation" - 'tis - that waits,
   But our unfurnished eyes -

501 The Robin is the One
   That interrupt the Morn
   With hurried - few - express Reports
   When March is scarcely on -

   The Robin is the One   5
   That overflow the Noon
   With her cherubic quantity -
   An April but begun -

   The Robin is the One
   That speechless from her Nest   10
   Submit that Home - and Certainty
   And Sanctity, are best

502 Life is death we're lengthy at,
   Death the hinge to life.

503 We'll pass without the parting
   So to spare
   Certificate of Absence -
   Deeming where

   I left Her I could find Her   5
   If I tried -
   This way, I keep from missing
   Those that died.

504   The Birds begun at Four o'clock -
Their period for Dawn -
A Music numerous as space -
But neighboring as Noon -

I could not count their Force -   5
Their numbers did expend
As Brook by Brook bestows itself
To multiply the Pond.

The Listener - was not -
Except Occasional Man -   10
In homely industry arrayed -
To overtake the Morn -

Nor was it for applause -
That I could ascertain -
But independent Extasy   15
Of Universe, and Men -

By Six, the Flood had done -
No tumult there had been
Of Dressing, or Departure -
Yet all the Band - was gone -   20

The Sun engrossed the East -
The Day Resumed the World -
The Miracle that introduced
Forgotten, as fulfilled.

505   They have a little Odor - that to me
Is metre - nay - 'tis Poesy -
And spiciest at fading - celebrate -
A Habit - of a Laureate -

506   Light is sufficient to itself -
If Others want to see
It can be had on Window Panes
Some Hours in the Day.

□

But not for compensation -
It holds as large a Glow
To Squirrel in the Himmaleh
Precisely, as to you.

507   Like Mighty Foot Lights - burned the Red
At Bases of the Trees -
The far Theatricals of Day
Exhibiting - to These -

'Twas Universe - that did applaud -
While Chiefest - of the Crowd -
Enabled by his Royal Dress -
Myself distinguished God -

508   A Pit - but Heaven over it -
And Heaven beside, and Heaven abroad;
And yet a Pit -
With Heaven over it.

To stir would be to slip -
To look would be to drop -
To dream - to sap the Prop
That holds my chances up.
Ah! Pit! With Heaven over it!

The depth is all my thought -
I dare not ask my feet -
'Twould start us where we sit
So straight you'd scarce suspect
It was a Pit - with fathoms under it
It's Circuit just the same
Whose Doom to whom
'Twould start them -
We - could tremble -
But since we got a Bomb -
And held it in our Bosom -
Nay - Hold it - it is calm -

509 A curious Cloud surprised the Sky,
   'Twas like a sheet with Horns;
   The sheet was Blue -
   The Antlers Gray -
   It almost touched the Lawns.   5

   So low it leaned - then statelier drew -
   And trailed like robes away;
   A Queen adown a satin aisle,
   Had not the majesty.

510 Of Brussels - it was not -
   Of Kidderminster? Nay -
   The Winds did buy it of the Woods -
   They - sold it unto me

   It was a gentle price -   5
   The poorest - could afford -
   It was within the frugal purse
   Of Beggar - or of Bird -

   Of small and spicy Yards -
   In hue - a mellow Dun -   10
   Of Sunshine - and of Sere - Composed -
   But, principally - of Sun -

   The Wind - unrolled it fast -
   And spread it on the Ground -
   Upholsterer of the Pines - is He -   15
   Upholsterer - of the Pond -

511 He found my Being - set it up -
   Adjusted it to place -
   Then carved his name - opon it -
   And bade it to the East

   Be faithful - in his absence -   5
   And he would come again -
   With Equipage of Amber -
   That time - to take it Home -

512   Unto my Books - so good to turn -
Far ends of tired Days -
It half endears the Abstinence -
And Pain - is missed - in Praise.

As Flavors - cheer Retarded Guests   5
With Banquettings to be -
So Spices - stimulate the time
Till my small Library -

It may be Wilderness - without -
Far feet of failing Men -   10
But Holiday - excludes the night -
And it is Bells - within -

I thank these Kinsmen of the Shelf -
Their Countenances Kid
Enamor - in Prospective -   15
And satisfy - obtained -

513   The Spider holds a Silver Ball
In unperceived Hands -
And dancing softly to Himself
His Yarn of Pearl - unwinds -

He plies from nought to nought -   5
In unsubstantial Trade -
Supplants our Tapestries with His -
In half the period -

An Hour to rear supreme
His Continents of Light -
Then dangle from the Housewife's Broom -   10
His Boundaries - forgot -

514   Three times - we parted - Breath - and I -
Three times - He would not go -
But strove to stir the lifeless Fan
The Waters - strove to stay.

□

Three times - the Billows threw me up -   5
Then caught me - like a Ball -
Then made Blue faces in my face -
And pushed away a sail

That crawled Leagues off - I liked to see -
For thinking - While I die -   10
How pleasant to behold a Thing
Where Human faces - be -

The Waves grew sleepy - Breath - did not -
The Winds - like Children - lulled -
Then Sunrise kissed my Chrysalis -   15
And I stood up - and lived -

515   There is a pain - so utter -
        It swallows substance up -
        Then covers the Abyss with Trance -
        So Memory can step
        Around - across - opon it -   5
        As One within a Swoon -
        Goes safely - where an open eye -
        Would drop Him - Bone by Bone -

516   It troubled me as once I was -
        For I was once a Child -
        Concluding how an atom - fell -
        And yet the Heavens - held -

        The Heavens weighed the most - by far -   5
        Yet Blue - and solid - stood -
        Without a Bolt - that I could prove -
        Would Giants - understand?

        Life set me larger - problems -
        Some I shall keep - to solve   10
        Till Algebra is easier -
        Or simpler proved - above -

                                                            □

Then - too - be comprehended -
What sorer - puzzled me -
Why Heaven did not break away -
And tumble - Blue - on me -   15

517   A still - Volcano - Life -
       That flickered in the night -
       When it was dark enough to do
       Without erasing sight -

       A quiet - Earthquake style -   5
       Too subtle to suspect
       By natures this side Naples -
       The North cannot detect

       The solemn - Torrid - Symbol -
       The lips that never lie -   10
       Whose hissing Corals part - and shut -
       And Cities - ooze away -

518   When I was small, a Woman died -
       Today - her Only Boy
       Went up from the Potomac -
       His face all Victory

       To look at her - How slowly   5
       The Seasons must have turned
       Till Bullets clipt an Angle
       And He passed quickly round -

       If pride shall be in Paradise -
       Ourself cannot decide -   10
       Of their imperial conduct -
       No person testified -

       But, proud in Apparition -
       That Woman and her Boy
       Pass back and forth, before my Brain   15
       As even in the sky -

                                                      □

I'm confident, that Bravoes -
Perpetual break abroad
For Braveries, remote as this
In Yonder Maryland -   20

519   This is my letter to the World
       That never wrote to Me -
       The simple News that Nature told -
       With tender Majesty

       Her Message is committed   5
       To Hands I cannot see -
       For love of Her - Sweet - countrymen -
       Judge tenderly - of Me

520   God made a little Gentian -
       It tried - to be a Rose -
       And failed - and all the Summer laughed -
       But just before the Snows

       There rose a Purple Creature -   5
       That ravished all the Hill -
       And Summer hid her Forehead -
       And Mockery - was still -

       The Frosts were her condition -
       The Tyrian would not come   10
       Until the North - invoke it -
       Creator - Shall I - bloom?

521   It always felt to me - a wrong
       To that Old Moses - done -
       To let him see - the Canaan -
       Without the entering -

       And tho' in soberer moments -   5
       No Moses there can be
       I'm satisfied - the Romance
       In point of injury -

                                                          □

Surpasses sharper stated -
Of Stephen - or of Paul -   10
For these - were only put to death -
While God's adroiter will

On Moses - seemed to fasten
With tantalizing Play
As Boy - should deal with lesser Boy -   15
To prove ability -

The fault - was doubtless Israel's -
Myself - had banned the Tribes -
And ushered Grand Old Moses
In Pentateuchal Robes   20

Opon the Broad Possession
'Twas little - He should see -
Old Man on Nebo! Late as this -
My justice bleeds - for Thee!

522   I tie my Hat - I crease my Shawl -
Life's little duties do - precisely -
As the very least
Were infinite - to me -

I put new Blossoms in the Glass -   5
And throw the Old - away -
I push a petal from my Gown
That anchored there - I weigh
The time 'twill be till six o'clock -
So much I have to do -   10
And yet - existence - some way back -
Stopped - struck - my ticking - through -

We cannot put Ourself away
As a completed Man
Or Woman - When the errand's done   15
We came to Flesh - opon -
There may be - Miles on Miles of Nought -
Of Action - sicker far -
To simulate - is stinging work -
To cover what we are   20

From Science - and from Surgery -
Too Telescopic eyes
To bear on us unshaded -
For their - sake - Not for Our's -

Therefore - we do life's labor -   25
Though life's Reward - be done -
With scrupulous exactness -
To hold our Senses - on -

523   The Trees like Tassels - hit - and swung -
There seemed to rise a Tune
From Miniature Creatures
Accompanying the Sun -

Far Psalteries of Summer -   5
Enamoring the Ear
They never yet did satisfy -
Remotest - when most fair

The Sun shone whole at intervals -
Then Half - then utter hid -   10
As if Himself were optional
And had Estates of Cloud

Sufficient to enfold Him
Eternally from view -
Except it were a whim of His   15
To let the Orchards grow -

A Bird sat careless on the fence -
One gossipped in the Lane
On silver matters charmed a Snake
Just winding round a stone -   20

Bright Flowers slit a Calyx
And soared opon a stem
Like Hindered Flags - Sweet hoisted -
With Spices - in the Hem -

'Twas more - I cannot mention -   25
How mean - to those that see -

Vandyke's Delineation
Of Nature's - Summer Day!

524   It feels a shame to be Alive -
When Men so brave - are dead -
One envies the Distinguished Dust -
Permitted - such a Head -

The Stone - that tells defending Whom   5
This Spartan put away
What little of Him we - possessed
In Pawn for Liberty -

The price is great - Sublimely paid -
Do we deserve - a Thing -   10
That lives - like Dollars - must be piled
Before we may obtain?

Are we that wait - sufficient worth -
That such Enormous Pearl
As life - dissolved be - for Us -   15
In Battle's - horrid Bowl?

It may be - a Renown to live -
I think the Men who die -
Those unsustained - Saviors -
Present Divinity -   20

525   My period had come for Prayer -
No other Art - would do -
My Tactics missed a rudiment -
Creator - Was it you?

God grows above - so those who pray   5
Horizons - must ascend -
And so I stepped opon the North
To see this Curious Friend -

His House was not - no sign had He -
By Chimney - nor by Door -   10

Could I infer his Residence -
Vast Prairies of Air

Unbroken by a Settler -
Were all that I could see -
Infinitude - Had'st Thou no Face   15
That I might look on Thee?

The Silence condescended -
Creation stopped - for me -
But awed beyond my errand -
I worshipped - did not "pray" -   20

526   I pay - in Satin Cash -
        You did not state - your price -
        A Petal, for a Paragraph
        Is near as I can guess -

527   One Anguish - in a Crowd -
        A minor thing - it sounds -
        And yet, unto the single Doe
        Attempted - of the Hounds

        'Tis Terror as consummate   5
        As Legions of Alarm
        Did leap, full flanked, opon the Host -
        'Tis Units - make the Swarm -

        A small Leech - on the Vitals -
        The sliver, in the Lung -   10
        The Bung out - of an Artery -
        Are scarce accounted - Harms -

        Yet mighty - by relation
        To that Repealless thing -
        A Being - impotent to end -   15
        When once it has begun -

528   'Tis not that Dying hurts us so -
      'Tis Living - hurts us more -
      But Dying - is a different way -
      A kind behind the Door -

      The Southern Custom - of the Bird -   5
      That ere the Frosts are due -
      Accepts a better Latitude -
      We - are the Birds - that stay.

      The Shiverers round Farmer's doors -
      For whose reluctant Crumb -   10
      We stipulate - till pitying Snows
      Persuade our Feathers Home

529   A Dying Tiger - moaned for Drink -
      I hunted all the Sand -
      I caught the Dripping of a Rock
      And bore it in my Hand -

      His mighty Balls - in death were thick -   5
      But searching - I could see
      A Vision on the Retina
      Of Water - and of me -

      'Twas not my blame - who sped too slow -
      'Twas not his blame - who died   10
      While I was reaching him -
      But 'twas - the fact that He was dead -

530   He gave away his Life -
      To Us - Gigantic Sum -
      A trifle - in his own esteem -
      But magnified - by Fame -

      Until it burst the Hearts   5
      That fancied they could hold -
      When swift it slipped it's limit -
      And on the Heavens - unrolled -

                                                            □

'Tis Our's - to wince - and weep -
And wonder - and decay 10
By Blossom's gradual process -
He chose - Maturity -

And quickening - as we sowed -
Just obviated Bud -
And when We turned to note the Growth - 15
Broke - perfect - from the Pod -

531 We learned the Whole of Love -
The Alphabet - the Words -
A Chapter - then the mighty Book -
Then - Revelation closed -

But in each Other's eyes 5
An Ignorance beheld -
Diviner than the Childhood's
And each to each, a Child -

Attempted to expound
What neither - understood - 10
Alas, that Wisdom is so large -
And Truth - so manifold!

532 The Winters are so short -
I'm hardly justified
In sending all the Birds away -
And moving into Pod -

Myself - for scarcely settled - 5
The Phebes have begun -
And then - it's time to strike my Tent -
And open House - again -

It's mostly, interruptions -
My Summer - is despoiled - 10
Because there was a Winter - once -
And all the Cattle - starved -

□

And so there was a Deluge -
And swept the World away -
But Ararat's a Legend - now -   15
And no one credits Noah -

533   I reckon - When I count at all -
First - Poets - Then the Sun -
Then Summer - Then the Heaven of God -
And then - the List is done -

But, looking back - the First so seems   5
To Comprehend the Whole -
The Others look a needless Show -
So I write - Poets - All -

Their Summer - lasts a solid Year -
They can afford a Sun   10
The East - would deem extravagant -
And if the Further Heaven -

Be Beautiful as they prepare
For Those who worship Them -
It is too difficult a Grace -   15
To justify the Dream -

534   How many Flowers fail in Wood -
Or perish from the Hill -
Without the privilege to know
That they are Beautiful -

How many cast a nameless Pod   5
Opon the nearest Breeze -
Unconscious of the Scarlet Freight -
It bear to other eyes -

535   It might be lonelier
Without the Loneliness -
I'm so accustomed to my Fate -
Perhaps the Other - Peace -

□

Would interrupt the Dark -   5
And crowd the little Room -
Too scant - by Cubits - to contain
The Sacrament - of Him -

I am not used to Hope -
It might intrude opon -   10
It's sweet parade - blaspheme the place -
Ordained to Suffering -

It might be easier
To fail - with Land in Sight -
Than gain - my Blue Peninsula -   15
To perish - of Delight -

536   Some - Work for Immortality -
       The Chiefer part, for Time -
       He - Compensates - immediately -
       The former - Checks - on Fame -

       Slow Gold - but Everlasting -   5
       The Bullion of Today -
       Contrasted with the Currency
       Of Immortality -

       A Beggar - Here and There -
       Is gifted to discern   10
       Beyond the Broker's insight -
       One's - Money - One's - the Mine -

537   I could die - to know -
       'Tis a trifling knowledge -
       News-Boys salute the Door -
       Carts - joggle by -
       Morning's bold face - stares in the window -   5
       Were but mine - the Charter of the least Fly -

       Houses hunch the House
       With their Brick shoulders -
       Coals - from a Rolling Load - rattle - how - near -

To the very Square - His foot is passing -   10
Possibly, this moment -
While I - dream - Here -

538   Must be a Wo -
        A loss or so -
        To bend the eye
        Best Beauty's way -

        But - once aslant   5
        It notes Delight
        As difficult
        As Stalactite -

        A Common Bliss
        Were had for less -   10
        The price - is
        Even as the Grace -

        Our Lord - thought no
        Extravagance
        To pay - a Cross -   15

539   Delight - becomes pictorial -
        When viewed through Pain -
        More fair - because impossible
        That any gain -

        The Mountain - at a given distance -   5
        In Amber - lies -
        Approached - the Amber flits - a little -
        And That's - the Skies -

540   If What we could - were what we would -
        Criterion - be small -
        It is the Ultimate of Talk -
        The Impotence to Tell -

541   The Test of Love - is Death -
           Our Lord - "so loved" - it saith -
           What Largest Lover - hath -
           Another - doth -

           If Smaller Patience - be -   5
           Through less Infinity -
           If Bravo, sometimes swerve -
           Through fainter Nerve -

           Accept it's Most -
           And overlook - the Dust -   10
           Last - Least -
           The Cross' - Request -

542   For Largest Woman's Heart I knew -
           'Tis little I can do -
           And yet the Largest Woman's Heart
           Can hold an Arrow, too,
           And so, instructed by my own -   5
           I tenderer - turn me to -

543   Unit, like Death, for Whom?
           True, like the Tomb,
           Who tells no secret
           Told to Him -
           The Grave is strict -   5
           Tickets admit
           Just two - the Bearer - and the Borne -
           And seat - just One -
           The Living - tell -
           The Dying - but a syllable -   10
           The Coy Dead - None -
           No Chatter - here - No Tea -
           So Babbler, and Bohea - stay there -
           But Gravity - and Expectation - and Fear -
           A tremor just, that all's not sure.   15

544   "Heaven" has different Signs - to me -
Sometimes, I think that Noon
Is but a symbol of the Place -
And when again, at Dawn,

A mighty look runs round the World   5
And settles in the Hills -
An Awe if it should be like that
Opon the Ignorance steals -

The Orchard, when the Sun is on -
The Triumph of the Birds   10
When they together Victory make -
Some Carnivals of Clouds -

The Rapture of a finished Day
Returning to the West -
All these - remind us of the place   15
That Men call "Paradise" -

Itself be fairer - we suppose -
But how Ourself, shall be
Adorned, for a Superior Grace -
Not yet, our eyes can see -   20

545   They dropped like Flakes -
They dropped like stars -
Like Petals from a Rose -
When suddenly across the June
A Wind with fingers - goes -   5

They perished in the seamless Grass -
No eye could find the place -
But God can summon every face
On his Repealless - List.

546   I prayed, at first, a little Girl,
Because they told me to -
But stopped, when qualified to guess
How prayer would feel - to me -

□

If I believed God looked around,
Each time my Childish eye
Fixed full, and steady, on his own
In Childish honesty -

And told him what I'd like, today,
And parts of his far plan
That baffled me -
The mingled side
Of his Divinity -

And often since, in Danger,
I count the force 'twould be
To have a God so strong as that
To hold my life for me

Till I could take the Balance
That tips so frequent, now,
It takes me all the while to poise -
And then - it does'nt stay -

547   There's been a Death, in the Opposite House,
As lately as Today -
I know it, by the numb look
Such Houses have - alway -

The Neighbors rustle in and out -
The Doctor - drives away -
A Window opens like a Pod -
Abrupt - mechanically -

Somebody flings a Mattrass out -
The Children hurry by -
They wonder if it died - on that -
I used to - when a Boy -

The Minister - goes stiffly in -
As if the House were His -
And He owned all the Mourners - now -
And little Boys - besides.

□

And then the Milliner - and the Man
Of the Appalling Trade -
To take the measure of the House -

There'll be that Dark Parade -   20

Of Tassels - and of Coaches - soon -
It's easy as a Sign -
The Intuition of the News -
In just a Country Town -

548   The Black Berry - wears a Thorn in his side -
        But no Man heard Him cry -
        He offers His Berry, just the same
        To Partridge - and to Boy -

        He sometimes holds opon the Fence -   5
        Or struggles to a Tree -
        Or clasps a Rock, with both His Hands -
        But not for sympathy -

        We - tell a Hurt - to cool it -
        This Mourner - to the Sky   10
        A little further reaches - instead -
        Brave Black Berry -

549   The One that could repeat the Summer Day -
        Were Greater than Itself - though He -
        Minutest of Mankind - should be -

        And He - could reproduce the Sun -
        At Period of Going down -   5
        The Lingering - and the Stain - I mean -

        When Orient - have been outgrown -
        And Occident - become Unknown -
        His Name - Remain -

550   I measure every Grief I meet
        With narrow, probing, eyes -

I wonder if It weighs like Mine -
Or has an Easier size -

I wonder if They bore it long -
Or did it just begin -
I could not tell the Date of Mine -
It feels so old a pain -

I wonder if it hurts to live -
And if They have to try -
And whether - could They choose between -
It would not be - to die -

I note that Some - gone patient long -
At length, renew their smile -
An imitation of a Light
That has so little Oil -

I wonder if when Years have piled -
Some Thousands - on the Harm -
That hurt them Early - such a lapse
Could give them any Balm -

Or would They go on aching still
Through Centuries of Nerve -
Enlightened to a larger Pain -
In Contrast with the Love -

The Grieved - are many - I am told -
There is the various Cause -
Death - is but one - and comes but once -
And only nails the Eyes -

There's Grief of Want - and Grief of Cold -
A sort they call "Despair" -
There's Banishment from native Eyes -
In sight of Native Air -

And though I may not guess the kind -
Correctly - yet to me
A piercing Comfort it affords
In passing Calvary -

To note the fashions - of the Cross -
And how they're mostly worn -

Still fascinated to presume
That Some - are like my own -   40

551   Conjecturing a Climate
        Of unsuspended Suns -
        Adds poignancy to Winter -
        The shivering Fancy turns

        To a fictitious Country   5
        To palliate a Cold -
        Not obviated of Degree -
        Nor eased - of Latitude -

552   There is a Languor of the Life
        More imminent than Pain -
        'Tis Pain's Successor - When the Soul
        Has suffered all it can -

        A Drowsiness - diffuses -   5
        A Dimness like a Fog
        Envelopes Consciousness -
        As Mists - obliterate a Crag.

        The Surgeon - does not blanch - at pain -
        His Habit - is severe -   10
        But tell him that it ceased to feel -
        The Creature lying there -

        And he will tell you - Skill is late -
        A Mightier than He -
        Has ministered before Him -   15
        There's no Vitality

553   When Diamonds are a Legend,
        And Diadems - a Tale -
        I Brooch and Earrings for Myself,
        Do sow, and Raise for sale -

                                                                 □

And tho' I'm scarce accounted,   5
My Art, a Summer Day - had Patrons -
Once - it was a Queen -
And once - a Butterfly -

554   I had not minded - Walls -
      Were Universe - one Rock -
      And far I heard his silver Call
      The other side the Block -

      I'd tunnel - till my Groove   5
      Pushed sudden thro' to his -
      Then my face take her Recompense -
      The looking in his Eyes -

      But 'tis a single Hair -
      A filament - a law -   10
      A Cobweb - wove in Adamant -
      A Battlement - of Straw -

      A limit like the Vail
      Unto the Lady's face -
      But every Mesh - a Citadel -   15
      And Dragons - in the Crease -

555   A House opon the Hight -
      That Wagon never reached -
      No Dead, were ever carried down -
      No Peddler's Cart - approached -

      Whose Chimney never smoked -   5
      Whose Windows - Night and Morn -
      Caught Sunrise first - and Sunset - last -
      Then - held an Empty Pane -

      Whose fate - Conjecture knew -
      No other neighbor - did -   10
      And what it was - we never lisped -
      Because He - never told -

556 It's Coming - the postponeless Creature -
It gains the Block - and now - it gains the Door -
Chooses it's latch, from all the other fastenings -
Enters - with a "You know me - Sir"?

Simple Salute - and Certain Recognition - 5
Bold - were it enemy - Brief - were it friend -
Dresses each House in Crape, and Icicle -
And Carries one - out of it - to God -

557 I send Two Sunsets -
Day and I - in competition ran -
I finished Two - and several Stars -
While He - was making One -

His own was ampler - but as I 5
Was saying to a friend -
Mine - is the more convenient
To Carry in the Hand -

558 A Visitor in Marl -
Who influences Flowers -
Till they are orderly as Busts -
And Elegant - as Glass -

Who visits in the Night - 5
And just before the Sun -
Concludes his glistening interview -
Caresses - and is gone -

But whom his fingers touched -
And where his feet have run - 10
And whatsoever Mouth he kissed -
Is as it had not been -

559 Through the Dark Sod - as Education -
The Lily passes sure -
Feels her White foot - no trepidation -
Her faith - no fear -

  □

Afterward - in the Meadow -   5
Swinging her Beryl Bell -
The Mold-life - all forgotten - now -
In Extasy - and Dell -

560   Did Our Best Moment last -
        'Twould supersede the Heaven -
        A few - and they by Risk - procure -
        So this Sort - are not given -

        Except as stimulants - in   5
        Cases of Despair -
        Or Stupor - The Reserve -
        These Heavenly moments are -

        A Grant of the Divine -
        That Certain as it Comes -   10
        Withdraws - and leaves the dazzled Soul
        In her unfurnished Rooms -

561   Trust in the Unexpected -
        By this - was William Kidd
        Persuaded of the Buried Gold -
        As One had testified -

        Through this - the old Philosopher -   5
        His Talismanic Stone
        Discerned - still witholden
        To effort undivine -

        'Twas this - allured Columbus -
        When Genoa - withdrew   10
        Before an Apparition
        Baptized America -

        The Same - afflicted Thomas -
        When Deity assured
        'Twas better - the perceiving not -   15
        Provided it believed -

562   'Twas Love - not me -
Oh punish - pray -
The Real One died for Thee -
Just Him - not me -

Such Guilt - to love Thee - most!   5
Doom it beyond the Rest -
Forgive it - last -
'Twas base as Jesus' - most!

Let Justice not mistake -
We Two - looked so alike -   10
Which was the Guilty Sake -
'Twas Love's - Now strike!

563   The Brain, within it's Groove
Runs evenly - and true -
But let a Splinter swerve -
'Twere easier for You -

To put a Current back -   5
When Floods have slit the Hills -
And scooped a Turnpike for Themselves -
And trodden out the Mills -

564   She hideth Her the last -
And is the first, to rise -
Her Night doth hardly recompense
The Closing of Her eyes -

She doth Her Purple Work -   5
And putteth Her away
In low apartments in the sod -
As Worthily as We.

To imitate Her life
As impotent would be   10
As make of Our imperfect Mints,
The Julep - of the Bee -

565   Reverse cannot befall
       That fine Prosperity
       Whose Sources are interior -
       As soon - Adversity

       A Diamond - overtake   5
       In far - Bolivian Ground -
       Misfortune hath no implement
       Could mar it - if it found -

566   But little Carmine hath her face -
       Of Emerald scant - her Gown -
       Her Beauty - is the love she doth -
       Itself - exhibit - mine -

567   It knew no Medicine -
       It was not Sickness - then -
       Nor any need of Surgery -
       And therefore - 'twas not Pain -

       It moved away the Cheeks -   5
       A Dimple at a time -
       And left the Profile - plainer -
       And in the place of Bloom

       It left the little Tint
       That never had a Name -
       You've seen it on a Cast's face -   10
       Was Paradise - to blame -

       If momently ajar -
       Temerity - drew near -
       And sickened - ever afterward   15
       For Somewhat that it saw?

568   It knew no lapse, nor Diminution -
       But large - serene -
       Burned on - until through Dissolution -
       It failed from Men -

                                                    □

I could not deem these Planetary forces
Annulled -
But suffered an Exchange of Territory -
Or World -

5

569   A precious - mouldering pleasure - 'tis -
To meet an Antique Book -
In just the Dress his Century wore -
A privilege - I think -

His venerable Hand to take -   5
And warming in our own -
A passage back - or two - to make -
To Times when he - was young -

His quaint opinions - to inspect -
His thought to ascertain   10
On Themes concern our mutual mind -
The Literature of Man -

What interested Scholars - most -
What Competitions ran -
When Plato - was a Certainty -   15
And Sophocles - a Man -

When Sappho - was a living Girl -
And Beatrice wore
The Gown that Dante - deified -
Facts Centuries before   20

He traverses - familiar -
As One should come to Town -
And tell you all your Dreams - were true -
He lived - where Dreams were born -

His presence is enchantment -   25
You beg him not to go -
Old Volumes shake their Vellum Heads
And tantalize - just so -

570   I tried to think a lonelier Thing
Than any I had seen -
Some Polar Expiation - An Omen in the Bone
Of Death's tremendous nearness -

I probed Retrieveless things   5
My Duplicate - to borrow -
A Haggard comfort springs

From the belief that Somewhere -
Within the Clutch of Thought -
There dwells one other Creature   10
Of Heavenly Love - forgot -

I plucked at our Partition -
As One should pry the Walls -
Between Himself - and Horror's Twin -
Within Opposing Cells. -   15

I almost strove to clasp his Hand,
Such Luxury - it grew -
That as Myself - could pity Him -
Perhaps he - pitied me -

571   Two Butterflies went out at Noon
And waltzed opon a Farm
And then espied Circumference
And caught a ride with him -
Then lost themselves and found themselves   5
In eddies of the sun
Till Gravitation missed them -
And Both were wrecked in Noon -
To all surviving Butterflies
Be this Fatuity   10
Example - and monition
To entomology -

572   The Day came slow - till Five o'clock -
Then sprang before the Hills

Like Hindered Rubies - or the Light
A Sudden Musket - spills -

The Purple could not keep the East - 5
The Sunrise shook abroad
Like Breadths of Topaz - packed a night -
The Lady just unrolled -

The Happy Winds - their Timbrels took -
The Birds - in docile Rows 10
Arranged themselves around their Prince
The Wind - is Prince of Those -

The Orchard sparkled like a Jew -
How mighty 'twas - to be
A Guest in this stupendous place - 15
The Parlor - of the Day -

573　　It was a quiet way -
He asked if I was his -
I made no answer of the Tongue
But answer of the Eyes -
And then He bore me on 5
Before this mortal noise
With swiftness, as of Chariots
And distance, as of Wheels -
This World did drop away
As Acres from the feet 10
Of one that leaneth from Balloon
Opon an Ether street.
The Gulf behind was not,
The Continents were new -
Eternity it was before 15
Eternity was due -
No Seasons were to us -
It was not Night nor Morn -
But Sunrise stopped opon the place
And fastened it in Dawn - 20

574   I know lives, I could miss
        Without a Misery -
        Others - whose instant's wanting -
        Would be Eternity -

        The last - a scanty Number -   5
        'Twould scarcely fill a Two -
        The first - a Gnat's Horizon
        Could easily outgrow -

575   I'm saying every day
        "If I should be a Queen, Tomorrow" -
        I'd do this way -
        And so I deck, a little,

        If it be, I wake a Bourbon,   5
        None on me - bend supercilious -
        With "This was she -
        Begged in the Market place - Yesterday."

        Court is a stately place -
        I've heard men say -   10
        So I loop my apron - against the Majesty
        With bright Pins of Buttercup -
        That not too plain -
        Rank - overtake me -

        And perch my Tongue   15
        On Twigs of singing - rather high -
        But this, might be my brief Term
        To qualify -

        Put from my simple speech all plain word -
        Take other accents, as such I heard,   20
        Though but for the Cricket - just,
        And but for the Bee -
        Not in all the Meadow -
        One accost me -

        Better to be ready -   25
        Than did next Morn

Meet me in Arragon -
My old Gown - on -

And the surprised Air
Rustics - wear -
Summoned - unexpectedly -   30
To Exeter -

576   The difference between Despair
      And Fear, is like the One
      Between the instant of a Wreck
      And when the Wreck has been -
      The Mind is smooth -   5
      No motion - Contented as the Eye
      Opon the Forehead of a Bust -
      That knows it cannot see -

577   I went to Heaven -
      'Twas a small Town -
      Lit - with a Ruby -
      Lathed - with Down -

      Stiller - than the fields   5
      At the full Dew -
      Beautiful - as Pictures -
      No Man drew -
      People - like the Moth -
      Of Mechlin - frames -   10
      Duties - of Gossamer -
      And Eider - names -
      Almost - contented -
      I - could be -
      'Mong such unique   15
      Society -

578   The Angle of a Landscape -
      That every time I wake -

Between my Curtain and the Wall
Opon an ample Crack -

Like a Venetian - Waiting - 5
Accosts my open eye -
Is just a Bough of Apples -
Held slanting, in the Sky -

The Pattern of a Chimney -
The Forehead of a Hill - 10
Sometimes - a Vane's Forefinger -
But that's - Occasional -

The Seasons - shift - my Picture -
Opon my Emerald Bough,
I wake - to find no - Emeralds - 15
Then - Diamonds - which the Snow

From Polar Caskets - fetched me -
The Chimney - and the Hill -
And just the Steeple's finger -
These - never stir at all - 20

579 The Soul unto itself
Is an imperial friend -
Or the most agonizing Spy -
An Enemy - could send -

Secure against it's own - 5
No treason it can fear -
Itself - it's Sovreign - Of itself
The Soul should stand in Awe -

580 We see - Comparatively -
The Thing so towering high
We could not grasp it's segment
Unaided - Yesterday -

This Morning's finer Verdict - 5
Makes scarcely worth the toil -

A furrow - Our Cordillera -
Our Appenine - a knoll -

Perhaps 'tis kindly - done us -
The Anguish - and the loss -   10
The wrenching - for His Firmament
The Thing belonged to us -

To spare these striding spirits
Some Morning of Chagrin -
The waking in a Gnat's - embrace -   15
Our Giants - further on -

581   Of Course - I prayed -
       And did God Care?
       He cared as much as on the Air
       A Bird - had stamped her foot -
       And cried "Give Me" -   5
       My Reason - Life -
       I had not had - but for Yourself -
       'Twere better Charity
       To leave me in the Atom's Tomb -
       Merry, and nought, and gay, and numb -   10
       Than this smart Misery.

582   I'm sorry for the Dead - Today -
       It's such congenial times
       Old neighbors have at fences -
       It's time o'year for Hay,

       And Broad - Sunburned Acquaintance   5
       Discourse between the Toil -
       And laugh, a homely species
       That makes the Fences smile -

       It seems so straight to lie away
       From all the noise of Fields -   10
       The Busy Carts - the fragrant Cocks -
       The Mower's metre - Steals

                                                               □

A Trouble lest they're homesick -
Those Farmers - and their Wives -
Set separate from the Farming -   15
And all the Neighbor's lives -

A Wonder if the Sepulchre
Dont feel a lonesome way -
When Men - and Boys - and Carts - and June,
Go down the Fields to "Hay" -   20

583   You cannot put a Fire out -
        A Thing that can ignite
        Can go, itself, without a Fan -
        Opon the slowest night -

        You cannot fold a Flood -   5
        And put it in a Drawer -
        Because the Winds would find it out -
        And tell your Cedar Floor -

584   We dream - it is good we are dreaming -
        It would hurt us - were we awake -
        But since it is playing - kill us,
        And we are playing - shriek -

        What harm? Men die - Externally -   5
        It is a truth - of Blood -
        But we - are dying in Drama -
        And Drama - is never dead -

        Cautious - We jar each other -
        And either - open the eyes -   10
        Lest the Phantasm - prove the mistake -
        And the livid Surprise

        Cool us to Shafts of Granite -
        With just an age - and name -
        And perhaps a phrase in Egyptian -   15
        It's prudenter - to dream -

585   If ever the lid gets off my head
        And lets the brain away
        The fellow will go where he belonged -
        Without a hint from me,

        And the world - if the world be looking on -   5
        Will see how far from home
        It is possible for sense to live
        The soul there - all the time.

586   Some say good night - at night -
        I say good night by day -
        Good bye - the Going utter me -
        Good night, I still reply -

        For parting, that is night,   5
        And presence, simply dawn -
        Itself, the purple on the hight
        Denominated morn.

587   She's happy - with a new Content -
        That feels to her - like Sacrament -
        She's busy - with an altered Care -
        As just apprenticed to the Air -

        She's tearful - if she weep at all -   5
        For blissful Causes - Most of all
        That Heaven permit so meek as her -
        To such a Fate - to minister -

588   The Heart asks Pleasure - first -
        And then - excuse from Pain -
        And then - those little Anodynes
        That deaden suffering -

        And then - to go to sleep -   5
        And then - if it should be
        The will of it's Inquisitor
        The privilege to die -

589   They called me to the Window, for
           "'Twas Sunset" - Some one said -
           I only saw a Sapphire Farm -
           And just a Single Herd -

           Of Opal Cattle - feeding far   5
           Opon so vain a Hill -
           As even while I looked - dissolved -
           Nor Cattle were - nor Soil -

           But in their Room - a Sea - displayed -
           And Ships - of such a size   10
           As Crew of Mountains - could afford -
           And Decks - to seat the Skies -

           This - too - the Showman rubbed away -
           And when I looked again -
           Nor Farm - nor Opal Herd - was there -   15
           Nor Mediterranean -

590   No Romance sold unto
           Could so enthrall a Man -
           As the perusal of
           His individual One -

           'Tis Fiction's - to dilute to plausibility   5
           Our - Novel. When 'tis small eno'
           To credit - 'Tis'nt true -

591   I heard a Fly buzz - when I died -
           The Stillness in the Room
           Was like the Stillness in the Air -
           Between the Heaves of Storm -

           The Eyes around - had wrung them dry -   5
           And Breaths were gathering firm
           For that last Onset - when the King
           Be witnessed - in the Room -

           I willed my Keepsakes - Signed away
           What portion of me be   10

Assignable - and then it was
There interposed a Fly -

With Blue - uncertain - stumbling Buzz -
Between the light - and me -
And then the Windows failed - and then   15
I could not see to see -

592   The Soul that hath a Guest,
        Doth seldom go abroad -
        Diviner Crowd - at Home -
        Obliterate the need -

        And Courtesy forbids   5
        The Host's departure - when
        Opon Himself - be visiting
        The Emperor of Men -

593   I watched the Moon around the House
        Until opon a Pane -
        She stopped - a Traveller's privilege - for Rest -
        And there opon

        I turned - as at a Stranger,   5
        The Lady in the Town
        Doth think no incivility
        To lift her Glass - opon -

        But never Stranger justified
        The Curiosity   10
        Like Mine - for not a Foot - nor Hand -
        Nor Formula - had she -

        But like a Head - a Guillotine
        Slid carelessly away -
        Did independent, Amber -   15
        Sustain her in the sky -

        Or like a Stemless Flower -
        Upheld in rolling Air

By finer Gravitations -
Than bind Philosopher -   20

No Hunger - had she - nor an Inn -
Her Toilette - to suffice -
Nor Avocation - nor Concern
For little Mysteries

As harass us - like Life - and Death -   25
And Afterward - or Nay -
But seemed engrossed to Absolute -
With Shining - and the Sky -

The privilege to scrutinize
Was scarce opon my Eyes   30
When, with a Silver practise -
She vaulted out of Gaze -

And next - I met her on a Cloud -
Myself too far below
To follow her Superior pace -   35
Or it's Advantage - Blue -

594   When I hoped I feared -
       Since I hoped I dared
       Everywhere alone
       As a Church remain -
       Spectre cannot harm -   5
       Serpent cannot charm -
       He deposes Doom
       Who hath suffered him -

595   The Lightning playeth - all the while -
       But when He singeth - then -
       Ourselves are conscious He exist -
       And we approach Him - stern -

       With Insulators - and a Glove -   5
       Whose short - sepulchral Bass

Alarms us - tho' His Yellow feet
May pass - and counterpass -

Opon the Ropes - above our Head -
Continual - with the News -   10
Nor We so much as check our speech -
Nor stop to cross Ourselves -

596   Ourselves were wed one summer - dear -
        Your Vision - was in June -
        And when Your little Lifetime failed,
        I wearied - too - of mine -

        And overtaken in the Dark -   5
        Where You had put me down -
        By Some one carrying a Light -
        I - too - received the Sign -

        'Tis true - Our Futures different lay -
        Your Cottage - faced the sun -   10
        While Oceans - and the North must be -
        On every side of mine

        'Tis true, Your Garden led the Bloom,
        For mine - in Frosts - was sown -
        And yet, one Summer, we were Queens -   15
        But You - were crowned in June -

597   'Tis little I - could care for Pearls -
        Who own the Ample sea -
        Or Brooches - when the Emperor -
        With Rubies - pelteth me -

        Or Gold - who am the Prince of Mines -   5
        Or Diamonds - when have I
        A Diadem to fit a Dome -
        Continual opon me -

598   The Brain - is wider than the Sky -
For - put them side by side -
The one the other will contain
With ease - and You - beside -

The Brain is deeper than the sea -   5
For - hold them - Blue to Blue -
The one the other will absorb -
As Sponges - Buckets - do -

The Brain is just the weight of God -
For - Heft them - Pound for Pound -   10
And they will differ - if they do -
As Syllable from Sound -

599   We do not play on Graves -
Because there is'nt Room -
Besides - it is'nt even - it slants
And People come -

And put a Flower on it -   5
And hang their faces so -
We're fearing that their Hearts will drop -
And crush our pretty play -

And so we move as far
As Enemies - away -   10
Just looking round to see how far
It is - Occasionally -

600   Her - last Poems -
Poets ended -
Silver - perished - with her Tongue -
Not on Record - bubbled Other -
Flute - or Woman - so divine -   5

Not unto it's Summer Morning -
Robin - uttered half the Tune
Gushed too full for the adoring -
From the Anglo-Florentine -

□

Late - the Praise - 'Tis dull - Conferring 10
On the Head too High - to Crown -
Diadem - or Ducal showing -
Be it's Grave - sufficient Sign -

Nought - that We - No Poet's Kinsman -
Suffocate - with easy Wo - 15
What - and if Ourself a Bridegroom -
Put Her down - in Italy?

601   When Bells stop ringing - Church - begins -
       The Positive - of Bells -
       When Cogs - stop - that's Circumference -
       The Ultimate - of Wheels -

602   The Manner of it's Death
       When Certain it must die -
       'Tis deemed a privilege to choose -
       'Twas Major Andre's Way -

       When Choice of Life - is past - 5
       There yet remains a Love
       It's little Fate to stipulate -

       How small in those who live -

       The Miracle to teaze
       With Babble of the styles - 10
       How "they are dying mostly - now" -
       And Customs at "St James"!

603   The Red - Blaze - is the Morning -
       The Violet - is Noon -
       The Yellow - Day - is falling -
       And after that - is None -

       But Miles of Sparks - at Evening - 5
       Reveal the Width that burned -
       The Territory Argent - that never yet - consumed -

604   You'll know Her - by Her Foot -
The smallest Gamboge Hand
With Fingers - where the Toes should be -
Would more affront the sand -

Than this Quaint Creature's Boot -   5
Adjusted by a stem -
Without a Button - I c'd vouch -
Unto a Velvet Limb -

You'll know Her - by Her Vest -
Tight fitting - Orange - Brown -   10
Inside a Jacket duller -
She wore when she was born -

Her Cap is small - and snug -
Constructed for the Winds -
She'd pass for Barehead - short way off -   15
But as she closer stands -

So finer 'tis than Wool -
You cannot feel the seam -
Nor is it clasped unto of Band -
Nor held opon - of Brim -   20

You'll know Her - by Her Voice -
At first - a doubtful Tone -
A sweet endeavor - but as March
To April - hurries on -

She squanders on your Head   25
Such Arguments of Pearl -
You beg the Robin in your Brain
To keep the other - still -

605   I am alive - I guess -
The Branches on my Hand
Are full of Morning Glory -
And at my finger's end -

The Carmine - tingles warm -   5
And if I hold a Glass

Across my mouth - it blurs it -
Physician's - proof of Breath -

I am alive - because
I am not in a Room -
The Parlor - commonly - it is -
So Visitors may come -

And lean - and view it sidewise -
And add "How cold - it grew" -
And "Was it conscious - when it stepped
In Immortality"?

I am alive - because
I do not own a House -
Entitled to myself - precise -
And fitting no one else -

And marked my Girlhood's name -
So Visitors may know
Which Door is mine - and not mistake -
And try another Key -

How good - to be alive!
How infinite - to be
Alive - two-fold - The Birth I had -
And this - besides, in Thee!

606   Except the smaller size
No lives are round -
These - hurry to a sphere
And show and end -
The larger - slower grow
And later hang -
The Summers of Hesperides
Are long.

607   I think the longest Hour of all
Is when the Cars have come -

And we are waiting for the Coach -
It seems as though the Time -

Indignant - that the Joy was come -   5
Did block the Gilded Hands -
And would not let the Seconds by -
But slowest instant - ends -

The Pendulum begins to count -
Like little Scholars - loud -   10
The steps grow thicker - in the Hall -
The Heart begins to crowd -

Then I - my timid service done -
Tho' service 'twas, of Love -
Take up my little Violin -   15
And further North - remove -

608   So glad we are - a stranger'd deem
       'Twas sorry - that we were -
       For where the Holiday - should be -
       There publishes - a Tear -

       Nor how Ourselves be justified -   5
       Since Grief and Joy are done
       So similar - an Optizan
       Could not decide between -

609   A Night - there lay the Days between -
       The Day that was Before -
       And Day that was Behind - were One -
       And now - 'twas Night - was here -

       Slow - Night - that must be watched away -   5
       As Grains opon a shore -
       Too imperceptible to note -
       Till it be Night - no more -

610   From Cocoon forth a Butterfly
As Lady from her Door
Emerged - a Summer Afternoon -
Repairing Everywhere -

Without Design - that I could trace   5
Except to stray abroad
On miscellaneous Enterprise
The Clovers - understood -

Her pretty Parasol be seen
Contracting in a Field   10
Where Men made Hay -
Then struggling hard
With an opposing Cloud -

Where Parties - Phantom as Herself -
To Nowhere - seemed to go   15
In purposeless Circumference -
As 'twere a Tropic Show -

And notwithstanding Bee - that worked -
And Flower - that zealous blew -
This Audience of Idleness   20
Disdained them, from the Sky -

Till Sundown crept - a steady Tide -
And Men that made the Hay -
And Afternoon - and Butterfly -
Extinguished - in the Sea -   25

611   Her sweet Weight on my Heart a Night
Had scarcely deigned to lie -
When, stirring, for Belief's delight,
My Bride had slipped away -

If 'twas a Dream - made solid - just   5
The Heaven to confirm -
Or if Myself were dreamed of Her -
The power to presume -

With Him remain - who unto Me -
Gave - even as to All -   10

A Fiction superseding Faith -
By so much - as 'twas real -

612   'Tis Opposites - Entice
Deformed Men - ponder Grace -
Bright fires - the Blanketless -
The Lost - Day's face -

The Blind - esteem it be   5
Enough Estate - to see -
The Captive - strangles new -
For deeming - Beggars - play -

To lack - enamor Thee -
Tho' the Divinity -   10
Be only
Me -

613   The Day that I was crowned
Was like the other Days -
Until the Coronation came -
And then - 'twas Otherwise -

As Carbon in the Coal   5
And Carbon in the Gem
Are One - and yet the former
Were dull for Diadem -

I rose, and all was plain -
But when the Day declined   10
Myself and It, in Majesty
Were equally - adorned -

The Grace that I - was chose -
To me - surpassed the Crown
That was the Witness for the Grace -   15
'Twas even that 'twas Mine -

614   'Twas warm - at first - like Us -
Until there crept opon
A Chill - like frost opon a Glass -
Till all the scene - be gone.

The Forehead copied stone -   5
The Fingers grew too cold
To ache - and like a Skater's Brook -
The busy eyes - congealed -

It straightened - that was all -
It crowded Cold to Cold -
It multiplied indifference -   10
As Pride were all it could -

And even when with Cords -
'Twas lowered, like a Weight -
It made no Signal, nor demurred,
But dropped like Adamant.   15

615   God is a distant - stately Lover -
Woos, as He states us - by His Son -
Verily, a Vicarious Courtship -
"Miles", and "Priscilla," were such an One -

But, lest the Soul - like fair "Priscilla"   5
Choose the Envoy - and spurn the 'Groom -
Vouches, with hyperbolic archness -
"Miles", and "John Alden" are Synonyme -

616   If any sink, assure that this, now standing -
Failed like Themselves - and conscious that it rose -
Grew by the Fact, and not the Understanding
How Weakness passed - or Force - arose -

Tell that the Worst, is easy in a Moment -   5
Dread, but the Whizzing, before the Ball -
When the Ball enters, enters Silence -
Dying - annuls the power to kill -

617 The Night was wide, and furnished scant
  With but a single Star -
  That often as a Cloud it met -
  Blew out itself - for fear -

  The Wind pursued the little Bush -   5
  And drove away the Leaves
  November left - then clambered up
  And fretted in the Eaves -

  No Squirrel went abroad -
  A Dog's belated feet   10
  Like intermittent Plush, be heard
  Adown the empty street -

  To feel if Blinds be fast -
  And closer to the fire -
  Her little Rocking Chair to draw -   15
  And shiver for the Poor -

  The Housewife's gentle Task -
  How pleasanter - said she
  Unto the Sofa opposite -
  The Sleet - than May, no Thee -   20

618 To love thee Year by Year -
  May less appear
  Than sacrifice, and cease -
  However, dear,
  Forever might be short, I thought to show - 5
  And so I pieced it, with a flower, now.

619 Did you ever stand in a Cavern's Mouth -
  Widths out of the Sun -
  And look - and shudder, and block your breath -
  And deem to be alone

  In such a place, what horror,   5
  How Goblin it would be -

And fly, as 'twere pursuing you?
Then Loneliness - looks so -

Did you ever look in a Cannon's face -
Between whose Yellow eye -
And your's - the Judgment intervened -
The Question of "To die" -

Extemporizing in your ear
As cool as Satyr's Drums -
If you remember, and were saved
It's liker so - it seems -

10

15

620   Much Madness is divinest Sense -
        To a discerning Eye -
        Much Sense - the starkest Madness -
        'Tis the Majority
        In this, as all, prevail -
        Assent - and you are sane -
        Demur - you're straightway dangerous -
        And handled with a Chain -

5

621   The Wind - tapped like a tired Man -
        And like a Host - "Come in"
        I boldly answered - entered then
        My Residence within

        A Rapid - footless Guest -
        To offer whom a Chair
        Were as impossible as hand
        A Sofa to the Air -

5

        No Bone had He to bind Him -
        His Speech was like the Push
        Of numerous Humming Birds at once
        From a superior Bush -

10

        His Countenance - a Billow -
        His Fingers, as He passed

Let go a music - as of tunes
Blown tremulous in Glass -

He visited - still flitting -
Then like a timid Man
Again, He tapped - 'twas flurriedly -
And I became alone -

622   To interrupt His Yellow Plan
       The Sun does not allow
       Caprices of the Atmosphere -
       And even when the Snow

       Heaves Balls of Specks, like Vicious Boy   5
       Directly in His Eye -
       Does not so much as turn His Head -
       Busy with Majesty -

       'Tis His to stimulate the Earth -
       And magnetize the Sea -   10
       And bind Astronomy, in place,
       Yet Any passing by

       Would deem Ourselves - the busier
       As the minutest Bee
       That rides - emits a Thunder -   15
       A Bomb - to justify -

623   Prayer is the little implement
       Through which Men reach
       Where Presence - is denied them -
       They fling their Speech

       By means of it - in God's Ear -   5
       If then He hear -
       This sums the Apparatus
       Comprised in Prayer -

624   What care the Dead, for Chanticleer -
What care the Dead for Day?
'Tis late your Sunrise vex their face -
And Purple Ribaldry - of Morning

Pour as blank on them   5
As on the Tier of Wall
The Mason builded, yesterday,
And equally as cool -

What care the Dead for Summer?
The Solstice had no Sun   10
Could waste the Snow before their Gate -
And knew One Bird a Tune -

Could thrill their Mortised Ear
Of all the Birds that be -
This One - beloved of Mankind   15
Henceforward cherished be -

What care the Dead for Winter?
Themselves as easy freeze -
June Noon - as January Night -
As soon the South - her Breeze   20
Of Sycamore - or Cinnamon -
Deposit in a Stone
And put a Stone to keep it Warm -
Give Spices - unto Men -

625   Forget! The lady with the Amulet
Forgot she wore it at her Heart
Because she breathed against
Was Treason twixt?

Deny! Did Rose her Bee -   5
For Privilege of Play
Or Wile of Butterfly
Or Opportunity - Her Lord away?

The lady with the Amulet - will fade -
The Bee - in Mausoleum laid -   10
Discard his Bride -

But longer than the little Rill -
That cooled the Forehead of the Hill -
While Other - went the Sea to fill -
And Other - went to turn the Mill -   15
I'll do thy Will -

626   Undue Significance a starving man attaches
        To Food -
        Far off - He sighs - and therefore - Hopeless -
        And therefore - Good -

        Partaken - it relieves - indeed -   5
        But proves us
        That Spices fly
        In the Receipt - It was the Distance -
        Was Savory -

627   I think I was enchanted
        When first a sombre Girl -
        I read that Foreign Lady -
        The Dark - felt beautiful -

        And whether it was noon at night -   5
        Or only Heaven - at noon -
        For very Lunacy of Light
        I had not power to tell -

        The Bees - became as Butterflies -
        The Butterflies - as Swans -   10
        Approached - and spurned the narrow Grass -
        And just the meanest Tunes

        That Nature murmured to herself
        To keep herself in Cheer -
        I took for Giants - practising   15
        Titanic Opera -

        The Days - to Mighty Metres stept -
        The Homeliest - adorned

As if unto a Jubilee
'Twere suddenly confirmed -

20

I could not have defined the change -
Conversion of the Mind
Like Sanctifying in the Soul -
Is witnessed - not explained -

'Twas a Divine Insanity -
The Danger to be sane
Should I again experience -
'Tis Antidote to turn -

25

To Tomes of Solid Witchcraft -
Magicians be asleep -
But Magic - hath an element
Like Deity - to keep -

30

628   'Tis Customary as we part
A Trinket - to confer -
It helps to stimulate the faith
When Lovers be afar -

'Tis various - as the various taste -
Clematis - journeying far -
Presents me with a single Curl
Of her Electric Hair -

5

629   The Battle fought between the Soul
And No Man - is the One
Of all the Battles prevalent -
By far the Greater One -

No News of it is had abroad -
It's Bodiless Campaign
Establishes, and terminates -
Invisible - Unknown -

5

Nor History - record it -
As Legions of a Night

10

The Sunrise scatters - These endure -
Enact - and terminate -

630   The Soul's Superior instants
       Occur to Her - Alone -
       When friend - and Earth's occasion
       Have infinite withdrawn -

       Or She - Herself - ascended   5
       To too remote a Hight
       For lower Recognition
       Than Her Omnipotent -

       This mortal Abolition
       Is seldom - but as fair   10
       As Apparition - subject
       To Autocratic Air -

       Eternity's disclosure
       To favorites - a few -
       Of the Colossal substance   15
       Of Immortality -

631   Me prove it now - Whoever doubt
       Me stop to prove it - now -
       Make haste - the Scruple! Death be scant
       For Opportunity -

       The River reaches to my feet -   5
       As yet - My Heart be dry -
       Oh Lover - Life could not convince -
       Might Death - enable Thee -

       The River reaches to My Breast -
       Still - still - My Hands above   10
       Proclaim with their remaining might -
       Dost recognize the Love?

       The River reaches to my Mouth -
       Remember - when the Sea

Swept by my searching eyes - the last -
Themselves were quick - with Thee!

632   To lose One's faith - surpass
        The loss of an Estate -
        Because Estates can be
        Replenished - faith cannot -

        Inherited with Life -   5
        Belief - but once - can be -
        Annihilate a single clause -
        And Being's - Beggary -

633   I saw no Way - The Heavens were stitched -
        I felt the Columns close -
        The Earth reversed her Hemispheres -
        I touched the Universe -

        And back it slid - and I alone -   5
        A speck opon a Ball -
        Went out opon Circumference -
        Beyond the Dip of Bell -

634   Had I presumed to hope -
        The loss had been to Me
        A Value - for the Greatness' Sake -
        As Giants - gone away -

        Had I presumed to gain   5
        A Favor so remote -
        The Failure but confirm the Grace
        In further Infinite -

        'Tis failure - not of Hope -
        But Confident Despair -   10
        Advancing on Celestial Lists -
        With faint - Terrestrial power -

                                                                 □

'Tis Honor - though I die -
For That no Man obtain
Till He be justified by Death -   15
This - is the Second Gain -

635   Just to be Rich
To waste my Guinea
On so broad a Heart!
Just to be Poor,
For Barefoot pleasure   5
You, Sir, shut me out!

636   It struck me - every Day -
The Lightning was as new
As if the Cloud that instant slit
And let the Fire through -

It burned Me - in the Night -   5
It Blistered to My Dream -
It sickened fresh opon my sight -
With every Morn that came -

I thought that Storm - was brief -
The Maddest - quickest by -   10
But Nature lost the Date of This -
And left it in the Sky -

637   I went to thank Her -
But She Slept -
Her Bed - a funneled Stone -
With Nosegays at the Head and Foot -
That Travellers - had thrown -   5

Who went to thank Her -
But She Slept -
'Twas Short - to cross the Sea -
To look opon Her like - alive -
But turning back - 'twas slow -   10

638   The Future never spoke -
           Nor will he like the Dumb
           Reveal by sign a Syllable
           Of his profound To Come -

           But when the News be ripe   5
           Presents it in the Act -
           Forestalling Preparation -
           Escape - or Substitute -

           Indifferent to him
           The Dower - as the Doom -   10
           His Office but to execute
           Fate's Telegram - to Him -

639   I gained it so -
           By Climbing slow -
           By catching at the Twigs that grow
           Between the Bliss - and me -
           It hung so high   5
           As well the Sky
           Attempt by Strategy -

           I said I gained it -
           This - was all -
           Look, how I clutch it   10
           Lest it fall -
           And I a Pauper go -
           Unfitted by an instant's Grace
           For the Contented - Beggar's face
           I wore - an hour ago -   15

640   Death sets a Thing significant
           The Eye had hurried by
           Except a perished Creature
           Entreat us tenderly

           To ponder little workmanships   5
           In Crayon - or in wool -

With "This was last Her fingers did" -
Industrious until -

The Thimble weighed too heavy -
The stitches stopped - themselves -   10
And then 'twas put among the Dust
Opon the Closet shelves -

A Book I have - a friend gave -
Whose Pencil - here and there -
Had notched the place that pleased Him -   15
At Rest - His fingers are -

Now - when I read - I read not -
For interrupting Tears -
Obliterate the Etchings
Too Costly for Repairs -   20

641   What I can do - I will -
       Though it be little as a Daffodil -
       That I cannot - must be
       Unknown to possibility -

642   There is a flower that Bees prefer -
       And Butterflies - desire -
       To gain the Purple Democrat
       The Humming Bird - aspire -   .

       And Whatsoever Insect pass -   5
       A Honey bear away
       Proportioned to his several dearth
       And her - capacity -

       Her face be rounder than the Moon
       And ruddier than the Gown   10
       Of Orchis in the Pasture -
       Or Rhododendron - worn -

       She doth not wait for June -
       Before the World be Green -

Her sturdy little Countenance   15
Against the Wind - be seen -

Contending with the Grass -
Near Kinsman to Herself -
For privilege of Sod and Sun -
Sweet Litigants for Life -   20

And when the Hills be full -
And newer fashions blow -
Doth not retract a single spice
For pang of jealousy -

Her Public - be the Noon -   25
Her Providence - the Sun -
Her Progress - by the Bee - proclaimed -
In sovreign - Swerveless Tune -

The Bravest - of the Host -
Surrendering - the last -   30
Nor even of Defeat - aware -
When cancelled by the Frost -

643   A Secret told -
        Ceases to be a Secret - then -
        A Secret - kept -
        That - can appall but One -

        Better of it - continual be afraid -   5.
        Than it -
        And Whom you told it to - beside -

644   For Death - or rather
        For the Things 'twould buy -
        This - put away
        Life's Opportunity -

        The Things that Death will buy   5
        Are Room -
        Escape from Circumstances -
        And a Name -

                                                        □

With Gifts of Life
How Death's Gifts may compare -   10
We know not -
For the Rates - lie Here -

645   Exhiliration - is within -
        There can no Outer Wine
        So royally intoxicate
        As that diviner Brand

        The Soul achieves - Herself -   5
        To drink - or set away
        For Visitor - or Sacrament -
        'Tis not of Holiday

        To stimulate a Man
        Who hath the Ample Rhine   10
        Within his Closet - Best you can
        Exhale in offering -

646   'Tis One by One - the Father counts -
        And then a Tract between
        Set Cypherless - to teach the Eye
        The Value of it's Ten -

        Until the peevish Student   5
        Acquire the Quick of Skill -
        Then Numerals are dowered back -
        Adorning all the Rule -

        'Tis mostly Slate and Pencil -
        And Darkness on the School   10
        Distracts the Children's fingers -
        Still the Eternal Rule

        Regards least Cypherer alike
        With Leader of the Band -
        And every separate Urchin's Sum -   15
        Is fashioned for his hand -

647 To fill a Gap
   Insert the Thing that caused it -
   Block it up
   With Other - and 'twill yawn the more -
   You cannot solder an Abyss   5
   With Air -

648 I've seen a Dying Eye
   Run round and round a Room -
   In search of Something - as it seemed -
   Then Cloudier become -
   And then - obscure with Fog -   5
   And then - be soldered down
   Without disclosing what it be
   'Twere blessed to have seen -

649 No Rack can torture me -
   My Soul - at Liberty -
   Behind this mortal Bone
   There knits a bolder One -

   You cannot prick with Saw -   5
   Nor pierce with Cimitar -
   Two Bodies - therefore be -
   Bind One - The Other fly -

   The Eagle of his Nest
   No easier divest -   10
   And gain the Sky
   Than mayest Thou -

   Except Thyself may be
   Thine Enemy -
   Captivity is Consciousness -   15
   So's Liberty -

650 Death is potential to that Man
   Who dies - and to his friend -

Beyond that - unconspicuous
To Anyone but God -

Of these Two - God remembers   5
The longest - for the friend -
Is integral - and therefore
Itself dissolved - of God -

651   Smiling back from Coronation
        May be Luxury -
        On the Heads that started with us -
        Being's Peasantry -

        Recognizing in Procession   5
        Ones We former knew -
        When Ourselves were also dusty -
        Centuries ago -

        Had the Triumph no Conviction
        Of how many be -   10
        Stimulated - by the Contrast -
        Unto Misery -

652   That I did always love
        I bring thee Proof
        That till I loved
        I never lived - Enough -

        That I shall love alway -   5
        I argue thee
        That love is life -
        And life hath Immortality -

        This - dost thou doubt - Sweet -
        Then have I   10
        Nothing to show
        But Calvary -

653   No Crowd that has occurred
        Exhibit - I suppose
        That General Attendance
        That Resurrection - does -

        Circumference be full -   5
        The long restricted Grave
        Assert her Vital Privilege -
        The Dust - connect - and live -

        On Atoms - features place -
        All Multitudes that were   10
        Efface in the Comparison -
        As Suns - dissolve a star -

        Solemnity - prevail -
        It's Individual Doom
        Possess each - separate Consciousness -   15
        August - Absorbed - Numb -

        What Duplicate - exist -
        What Parallel can be -
        Of the Significance of This -
        To Universe - and Me?   20

654   Beauty - be not caused - It Is -
        Chase it, and it ceases -
        Chase it not, and it abides -

        Overtake the Creases

        In the Meadow - when the Wind   5
        Runs his fingers thro' it -
        Deity will see to it
        That You never do it -

655   He parts Himself - like Leaves -
        And then - He closes up -
        Then stands opon the Bonnet
        Of Any Buttercup -

                                                            □

And then He runs against   5
And oversets a Rose -
And then does Nothing -
Then away opon a Jib - He goes -

And dangles like a Mote
Suspended in the Noon -   10
Uncertain - to return Below -
Or settle in the Moon -

What come of Him at Night -
The privilege to say
Be limited by Ignorance -   15
What come of Him - That Day -

The Frost - possess the World -
In Cabinets - be shown -
A Sepulchre of quaintest Floss -
An Abbey - a Cocoon -   20

656   I started Early - Took my Dog -
        And visited the Sea -
        The Mermaids in the Basement
        Came out to look at me -

        And Frigates - in the Upper Floor   5
        Extended Hempen Hands -
        Presuming Me to be a Mouse -
        Aground - opon the Sands -

        But no Man moved Me - till the Tide
        Went past my simple Shoe -   10
        And past my Apron - and my Belt
        And past my Boddice - too -

        And made as He would eat me up -
        As wholly as a Dew
        Opon a Dandelion's Sleeve -   15
        And then - I started - too -

        And He - He followed - close behind -
        I felt His Silver Heel

Opon my Ancle - Then My Shoes
Would overflow with Pearl -   20

Until We met the Solid Town -
No One He seemed to know -
And bowing - with a Mighty look -
At me - The Sea withdrew -

657   Endow the Living - with the Tears -
       You squander on the Dead,
       And They were Men and Women - now,
       Around Your Fireside -

       Instead of Passive Creatures,   5
       Denied the Cherishing
       Till They - the Cherishing deny -
       With Death's Etherial Scorn -

658   'Tis true - They shut me in the Cold -
       But then - Themselves were warm
       And could not know the feeling 'twas -
       Forget it - Lord - of Them -

       Let not my Witness hinder Them   5
       In Heavenly esteem -
       No Paradise could be - Conferred
       Through Their beloved Blame -

       The Harm They did - was short - And since
       Myself - who bore it - do -   10
       Forgive Them - Even as Myself -
       Or else - forgive not me -

659   The Province of the Saved
       Should be the Art - To Save -
       Through Skill obtained in Themselves -
       The Science of the Grave

                                                               □

No Man can understand 5
But He that hath endured
The Dissolution - in Himself -
That Man - be qualified

To qualify Despair
To Those who failing new - 10
Mistake Defeat for Death - Each time -
Till acclimated - to -

660   I took my Power in my Hand -
And went against the World -
'Twas not so much as David - had -
But I - was twice as bold -

I aimed my Pebble - but Myself 5
Was all the one that fell -
Was it Goliah - was too large -
Or was myself - too small?

661   Some such Butterfly be seen
On Brazilian Pampas -
Just at noon - no later - Sweet -
Then - the License closes -

Some such Spice - express - and pass - 5
Subject to Your Plucking -
As the Stars - You knew last Night -
Foreigners - This Morning -

662   I had no Cause to be awake -
My Best - was gone to sleep -
And Morn a new politeness took -
And failed to wake them up -
But called the others - clear - 5
And passed their Curtains by -
Sweet Morning - When I oversleep -
Knock - Recollect - to Me -

□

I looked at Sunrise - Once -
And then I looked at Them -
And wishfulness in me arose -
For Circumstance the same -

'Twas such an Ample Peace -
It could not hold a Sigh -
'Twas Sabbath - with the Bells divorced -
'Twas Sunset - all the Day -

So choosing but a Gown -
And taking but a Prayer -
The Only Raiment I should need -
I struggled - and was There -

663   I fear a Man of frugal speech -
I fear a Silent Man -
Haranguer - I can overtake -
Or Babbler - entertain -

But He who weigheth - While the Rest -
Expend their furthest pound -
Of this Man - I am wary -
I fear that He is Grand -

664   Rehearsal to Ourselves
Of a Withdrawn Delight -
Affords a Bliss like Murder -
Omnipotent - Acute -

We will not drop the Dirk -
Because We love the Wound
The Dirk Commemorate - Itself
Remind Us that We died -

665   The Martyr Poets - did not tell -
But wrought their Pang in syllable -
That when their mortal name be numb -
Their mortal fate - encourage Some -

The Martyr Painters - never spoke -
Bequeathing - rather - to their Work -
That when their conscious fingers cease -
Some seek in Art - the Art of Peace -

666   I cross till I am weary
        A Mountain - in my mind -
        More Mountains - then a Sea -
        More Seas - And then
        A Desert - find -   5

        And my Horizon blocks
        With steady - drifting - Grains
        Of unconjectured quantity -
        As Asiatic Rains -

        Nor this - defeat my Pace -   10
        It hinder from the West
        But as an Enemy's salute
        One hurrying to Rest -

        What merit had the Goal -
        Except there intervene   15
        Faint Doubt - and far Competitor -
        To jeopardize the Gain?

        At last - the Grace in sight -
        I shout unto my feet -
        I offer them the Whole of Heaven   20
        The instant that we meet -

        They strive - and yet delay -
        They perish - Do we die -
        Or is this Death's experiment -
        Reversed - in Victory?   25

667   Answer July
        Where is the Bee -
        Where is the Blush -
        Where is the Hay?

                                                        □

Ah, said July -   5
Where is the Seed -
Where is the Bud -
Where is the May -
Answer Thee - me -

Nay - said the May -   10
Show me the Snow -
Show me the Bells -
Show me the Jay!

Quibbled the Jay -
Where be the Maise -   15
Where be the Haze -
Where be the Bur?
Here - said the Year -

668   There is a Shame of Nobleness -
           Confronting Sudden Pelf -
           A finer Shame of Extasy -
           Convicted of Itself -

           A best Disgrace - a Brave Man feels -   5
           Acknowledged - of the Brave -
           One more - "Ye Blessed" - to be told -
           But that's - Behind the Grave -

669   An ignorance a Sunset
           Confer opon the Eye -
           Of Territory - Color -
           Circumference - Decay -

           It's Amber Revelation   5
           Exhilirate - Debase -
           Omnipotence' inspection
           Of Our inferior face -

           And when the solemn features
           Confirm - in Victory -   10

We start - as if detected
In Immortality -

670   One Crucifixion is recorded - only -
       How many be
       Is not affirmed of Mathematics -
       Or History -

       One Calvary - exhibited to stranger -   5
       As many be
       As Persons - or Peninsulas -
       Gethsemane -

       Is but a Province - in the Being's Centre -
       Judea -   10
       For Journey - or Crusade's Achieving -
       Too near -

       Our Lord - indeed - made Compound Witness -
       And yet -
       There's newer - nearer Crucifixion   15
       Than That -

671   The Sweetest Heresy received
       That Man and Woman know -
       Each Other's Convert -
       Though the Faith accommodate but Two -

       The Churches are so frequent -   5
       The Ritual - so small -
       The Grace so unavoidable -
       To fail - is Infidel -

672   Take Your Heaven further on -
       This - to Heaven divine Has gone -
       Had You earlier blundered in
       Possibly, e'en You had seen
       An Eternity - put on -   5
       Now - to ring a Door beyond

Is the utmost of Your Hand -
To the Skies - apologize -
Nearer to Your Courtesies
Than this Sufferer polite -   10
Dressed to meet You -
See - in White!

673   A Tongue - to tell Him I am true!
         It's fee - to be of Gold -
         Had Nature - in Her monstrous House
         A single Ragged Child -

         To earn a Mine - would run   5
         That Interdicted Way,
         And tell Him - Charge Thee speak it plain -
         That so far - Truth is True?

         And answer What I do -
         Beginning with the Day   10
         That Night - begun -
         Nay - Midnight - 'twas -
         Since Midnight - happened - say -

         If once more - Pardon - Boy -
         The Magnitude thou may   15
         Enlarge my Message - If too vast
         Another Lad - help Thee -

         Thy Pay - in Diamonds - be -
         And His - in solid Gold -
         Say Rubies - if He hesitate -   20
         My Message - must be told -

         Say - last I said - was This -
         That when the Hills - come down -
         And hold no higher than the Plain -
         My Bond - have just begun -   25

         And when the Heavens - disband -
         And Deity conclude -
         Then - look for me - Be sure you say -
         Least Figure - on the Road -

674   I could not prove the Years had feet -
Yet confident they run
Am I, from symptoms that are past
And Series that are done -

I find my feet have further Goals -   5
I smile opon the Aims
That felt so ample - Yesterday -
Today's - have vaster claims -

I do not doubt the Self I was
Was competent to me -   10
But something awkward in the fit -
Proves that - outgrown - I see -

675   What Soft - Cherubic Creatures -
These Gentlewomen are -
One would as soon assault a Plush -
Or violate a Star -

Such Dimity Convictions -   5
A Horror so refined
Of freckled Human Nature -
Of Deity - Ashamed -

It's such a common - Glory -
A Fisherman's - Degree -   10
Redemption - Brittle Lady -
Be so - ashamed of Thee -

676   You know that Portrait in the Moon -
So tell me Who 'tis like -
The very Brow - the stooping eyes -
A'fog for - Say - Whose Sake?

The very Pattern of the Cheek -   5
It varies - in the Chin -
But - Ishmael - since we met - 'tis long -
And fashions - intervene -

☐

When Moon's at full - 'Tis Thou - I say -
My lips just hold the name -   10
When crescent - Thou art worn - I note -
But - there - the Golden Same -

And when - Some Night - Bold - slashing Clouds
Cut Thee away from Me -
That's easier - than the other film   15
That glazes Holiday -

677   Funny - to be a Century -
        And see the People - going by -
        I - should die of the oddity -
        But then - I'm not so staid - as He -

        He keeps His Secrets safely - very -   5
        Were He to tell - extremely sorry
        This Bashful Globe of Our's would be -
        So dainty of Publicity -

678   Not probable - The barest Chance -
        A smile too few - a word too much
        And far from Heaven as the Rest -
        The Soul so close on Paradise -

        What if the Bird - from journey far -   5
        Confused by Sweets - as Mortals - are -
        Forget the secret of His wing
        And perish - but a Bough between -
        Oh, Groping feet -
        Oh Phantom Queen!   10

679   When Night is almost done -
        And Sunrise grows so near
        That We can touch the Spaces -
        It's time to smooth the Hair -

        And get the Dimples ready -   5
        And wonder We could care

For that Old - faded Midnight -
That frightened - but an Hour -

680   Triumph - may be of several kinds -
There's Triumph in the Room
When that Old Imperator - Death -
By Faith - be overcome -

There's Triumph of the finer mind   5
When Truth - affronted long -
Advance unmoved - to Her Supreme -
Her God - Her only Throng -

A Triumph - when Temptation's Bribe
Be slowly handed back -   10
One eye opon the Heaven renounced -
And One - opon the Rack -

Severer Triumph - by Himself
Experienced - who pass
Acquitted - from that Naked Bar -   15
Jehovah's Countenance -

681   Dont put up my Thread & Needle -
I'll begin to Sow
When the Birds begin to whistle -
Better stitches - so -

These were bent - my sight got crooked -   5
When my mind - is plain
I'll do seams - a Queen's endeavor
Would not blush to own -

Hems - too fine for Lady's tracing
To the sightless knot -   10
Tucks - of dainty interspersion -
Like a dotted Dot -

Leave my Needle in the furrow -
Where I put it down -

I can make the zigzag stitches   15
Straight - when I am strong -

Till then - dreaming I am sowing
Fetch the seam I missed -
Closer - so I - at my sleeping -
Still surmise I stitch -   20

682   So well that I can live without -
I love thee - then How well is that?
As well as Jesus?
Prove it me
That He - loved Men -   5
As I - love thee -

683   At leisure is the Soul
That gets a staggering Blow -
The Width of Life - before it spreads
Without a thing to do -

It begs you give it Work -   5
But just the placing Pins -
Or humblest Patchwork - Children do -
To still it's noisy Hands -

684   Sweet - safe - Houses -
Glad - gay - Houses -
Sealed so stately tight -
Lids of Steel - on Lids of Marble -
Locking Barefeet out -   5

Brooks of Plush - in Banks of Satin
Not so softly fall
As the laughter - and the whisper -
From their People Pearl -

No Bald Death - affront their Parlors -   10
No Bold Sickness come

To deface their stately Treasures -
Anguish - and the Tomb -

Hum by - in muffled Coaches -
Lest they - wonder Why -   15
Any - for the Press of Smiling -
Interrupt - to die -

685   Glee - The great storm is over -
Four - have recovered the Land -
Forty - gone down together -
Into the boiling Sand -

Ring - for the scant Salvation -   5
Toll - for the bonnie Souls -
Neighbor - and friend - and Bridegroom -
Spinning opon the Shoals -

How they will tell the story -
When Winter shake the Door -   10
Till the Children urge -
But the Forty -
Did they - Come back no more?

Then a silence - suffuse the story -
And a softness - the Teller's eye -   15
And the Children - no further question -
And only the Sea - reply -

686   It makes no difference abroad -
The Seasons - fit - the same -
The Mornings blossom into Noons -
And split their Pods of Flame -

Wild flowers - kindle in the Woods -   5
The Brooks slam - all the Day -
No Black bird bates His Banjo -
For passing Calvary -

Auto da Fe - and Judgment -
Are nothing to the Bee -   10

His separation from His Rose -
To Him - sums Misery -

687   I asked no other thing -
No other - was denied -
I offered Being - for it -
The Mighty Merchant sneered -

Brazil? He twirled a Button -   5
Without a glance my way -
"But - Madam - is there nothing else -
That We can show - Today"?

688   To know just how He suffered - would be dear -
To know if any Human eyes were near
To whom He could entrust His wavering gaze -
Until it settled broad - on Paradise -

To know if He was patient - part content -   5
Was Dying as He thought - or different -
Was it a pleasant Day to die -
And did the Sunshine face His way -

What was His furthest mind - of Home - or God -
Or What the Distant say -   10
At News that He ceased Human Nature
Such a Day -

And Wishes - Had He any -
Just His Sigh - accented -
Had been legible - to Me -   15
And was He Confident until
Ill fluttered out - in Everlasting Well -

And if He spoke - What name was Best -
What last
What one broke off with   20
At the Drowsiest -

Was he afraid - or tranquil -
Might He know

How Conscious Consciousness - could grow -
Till Love that was - and Love too best to be -   25
Meet - and the Junction be Eternity

689   It was too late for Man -
        But early, yet, for God -
        Creation - impotent to help -
        But Prayer - remained - Our side -

        How excellent the Heaven -   5
        When Earth - cannot be had -
        How hospitable - then - the face
        Of Our Old Neighbor - God -

690   Forever - is composed of Nows -
        'Tis not a different time -
        Except for Infiniteness -
        And Latitude of Home -

        From this - experienced Here -   5
        Remove the Dates - to These -
        Let Months dissolve in further Months -
        And Years - exhale in Years -

        Without Debate - or Pause -
        Or Celebrated Days -   10
        No different Our Years would be
        From Anno Dominies -

691   'Twas a long Parting - but the time
        For Interview - had Come -
        Before the Judgment Seat of God -
        The last - and second time

        These Fleshless Lovers met -   5
        A Heaven in a Gaze -
        A Heaven of Heavens - the Privilege
        Of One another's Eyes -

                                                                 □

No Lifetime set - on Them -
Appareled as the new
Unborn - except They had beheld -
Born infiniter - now -

Was Bridal - e'er like This?
A Paradise - the Host -
And Cherubim - and Seraphim -
The unobtrusive Guest -

692 Only God - detect the Sorrow -
Only God -
The Jehovahs - are no Babblers -
Unto God -

God the Son - confide it -
Still secure -
God the Spirit's Honor -
Just as sure -

693 Like Eyes that looked on Wastes -
Incredulous of Ought
But Blank - and steady Wilderness -
Diversified by Night -

Just Infinites of Nought -
As far as it could see -
So looked the face I looked opon -
So looked itself - on Me -

I offered it no Help -
Because the Cause was Mine -
The Misery a Compact
As hopeless - as divine -

Neither - would be absolved -
Neither would be a Queen
Without the Other - Therefore -
We perish - tho' We reign -

694   A Tooth opon Our Peace
       The Peace cannot deface -
       Then Wherefore be the Tooth?
       To vitalize the Grace -

       The Heaven hath a Hell -   5
       Itself to signalize -
       And every sign before the Place -
       Is Gilt with Sacrifice -

695   I know Where Wells grow - Droughtless Wells -
       Deep dug - for Summer days -
       Where Mosses go no more away -
       And Pebble - safely plays -

       It's made of Fathoms - and a Belt -   5
       A Belt of jagged Stone -
       Inlaid with Emerald - half way down -
       And Diamonds - jumbled on -

       It has no Bucket - were I rich
       A Bucket I would buy -   10
       I'm often thirsty - but my lips
       Are so high up - You see -

       I read in an Old fashioned Book
       That People "thirst no more" -
       The Wells have Buckets to them there -   15
       It must mean that - I'm sure -

       Shall We remember Parching - then?
       Those Waters sound so grand -
       I think a little Well - like Mine -
       Dearer to understand -   20

696   The Tint I cannot take - is best -
       The Color too remote
       That I could show it in Bazaar -
       A Guinea at a sight -

                                                             □

The fine - impalpable Array -   5
That swaggers on the eye
Like Cleopatra's Company -
Repeated - in the sky -

The Moments of Dominion
That happen on the Soul   10
And leave it with a Discontent
Too exquisite - to tell -

The eager look - on Landscapes -
As if they just repressed
Some secret - that was pushing   15
Like Chariots - in the Vest -

The Pleading of the Summer -
That other Prank - of Snow -
That Cushions Mystery with Tulle,
For fear the Squirrels - know.   20

Their Graspless manners - mock us -
Until the Cheated Eye
Shuts arrogantly - in the Grave -
Another way - to see -

697   Why make it doubt - it hurts it so -
       So sick - to guess -
       So strong - to know -
       So brave - opon it's little Bed
       To tell the very last They said   5
       Unto Itself - and smile - And shake -
       For that dear - distant - dangerous - sake -
       But - the Instead - the Pinching fear
       That Something - it did do - or dare -
       Offend the Vision - and it flee -   10
       And They no more remember me -
       Nor ever turn to tell me why -
       Oh, Master, This is Misery -

698   I live with Him - I see His face -
       I go no more away
       For Visitor - or Sundown -
       Death's single privacy

       The Only One - forestalling Mine -   5
       And that - by Right that He
       Presents a Claim invisible -
       No Wedlock - granted Me -

       I live with Him - I hear His Voice -
       I stand alive - Today -   10
       To witness to the Certainty
       Of Immortality -

       Taught Me - by Time - the lower Way -
       Conviction - every day -
       That Life like This - is stopless -   15
       Be Judgment - what it may -

699   The power to be true to You,
       Until opon my face
       The Judgment push His Picture -
       Presumptuous of Your Place -

       Of This - Could Man deprive Me -   5
       Himself - the Heaven excel -
       Whose invitation - Your's reduced
       Until it showed too small -

700   The Way I read a Letter's - this -
       'Tis first - I lock the Door -
       And push it with my fingers - next -
       For transport it be sure -

       And then I go the furthest off   5
       To counteract a knock -
       Then draw my little Letter forth
       And slowly pick the lock -

                                                             □

Then - glancing narrow, at the Wall -
And narrow at the floor   10
For firm Conviction of a Mouse
Not exorcised before -

Peruse how infinite I am
To no one that You - know -
And sigh for lack of Heaven - but not   15
The Heaven God bestow -

701   The Child's faith is new -
Whole - like His Principle -
Wide - like the Sunrise
On fresh Eyes -
Never had a Doubt -   5
Laughs - at a scruple -
Believes all sham
But Paradise -

Credits the World -
Deems His Dominion   10
Broadest of Sovreignties -
And Caesar - mean -
In the Comparison -
Baseless Emperor -
Ruler of nought,   15
Yet swaying all -

Grown bye and bye
To hold mistaken
His pretty estimates
Of Prickly Things   20
He gains the skill
Sorrowful - as certain -
Men - to anticipate
Instead of Kings -

702   Except the Heaven had come so near -
So seemed to choose My Door -

The Distance would not haunt me so -
I had not hoped - before -

But just to hear the Grace depart -   5
I never thought to see -
Afflicts me with a Double loss -
'Tis lost - And lost to me -

703   To My Small Hearth His fire came -
        And all My House a'glow
        Did fan and rock, with sudden light -
        'Twas Sunrise - 'twas the Sky -

        Impanelled from no Summer brief -   5
        With limit of Decay -
        'Twas Noon - without the News of Night -
        Nay, Nature, it was Day -

704   My Portion is Defeat - today -
        A paler luck than Victory -
        Less Paeans - fewer Bells -
        The Drums dont follow Me - with tunes -
        Defeat - a somewhat slower - means -   5
        More Arduous than Balls -

        'Tis populous with Bone and stain -
        And Men too straight to stoop again -
        And Piles of solid Moan -
        And Chips of Blank - in Boyish Eyes -   10
        And scraps of Prayer -
        And Death's surprise,
        Stamped visible - in stone -

        There's somewhat prouder, Over there -
        The Trumpets tell it to the Air -   15
        How different Victory
        To Him who has it - and the One
        Who to have had it, would have been
        Contenteder - to die -

705   I am ashamed - I hide -
           What right have I - to be a Bride -
           So late a Dowerless Girl -
           Nowhere to hide my dazzled Face -
           No one to teach me that new Grace -   5
           Nor introduce - My soul -

           Me to adorn - How - tell -
           Trinket - to make Me beautiful -
           Fabrics of Cashmere -
           Never a Gown of Dun - more -   10
           Raiment instead - of Pompadour -
           For Me - My soul - to wear -

           Fingers - to frame - my Round Hair
           Oval - as Feudal Ladies wore -
           Far Fashions - Fair -   15
           Skill - to hold my Brow like an Earl -
           Plead - like a Whippowil -
           Prove - like a Pearl -
           Then, for Character -

           Fashion My Spirit quaint - white -   20
           Quick - like a Liquor -
           Gay - like Light -
           Bring Me my best Pride -
           No more ashamed -
           No more to hide -   25
           Meek - let it be - too proud - for Pride -
           Baptized - this Day - A Bride -

706   I cannot live with You -
           It would be Life -
           And Life is over there -
           Behind the Shelf

           The Sexton keeps the key to -   5
           Putting up
           Our Life - His Porcelain -
           Like a Cup -

□

Discarded of the Housewife -
Quaint - or Broke -
A newer Sevres pleases -
Old Ones crack -

I could not die - with You -
For One must wait
To shut the Other's Gaze down -
You - could not -

And I - Could I stand by
And see You - freeze -
Without my Right of Frost -
Death's privilege?

Nor could I rise - with You -
Because Your Face
Would put out Jesus' -
That New Grace

Glow plain - and foreign
On my homesick eye -
Except that You than He
Shone closer by -

They'd judge Us - How -
For You - served Heaven - You know,
Or sought to -
I could not -

Because You saturated sight -
And I had no more eyes
For sordid excellence
As Paradise

And were You lost, I would be -
Though my name
Rang loudest
On the Heavenly fame -

And were You - saved -
And I - condemned to be
Where You were not
That self - were Hell to me -

☐

So we must meet apart -
You there - I - here -
With just the Door ajar
That Oceans are - and Prayer -
And that White Sustenance -
Despair -

45

50

707   Size circumscribes - it has no room
For petty furniture -
The Giant tolerates no Gnat
For Ease of Gianture -

Repudiates it, all the more -
Because intrinsic size
Ignores the possibility
Of Calumnies - or Flies -

5

708   They put Us far apart -
As separate as Sea
And Her unsown Peninsula -
We signified "These see" -

They took away our eyes -
They thwarted Us with Guns -
"I see Thee" Each responded straight
Through Telegraphic Signs -

5

With Dungeons - They devised -
But through their thickest skill -
And their opaquest Adamant -
Our Souls saw - just as well -

10

They summoned Us to die -
With sweet alacrity
We stood upon our stapled feet -
Condemned - but just - to see -

15

Permission to recant -
Permission to forget -

We turned our backs opon the Sun
For perjury of that -   20

Not Either - noticed Death -
Of Paradise - aware -
Each other's Face - was all the Disc
Each other's setting - saw -

709   Me from Myself - to banish -
Had I Art -
Invincible My Fortress
Unto All Heart -

But since Myself - assault Me -   5
How have I peace
Except by subjugating
Consciousness?

And since We're Mutual Monarch
How this be   10
Except by Abdication -
Me - of Me - ?

710   Doom is the House without the Door -
'Tis entered from the Sun -
And then the Ladder's thrown away,
Because Escape - is done -

'Tis varied by the Dream   5
Of what they do outside -
Where Squirrels play - and Berries dye -
And Hemlocks - bow - to God -

711   I meant to have but modest needs -
Such as Content - and Heaven -
Within my income - these could lie
And Life and I - keep even -

□

But since the last - included both -
It would suffice my Prayer
But just for one - to stipulate -
And Grace would grant the Pair -

And so - opon this wise - I prayed -
Great Spirit - Give to me
A Heaven not so large as Your's,
But large enough - for me -

A Smile suffused Jehovah's face -
The Cherubim - withdrew -
Grave Saints stole out to look at me -
And showed their dimples - too -

I left the Place - with all my might -
I threw my Prayer away -
The Quiet Ages picked it up -
And Judgment - twinkled - too -
That one so honest - be extant -
It take the Tale for true -
That "Whatsoever Ye shall ask -
Itself be given You" -

But I, grown shrewder - scan the Skies
With a suspicious Air -
As Children - swindled for the first
All Swindlers - be - infer -

712   I could suffice for Him, I knew -
        He - could suffice for Me -
        Yet Hesitating Fractions - Both
        Surveyed Infinity -

        "Would I be Whole" He sudden broached -
        My Syllable rebelled -
        'Twas face to face with Nature - forced -
        'Twas face to face with God -

        Withdrew the Sun - to other Wests -
        Withdrew the furthest Star

Before Decision - stooped to speech -
And then - be audibler

The Answer of the Sea unto
The Motion of the Moon -
Herself adjust Her Tides - unto -   15
Could I - do else - with Mine?

713   You left me - Sire - two Legacies -
      A Legacy of Love
      A Heavenly Father would suffice
      Had He the offer of -

      You left me Boundaries of Pain -   5
      Capacious as the Sea -
      Between Eternity and Time -
      Your Consciousness - and me -

714   No Man can compass a Despair -
      As round a Goalless Road
      No faster than a mile at once
      The Traveller proceed -

      Unconscious of the Width -   5
      Unconscious that the Sun
      Be setting on His progress -
      So accurate the one

      At estimating Pain -
      Whose own - has just begun -   10
      His ignorance - the Angel
      That pilot Him along -

715   The Sun kept setting - setting - still
      No Hue of Afternoon -
      Opon the Village I perceived -
      From House to House 'twas Noon -

                                                            □

The Dusk kept dropping - dropping - still   5
No Dew opon the Grass -
But only on my Forehead stopped -
And wandered in my Face -

My Feet kept drowsing - drowsing - still
My fingers were awake -   10
Yet why so little sound - Myself
Unto my seeming - make?

How well I knew the Light before -
I could not see it now -
'Tis Dying - I am doing - but   15
I'm not afraid to know -

716   Shells from the Coast mistaking -
       I cherished them for all -
       Happening in After Ages
       To entertain a Pearl -

       Wherefore so late - I murmured -   5
       My need of Thee - be done -
       Therefore - the Pearl responded -
       My Period begin

717   The Heaven vests for Each
       In that small Deity
       It craved the grace to worship
       Some bashful Summer's Day -

       Half shrinking from the Glory   5
       It importuned to see
       Till these faint Tabernacles drop
       In full Eternity -

       How imminent the Venture -
       As One should sue a Star -   10
       For His mean sake to leave the Row
       And entertain Despair -

                                                   □

A Clemency so common -
We almost cease to fear -
Enabling the minutest -   15
And furthest - to adore -

718   The Spirit is the Conscious Ear -
       We actually Hear
       When We inspect - that's audible -
       That is admitted - Here -

       For other Services - as Sound -   5
       There hangs a smaller Ear
       Outside the Castle - that Contain -
       The other - only - Hear -

719   If He were living - dare I ask -
       And how if He be dead -
       And so around the Words I went -
       Of meeting them - afraid -

       I hinted Changes - Lapse of Time -   5
       The Surfaces of Years -
       I touched with Caution - lest they crack -
       And show me to my fears -

       Reverted to adjoining Lives -
       Adroitly turning out   10
       Wherever I suspected Graves -
       'Twas prudenter - I thought -

       And He - I pushed - with sudden force -
       In face of the Suspense -
       "Was buried" - "Buried"! "He!"   15
       My Life just holds the Trench -

720   As if the Sea should part
       And show a further Sea -
       And that - a further - and the Three
       But a Presumption be -

                                                           □

Of Periods of Seas -
Unvisited of Shores -
Themselves the Verge of Seas to be -
Eternity - is Those -

5

721   "Nature" is what We see -
       The Hill - the Afternoon -
       Squirrel - Eclipse - the Bumble bee -
       Nay - Nature is Heaven -

       "Nature" is what We hear -
       The Bobolink - the Sea -
       Thunder - the Cricket -
       Nay - Nature is Harmony -

5

       "Nature" is what We know -
       But have no Art to say -
       So impotent our Wisdom is
       To Her Sincerity -

10

722   Opon Concluded Lives
       There's nothing cooler falls -
       Than Life's sweet Calculations -
       The mixing Bells and Palls -

       Makes Lacerating Tune -
       To Ears the Dying side -
       'Tis Coronal - and Funeral -
       Saluting - in the Road -

5

723   Have any like Myself
       Investigating March,
       New Houses on the Hill descried -
       And possibly a Church -

       That were not, We are sure -
       As lately as the Snow -
       And are Today - if We exist -
       Though how may this be so?

5

□

Have any like Myself
Conjectured Who may be   10
The Occupants of these Abodes -
So easy to the Sky -

'Twould seem that God should be
The nearest Neighbor to -
And Heaven - a convenient Grace   15
For Show, or Company?

Have any like Myself
Preserved the Charm secure
By shunning carefully the Place
All Seasons of the Year,   20

Excepting March - 'Tis then
My Villages be seen -
And possibly a Steeple -
Not afterward - by Men -

724   Each Life converges to some Centre -
       Expressed - or still -
       Exists in every Human Nature
       A Goal -

       Embodied scarcely to itself - it may be -   5
       Too fair
       For Credibility's presumption
       To mar -

       Adored with caution - as a Brittle Heaven -
       To reach   10
       Were hopeless, as the Rainbow's Raiment
       To touch -   .

       Yet persevered toward - surer - for the Distance -
       How high -
       Unto the Saints' slow diligence -   15
       The Sky -

       Ungained - it may be - by a Life's low Venture -
       But then -

And cease to recollect
The Augur and the Carpenter -
Just such a retrospect
Hath the perfected Life -
A Past of Plank and Nail   10
And slowness - then the scaffolds drop
Affirming it a Soul -

730   You've seen Balloons set - Hav'nt You?
So stately they ascend -
It is as Swans - discarded You,
For Duties Diamond -

Their Liquid Feet go softly out   5
Opon a Sea of Blonde -
They spurn the Air, as 'twere too mean
For Creatures so renowned -

Their Ribbons just beyond the eye -
They struggle - some - for Breath -   10
And yet the Crowd applaud, below -
They would not encore - Death -

The Gilded Creature strains - and spins -
Trips frantic in a Tree -
Tears open her imperial Veins -   15
And tumbles in the Sea -

The Crowd - retire with an Oath -
The Dust in Streets - go down -
And Clerks in Counting Rooms
Observe - "'Twas only a Balloon" -   20

731   A Thought went up my mind today -
That I have had before -
But did not finish - some way back -
I could not fix the Year -

Nor Where it went - nor why it came   5
The second time to me -

Nor definitely, what it was -
Have I the Art to say -

But somewhere - in my soul - I know -
I've met the Thing before -   10
It just reminded me - 'twas all -
And came my way no more -

732   A first Mute Coming -
       In the Stranger's House -
       A first fair Going -
       When the Bells rejoice -

       A first Exchange - of   5
       What hath mingled - been -
       For Lot - exhibited to
       Faith - alone -

733   Out of sight? What of that?
       See the Bird - reach it!
       Curve by Curve - Sweep by Sweep -
       Round the Steep Air -
       Danger! What is that to Her?   5
       Better 'tis to fail - there -
       Than debate - here -

       Blue is Blue - the World through -
       Amber - Amber - Dew - Dew -
       Seek - Friend - and see -   10
       Heaven is shy of Earth - that's all -
       Bashful Heaven - thy Lovers small -
       Hide - too - from thee -

734   No matter - now - Sweet -
       But when I'm Earl -
       Wont you wish you'd spoken
       To that dull Girl?

                                                                □

Trivial a Word - just -
Trivial - a Smile -
But wont you wish you'd spared one
When I'm Earl?

I shant need it - then -
Crests - will do -
Eagles on my Buckles -
On my Belt - too -

Ermine - my familiar Gown -
Say - Sweet - then
Wont you wish you'd smiled - just -
Me opon?

735   The Moon was but a Chin of Gold
A night or two ago -
And now she turns Her perfect Face
Opon the World below -

Her Forehead is of Amplest Blonde -
Her Cheek - a Beryl hewn -
Her Eye unto the Summer Dew
The likest I have known -

Her Lips of Amber never part -
But what must be the smile
Opon Her Friend she could confer
Were such Her silver will -

And what a privilege to be
But the remotest star -
For Certainty she take Her way
Beside Your Palace Door -

Her Bonnet is the Firmament -
The Universe - Her shoe -
The Stars - the Trinkets at Her Belt -
Her Dimities - of Blue -

736   You said that I "was Great" - one Day -
       Then "Great" it be - if that please Thee -
       Or Small, or any size at all -
       Nay - I'm the size suit Thee -

       Tall - like the Stag - would that?   5
       Or lower - like the Wren -
       Or other hights of other ones
       I've seen?

       Tell which - it's dull to guess -
       And I must be Rhinoceros   10
       Or Mouse
       At once - for Thee -

       So say - if Queen it be -
       Or Page - please Thee -
       I'm that - or nought -   15
       Or other thing - if other thing there be -
       With just this stipulus -
       I suit Thee -

737   I many times thought Peace had come
       When Peace was far away -
       As Wrecked Men - deem they sight the Land -
       At Centre of the Sea -

       And struggle slacker - but to prove   5
       As hopelessly as I -
       How many the fictitious Shores -
       Or any Harbor be -

738   No other can reduce
       Our mortal Consequence
       Like the remembering it be nought
       A period from hence

       But Contemplation for   5
       Cotemporaneous nought -

Our only Competition
Jehovah's Estimate.

739   Joy to have merited the Pain -
To merit the Release -
Joy to have perished every step -
To Compass Paradise -

Pardon - to look opon thy face -   5
With these old fashioned Eyes -
Better than new - could be - for that -
Though bought in Paradise -

Because they looked on thee before -
And thou hast looked on them -   10
Prove Me - My Hazel Witnesses
The features are the same -

So fleet thou wert, when present -
So infinite - when gone -
An Orient's Apparition -   15
Remanded of the Morn -

The Hight I recollect -
'Twas even with the Hills -
The Depth opon my Soul was notched -
As Floods - on Whites of Wheels -   20

To Haunt - till Time have dropped
His last Decade away,
And Haunting actualize - to last
At least - Eternity -

740   On a Columnar Self -
How ample to rely
In Tumult - or Extremity -
How good the Certainty

That Lever cannot pry -   5
And Wedge cannot divide

Conviction - That Granitic Base -
Though none be on our side -

Suffice Us - for a Crowd -
Ourself - and Rectitude -   10
And that Assembly - not far off
From furthest Spirit - God -

741   Nature - the Gentlest Mother is,
        Impatient of no Child -
        The feeblest - or the Waywardest -
        Her Admonition mild -

        In Forest - and the Hill -   5
        By Traveller - be heard -
        Restraining Rampant Squirrel -
        Or too impetuous Bird -

        How fair Her Conversation -
        A Summer Afternoon -   10
        Her Household - Her Assembly -
        And when the Sun go down -

        Her Voice among the Aisles
        Incite the timid prayer
        Of the minutest Cricket -   15
        The most unworthy Flower -

        When all the Children sleep -
        She turns as long away
        As will suffice to light Her lamps -
        Then bending from the Sky -   20

        With infinite Affection -
        And infiniter Care -
        Her Golden finger on Her lip -
        Wills Silence - Everywhere -

742   No Prisoner be -
        Where Liberty -
        Himself - abide with Thee -

743   Behind Me - dips Eternity -
       Before Me - Immortality -
       Myself - the Term between -
       Death but the Drift of Eastern Gray,
       Dissolving into Dawn away,   5
       Before the West begin -

       'Tis Kingdoms - afterward - they say -
       In perfect - pauseless Monarchy -
       Whose Prince - is Son of none -
       Himself - His Dateless Dynasty -   10
       Himself - Himself diversify -
       In Duplicate divine -

       'Tis Miracle before Me - then -
       'Tis Miracle behind - between -
       A Crescent in the Sea -   15
       With Midnight to the North of Her -
       And Midnight to the South of Her -
       And Maelstrom - in the Sky -

744   She dwelleth in the Ground -
       Where Daffodils - abide -
       Her Maker - Her Metropolis -
       The Universe - Her Maid -

       To fetch Her Grace - and Hue -   5
       And Fairness - and Renown -
       The Firmament's - To pluck Her -
       And fetch Her Thee - be mine -

745   Sweet Mountains - Ye tell Me no lie -
       Never deny Me - Never fly -
       Those same unvarying Eyes
       Turn on Me - When I fail - or feign,
       Or take the Royal names in vain -   5
       Their far - slow - Violet Gaze -

       My Strong Madonnas - Cherish still -
       The Wayward Nun - beneath the Hill -

Whose service - is to You -
Her latest Worship - When the Day
Fades from the Firmament away -
To lift Her Brows on You -

746   It tossed - and tossed -
        A little Brig I knew - o'ertook by Blast -
        It spun - and spun -
        And groped delirious, for Morn -

        It slipped - and slipped -   5
        As One that drunken - stept -
        It's white foot tripped -
        Then dropped from sight -

        Ah, Brig - Good Night
        To crew and You -   10
        The Ocean's Heart too smooth - too Blue -
        To break for You -

747   It's easy to invent a Life -
        God does it - every Day -
        Creation - but the Gambol
        Of His Authority -

        It's easy to efface it -   5
        The thrifty Deity
        Could scarce afford Eternity
        To Spontaneity -

        The Perished Patterns murmur -
        But His Perturbless Plan   10
        Proceed - inserting Here - a Sun -
        There - leaving out a Man -

748   God gave a Loaf to every Bird -
        But just a Crumb - to Me -
        I dare not eat it - tho' I starve -
        My poignant luxury -

                                                      □

To own it - touch it -   5
Prove the feat - that made the Pellet mine -
Too happy - for my Sparrow's chance -
For Ampler Coveting -

It might be Famine - all around -
I could not miss an Ear -   10
Such Plenty smiles opon my Board -
My Garner shows so fair -

I wonder how the Rich - may feel -
An Indiaman - An Earl -
I deem that I - with but a Crumb -   15
Am Sovreign of them all -

749   Where Thou art - that - is Home -
         Cashmere - or Calvary - the same -
         Degree - or Shame -
         I scarce esteem Location's Name -
         So I may Come -   5

         What Thou dost - is Delight -
         Bondage as Play - be sweet -
         Imprisonment - Content -
         And Sentence - Sacrament -
         Just We two - meet -   10

         Where Thou art not - is Wo -
         Tho' Bands of Spices - row -
         What Thou dost not - Despair -
         Tho' Gabriel - praise me - Sir -

750   We thirst at first - 'tis Nature's Act -
         And later - when we die -
         A little Water supplicate -
         Of fingers going by -

         It intimates the finer want -   5
         Whose adequate supply

Is that Great Water in the West -
Termed Immortality -

751   Precious to Me - She still shall be -
        Though She forget the name I bear -
        The fashion of the Gown I wear -
        The very Color of My Hair -

        So like the Meadows - now -   5
        I dared to show a Tress of Their's
        If haply - She might not despise
        A Buttercup's Array -

        I know the Whole - obscures the Part -
        The fraction - that appeased the Heart   10
        Till Number's Empery -
        Remembered - as the Milliner's flower
        When Summer's Everlasting Dower -
        Confronts the dazzled Bee -

752   Ah, Teneriffe - Receding Mountain -
        Purples of Ages halt for You -   .
        Sunset reviews Her Sapphire Regiments -
        Day - drops You His Red Adieu -
        Still clad in Your Mail of Ices -   5
        Eye of Granite - and Ear of Steel -
        Passive alike - to Pomp - and Parting -
        Ah, Teneriffe - We're pleading still -

753   Grief is a Mouse -
        And chooses Wainscot in the Breast
        For His shy House -
        And baffles quest -

        Grief is a Thief - quick startled -   5
        Pricks His Ear - report to hear
        Of that Vast Dark -
        That swept His Being - back -

                                                        □

Grief is a Juggler - boldest at the Play -
Lest if He flinch - the eye that way   10
Pounce on His Bruises - One - say - or Three -
Grief is a Gourmand - spare His luxury -

Best Grief is Tongueless - before He'll tell -
Burn Him in the Public square -
His Ashes - will   15
Possibly - if they refuse - How then know -
Since a Rack could'nt coax a syllable - now

754   Let Us play Yesterday -
        I - the Girl at School -
        You - and Eternity - the untold Tale -

        Easing my famine
        At my Lexicon -   5
        Logarithm - had I - for Drink -
        'Twas a dry Wine -

        Somewhat different - must be -
        Dreams tint the Sleep -
        Cunning Reds of Morning   10
        Make the Blind - leap -

        Still at the Egg-life -
        Chafing the Shell -
        When you troubled the Ellipse -
        And the Bird fell -   15

        Manacles be dim - they say -
        To the new Free -
        Liberty - commoner -
        Never could - to me -

        'Twas my last gratitude   20
        When I slept - at night -
        'Twas the first Miracle
        Let in - with Light -

        Can the Lark resume the Shell -
        Easier - for the Sky -   25

Would'nt Bonds hurt more
Than Yesterday?

Would'nt Dungeons sorer grate
On the Man - free -
Just long enough to taste -   30
Then - doomed new -

God of the Manacle
As of the Free -
Take not my Liberty
Away from Me -   35

755   Alter! When the Hills do -
       Falter! When the Sun
       Question if His Glory
       Be the Perfect One -

       Surfeit! When the Daffodil   5
       Doth of the Dew -
       Even as Herself - Sir -
       I will - Of You -

756   Bereavement in their death to feel
       Whom We have never seen -
       A Vital Kinsmanship import
       Our Soul and their's between -

       For Stranger - Strangers do not mourn -   5
       There be Immortal friends
       Whom Death see first - 'tis news of this
       That paralyze Ourselves -

       Who - vital only to Our Thought -
       Such Presence bear away   10
       In dying - 'tis as if Our souls
       Absconded - suddenly -

757   I think To Live - may be a Bliss
       To those who dare to try -
       Beyond my limit - to conceive -
       My lip - to testify -

       I think the Heart I former wore   5
       Could widen - till to me
       The Other, like the little Bank
       Appear - unto the Sea -

       I think the Days - could every one
       In Ordination stand -   10
       And Majesty - be easier -
       Than an inferior kind -

       No numb alarm - lest Difference come -
       No Goblin - on the Bloom -
       No start in Apprehension's Ear,   15
       No Bankruptcy - no Doom -

       But Certainties of Sun -
       Midsummer - in the Mind -
       A steadfast South - opon the Soul -
       Her Polar time - behind -   20

       The Vision - pondered long -
       So plausible becomes
       That I esteem the fiction - real -
       The Real - fictitious seems -

       How bountiful the Dream -   25
       What Plenty - it would be
       Had all my Life but been Mistake
       Just rectified - in Thee

758   A little Road - not made of Man -
       Enabled of the Eye -
       Accessible to Thill of Bee -
       Or Cart of Butterfly -

       If Town it have - beyond itself -   5
       'Tis that - I cannot say -

I only know - no Curricle that rumble there
Bear me -

759 Her Sweet turn to leave the Homestead
Came the Darker Way -
Carriages - Be Sure - and Guests - True -
But for Holiday

'Twas more pitiful Endeavor   5
Than did Loaded Sea
O'er the Curls attempt to caper
It had cast away -

Never Bride had such Assembling -
Never kinsmen kneeled   10
To salute so fair a Forehead -
Garland be indeed -

Fitter Feet - of Her before us -
Than whatever Brow
Art of Snow - or Trick of Lily   15
Possibly bestow

Of Her Father - Whoso ask Her -
He shall seek as high
As the Palm - that serve the Desert -
To obtain the sky -   20

Distance - be Her only Motion -
If 'tis Nay - or Yes -
Acquiescence - or Demurral -
Whosoever guess -

He - must pass the Crystal Angle   25
That obscure Her face -
He - must have achieved in person
Equal Paradise -

760 Pain - has an Element of Blank -
It cannot recollect

When it begun - Or if there were
A time when it was not -

It has no Future - but itself -   5
It's Infinite contain
It's Past - enlightened to perceive
New Periods - Of Pain.

761   So much Summer
        Me for showing
        Illegitimate -
        Would a Smile's minute bestowing
        Too exorbitant   5

        To the Lady
        With the Guinea
        Look - if she should know
        Crumb of Mine
        A Robin's Larder   10
        Would suffice to stow -

762   Promise This - When You be Dying -
        Some shall summon Me -
        Mine belong Your latest Sighing -
        Mine - to Belt Your Eye -

        Not with Coins - though they be Minted   5
        From An Emperor's Hand -
        Be my lips - the only Buckle
        Your low Eyes - demand -

        Mine to stay - when all have wandered -
        To devise once more   10
        If the Life be too surrendered -
        Life of Mine - restore -

        Poured like this - My Whole Libation -
        Just that You should see
        Bliss of Death - Life's Bliss extol thro'   15
        Imitating You -

                                                                  □

Mine - to guard Your Narrow Precinct -
To seduce the Sun
Longest on Your South, to linger,
Largest Dews of Morn   20

To demand, in Your low favor -
Lest the Jealous Grass
Greener lean - Or fonder cluster
Round some other face -

Mine to supplicate Madonna -   25
If Madonna be
Could behold so far a Creature -
Christ - omitted - Me -

Just to follow Your dear feature -
Ne'er so far behind -   30
For My Heaven -
Had I not been
Most enough - denied?

763   I had no time to Hate -
Because
The Grave would hinder me -
And Life was not so
Ample I   5
Could finish - Enmity -

Nor had I time to Love -
But since
Some Industry must be -
The little Toil of Love -   10
I thought
Be large enough for Me -

764   My Life had stood - a Loaded Gun -
In Corners - till a Day
The Owner passed - identified -
And carried Me away -

☐

And now We roam in Sovreign Woods -   5
And now We hunt the Doe -
And every time I speak for Him
The Mountains straight reply -

And do I smile, such cordial light
Opon the Valley glow -   10
It is as a Vesuvian face
Had let it's pleasure through -

And when at Night - Our good Day done -
I guard My Master's Head -
'Tis better than the Eider Duck's   15
Deep Pillow - to have shared -

To foe of His - I'm deadly foe -
None stir the second time -
On whom I lay a Yellow Eye -
Or an emphatic Thumb -   20

Though I than He - may longer live
He longer must - than I -
For I have but the power to kill,
Without - the power to die -

765   The Sunrise runs for Both -
        The East - Her Purple Troth
        Keeps with the Hill -
        The Noon unwinds Her Blue
        Till One Breadth cover Two -   5
        Remotest - still -

        Nor does the Night forget
        A Lamp for Each - to set -
        Wicks wide away -
        The North - Her blazing Sign   10
        Erects in Iodine -
        Till Both - can see -

        The Midnight's Dusky Arms
        Clasp Hemispheres, and Homes
        And so   15

Opon Her Bosom - One -
And One opon Her Hem -
Both lie -

766   No Bobolink - reverse His Singing
When the only Tree
Ever He minded occupying
By the Farmer be -

Clove to the Root -   5
His Spacious Future -
Best Horizon - gone -
Brave Bobolink -
Whose Music be His
Only Anodyne -   10

767   One Blessing had I than the rest
So larger to my Eyes
That I stopped guaging - satisfied -
For this enchanted size -

It was the limit of my Dream -   5
The focus of my Prayer -
A perfect - paralyzing Bliss -
Contented as Despair -

I knew no more of Want - or Cold -
Phantasms both become   10
For this new Value in the Soul -
Supremest Earthly Sum -

The Heaven below the Heaven above -
Obscured with ruddier Blue -
Life's Latitudes leant over - full -   15
The Judgment perished - too -

Why Bliss so scantily disburse -
Why Paradise defer -
Why Floods be served to Us - in Bowls -
I speculate no more -   20

768   The Mountains - grow unnoticed -
Their Purple figures rise
Without attempt - Exhaustion -
Assistance - or Applause -

In Their Eternal Faces   5
The Sun - with just delight
Looks long - and last - and golden -
For fellowship - at night -

769   These - saw Visions -
Latch them softly -
These - held Dimples -
Smooth them slow -
This - addressed departing accents -   5
Quick - Sweet Mouth - to miss thee so -

This - we stroked -
Unnumbered - Satin -
These - we held among our own -
Fingers of the Slim Aurora -   10
Not so arrogant - this Noon -

These - adjust - that ran to meet Us -
Pearl - for stocking - Pearl for Shoe -
Paradise - the only Palace
Fit for Her reception - now -   15

770   Strong Draughts of Their Refreshing Minds
To drink - enables Mine
Through Desert or the Wilderness
As bore it sealed Wine -

To go elastic - Or as One   5
The Camel's trait - attained -
How powerful the stimulus
Of an Hermetic Mind -

771   We miss Her - not because We see -
       The Absence of an Eye -
       Except it's Mind accompany -
       Abridge Society

       As slightly as the Routes of Stars -   5
       Ourselves - asleep below -
       We know that their superior Eyes
       Include Us - as they go -

772   Essential Oils - are wrung -
       The Attar from the Rose
       Be not expressed by Suns - alone -
       It is the gift of Screws -

       The General Rose - decay -   5
       But this - in Lady's Drawer
       Make Summer - When the Lady lie
       In Ceaseless Rosemary -

773   Conscious am I in my Chamber -
       Of a shapeless friend -
       He doth not attest by Posture -
       Nor confirm - by Word -

       Neither Place - need I present Him -   5
       Fitter Courtesy
       Hospitable intuition
       Of His Company -

       Presence - is His furthest license -
       Neither He to Me   10
       Nor Myself to Him - by Accent -
       Forfeit Probity -

       Weariness of Him, were quainter
       Than Monotony
       Knew a Particle - of Space's   15
       Vast Society -

                                                            □

Neither if He visit Other -
Do He dwell - or Nay - know I -
But Instinct esteem Him
Immortality -   20

774   You taught me Waiting with Myself -
        Appointment strictly kept -
        You taught Me fortitude of Fate -
        This - also - I have learnt -

        An Altitude of Death, that could   5
        No bitterer debar
        Than Life - had done - before it -
        Yet - there is a Science more -

        The Heaven you know - to understand
        That you be not ashamed   10
        Of Me - in Christ's bright Audience
        Opon the further Hand -

775   Suspense - is Hostiler than Death -
        Death - tho'soever Broad,
        Is just Death, and cannot increase -
        Suspense - does not conclude -

        But perishes - to live anew -   5
        But just anew to die -
        Annihilation - plated fresh
        With Immortality -

776   Drama's Vitallest Expression is the Common Day
        That arise and set about Us -
        Other Tragedy

        Perish in the Recitation -
        This - the best enact   5
        When the Audience is scattered
        And the Boxes shut -

                                                   □

"Hamlet" to Himself were Hamlet -
Had not Shakespeare wrote -
Though the "Romeo" left no Record   10
Of his Juliet,

It were infinite enacted
In the Human Heart -
Only Theatre recorded
Owner cannot shut -   15

777   Life, and Death, and Giants -
       Such as These - are still -
       Minor - Apparatus - Hopper of the Mill -
       Beetle at the Candle -
       Or a Fife's Fame -   5
       Maintain - by Accident that they proclaim -

778   Four Trees - opon a solitary Acre -
       Without Design
       Or Order, or Apparent Action -
       Maintain -

       The Sun - opon a Morning meets them -   5
       The Wind -
       No nearer Neighbor - have they -
       But God -

       The Acre gives them - Place -
       They - Him - Attention of Passer by -   10
       Of Shadow, or of Squirrel, haply -
       Or Boy -

       What Deed is Their's unto the General Nature -
       What Plan
       They severally - retard - or further -   15
       Unknown -

779   The Grace - Myself - might not obtain -
       Confer opon my flower -

Refracted but a Countenance -
For I - inhabit Her -

780   The Birds reported from the South -
A News express to Me -
A spicy Charge, My little Posts -
But I am deaf - Today -

The Flowers - appealed - a timid Throng -   5
I reinforced the Door -
Go blossom to the Bees - I said -
And trouble Me - no More -

The Summer Grace, for notice strove -
Remote - Her best Array -   10
The Heart - to stimulate the Eye
Refused too utterly -

At length, a Mourner, like Myself,
She drew away austere -
Her frosts to ponder - then it was   15
I recollected Her -

She suffered Me, for I had mourned -
I offered Her no word -
My Witness - was the Crape I bore -
Her - Witness - was Her Dead -   20

Thenceforward - We - together dwelt -
She - never questioned Me -
Nor I - Herself -
Our Contract
A Wiser Sympathy   25

781   Remorse - is Memory - awake -
Her Parties all astir -
A Presence of Departed Acts -
At window - and at Door -

It's Past - set down before the Soul   5
And lighted with a match -

Perusal - to facilitate -
And help Belief to stretch -

Remorse is cureless - the Disease
Not even God - can heal -   10
For 'tis His institution - and
The Adequate of Hell -

782   Renunciation - is a piercing Virtue -
           The letting go
           A Presence - for an Expectation -
           Not now -
           The putting out of Eyes -   5
           Just Sunrise -
           Lest Day -
           Day's Great Progenitor -
           Outvie
           Renunciation - is the Choosing   10
           Against itself -
           Itself to justify
           Unto itself -
           When larger function -
           Make that appear -   15
           Smaller - that Covered Vision - Here -

783   Never for Society
           He shall seek in vain -
           Who His own acquaintance
           Cultivate - Of Men
           Wiser Men may weary -   5
           But the Man within

           Never knew Satiety -
           Better entertain
           Than could Border Ballad -
           Or Biscayan Hymn -   10
           Neither introduction
           Need You - unto Him -

784   I sometimes drop it, for a Quick -
       The Thought to be alive -
       Anonymous Delight to know -
       And madder - to conceive -

       Consoles a wo so monstrous   5
       That did it tear all Day,
       Without an instant's Respite -
       'Twould look too far - to Die -

       Delirium - diverts the Wretch
       For Whom the Scaffold neighs -   10
       The Hammock's motion lulls the Heads
       So close on Paradise -

       A Reef - crawled easy from the Sea
       Eats off the Brittle Line -
       The Sailor does'nt know the Stroke -   15
       Until He's past the Pain -

785   It dropped so low - in my Regard -
       I heard it hit the Ground -
       And go to pieces on the Stones
       At bottom of my mind -

       Yet blamed the Fate that flung it - less   5
       Than I denounced Myself,
       For entertaining Plated Wares
       Opon my Silver Shelf -

786   Autumn - overlooked my Knitting -
       Dyes - said He - have I -
       Could disparage a Flamingo -
       Show Me them - said I -

       Cochineal - I chose - for deeming   5
       It resemble Thee -
       And the little Border - Dusker -
       For resembling Me -

787   Bloom opon the Mountain stated -
Blameless of a name -
Efflorescence of a Sunset -
Reproduced - the same -

Seed had I, my Purple Sowing   5
Should endow the Day -
Not - a Tropic of a Twilight -
Show itself away -

Who for tilling - to the Mountain
Come - and disappear -   10
Whose be her Renown - or fading -
Witness is not here -

While I state - the Solemn Petals -
Far as North - and East -
Far as South - and West expanding -   15
Culminate - in Rest -

And the Mountain to the Evening
Fit His Countenance -
Indicating by no Muscle
The Experience -   20

788   Publication - is the Auction
Of the Mind of Man -
Poverty - be justifying
For so foul a thing

Possibly - but We - would rather   5
From Our Garret go
White - unto the White Creator -
Than invest - Our Snow -

Thought belong to Him who gave it -
Then - to Him Who bear   10
It's Corporeal illustration - sell
The Royal Air -

In the Parcel - Be the Merchant
Of the Heavenly Grace -

But reduce no Human Spirit
To Disgrace of Price -

789 All but Death, Can be adjusted
Dynasties repaired -
Systems - settled in their Sockets -
Citadels - dissolved -

Wastes of Lives - resown with Colors 5
By Succeeding Springs -
Death - unto itself - Exception -
Is exempt from Change -

790 Growth of Man - like Growth of Nature -
Gravitates within -
Atmosphere, and Sun endorse it -
But it stir - alone -

Each - it's difficult Ideal 5
Must achieve - Itself -
Through the solitary prowess
Of a Silent Life -

Effort - is the sole condition -
Patience of Itself - 10
Patience of opposing forces -
And intact Belief -

Looking on - is the Department
Of it's Audience -
But Transaction - is assisted 15
By no Countenance -

791 My Worthiness is all my Doubt -
His Merit - all my fear -
Contrasting which, my quality
Do lowlier - appear -

□

Lest I should insufficient prove   5
For His beloved Need -
The Chiefest Apprehension
Opon my thronging Mind -

'Tis true - that Deity to stoop
Inherently incline -   10
For nothing higher than Itself
Itself can rest opon -

So I - the Undivine Abode
Of His Elect Content -
Conform my Soul - as 'twere a Church,   15
Unto Her Sacrament -

792 So the Eyes accost - and sunder
In an Audience -
Stamped - occasionally - forever -
So may Countenance

Entertain - without addressing   5
Countenance of One
In a Neighboring Horizon -
Gone - as soon as known -

793 My Soul - accused Me - And I quailed -
As Tongues of Diamond had reviled
All Else accused Me - and I smiled -
My Soul - that Morning - was My friend -

Her favor - is the best Disdain   5
Toward Artifice of Time - or Men -
But Her Disdain - 'twere lighter bear
A finger of Enamelled Fire -

794   From Us She wandered now a Year,
      Her tarrying, unknown,
      If Wilderness prevent her feet
      Or that Etherial Zone

      No Eye hath seen and lived   5
      We ignorant must be -
      We only know what time of Year
      We took the Mystery.

795   Truth - is as old as God -
      His Twin identity
      And will endure as long as He
      A Co-Eternity -

      And perish on the Day   5
      Himself is borne away
      From Mansion of the Universe
      A lifeless Deity.

796   The Wind begun to rock the Grass
      With threatening Tunes and low -
      He threw a Menace at the Earth -
      Another, at the Sky -
      The Leaves unhooked themselves from Trees   5
      And started all abroad -
      The Dust did scoop itself like Hands
      And throw away the Road -
      The Wagons quickened on the streets
      The Thunder hurried slow -   10
      The Lightning showed a yellow Beak
      And then a livid Claw -
      The Birds put up the Bars to Nests -
      The Cattle clung to Barns -
      Then came one Drop of Giant Rain   15
      And then as if the Hands

That held the Dams, had parted hold,
The Waters wrecked the Sky,
But overlooked My Father's House -
Just quartering a Tree -

797   The Definition of Beauty is
       That Definition is none -
       Of Heaven, easing Analysis,
       Since Heaven and He are One.

798   The Veins of other Flowers
       The Scarlet Flowers are
       Till Nature leisure has for Terms
       As "Branch", and "Jugular".

       We pass, and she abides.   5
       We conjugate Her Skill
       While She creates and federates
       Without a syllable -

799   All I may, if small,
       Do it not display
       Larger for the Totalness -
       'Tis Economy

       To bestow a World   5
       And withold a Star -
       Utmost, is Munificence -
       Less, tho' larger, poor -

800   I never saw a Moor.
       I never saw the Sea -
       Yet know I how the Heather looks
       And what a Billow be -

       I never spoke with God   5
       Nor visited in Heaven -

Yet certain am I of the spot
As if the Checks were given -

801   As Sleigh Bells seem in Summer
Or Bees, at Christmas show -
So fairy - so fictitious -
The individuals do
Repealed from Observation -   5
A Party that we knew -
More distant in an instant
Than Dawn in Timbuctoo -

802   The spry Arms of the Wind
If I could crawl between
I have an errand imminent
To an adjoining Zone -
I should not care to stop,   5
My Process is not long
The Wind could wait without the Gate
Or stroll the Town among.

To ascertain the House
And is the Soul at Home   10
And hold the Wick of mine to it
To light, and then return -

803   Nature and God - I neither knew
Yet Both so well knew Me
They startled, like Executors
Of My identity -

Yet Neither told - that I could learn -   5
My Secret as secure
As Herschel's private interest
Or Mercury's Affair -

804   Ample make this Bed -
       Make this Bed with Awe -
       In it wait till Judgment break
       Excellent and Fair.

       Be it's Mattrass straight -   5
       Be it's Pillow round -
       Let no Sunrise' yellow noise
       Interrupt this Ground -

805   These Strangers, in a foreign World,
       Protection asked of me -
       Befriend them, lest yourself in Heaven
       Be found a Refugee -

806   Partake as doth the Bee -
       Abstemiously -
       A Rose is an Estate
       In Sicily -

807   Away from Home are some and I -
       An Emigrant to be
       In a metropolis of Homes
       Is easy possibly -

       The Habit of a Foreign Sky   5
       We - difficult acquire
       As Children, who remain in Face
       The more their Feet retire.

808   The lovely flowers embarrass me,
       They make me regret I am not a Bee -

809   Good to have had them lost
       For News that they be saved!

The nearer they departed Us
The nearer they, restored,

Shall stand to Our Right Hand -   5
Most precious - are the Dead -
Next precious, those that rose to go
Then thought of Us, and stayed -

810   The Robin for the Crumb
Returns no syllable
But long records the Lady's name
In Silver Chronicle.

811   There is a June when Corn is cut
And Roses in the Seed -
A Summer briefer than the first
But tenderer indeed

As should a Face supposed the Grave's   5
Emerge a single Noon
In the Vermillion that it wore
Affect us, and return -

Two Seasons, it is said, exist -
The Summer of the Just,   10
And this of our's, diversified
With Prospect - and with Frost -

May not our Second with it's First
So infinite compare
That We but recollect the one   15
The other to prefer?

812   Love reckons by itself - alone -
"As large as I" - relate the Sun
To One who never felt it blaze -
Itself is all the like it has -

813   How well I knew her not
       Whom not to know - has been
       A Bounty in prospective, now
       Next Door to mine the Pain -

814   Soto! Explore thyself!
       Therein thyself shalt find
       The "Undiscovered Continent" -
       No Settler had the Mind.

815   To this World she returned
       But with a tinge of that
       A Compound manner as a Sod
       Espoused a Violet -

       That chiefer to the Skies   5
       Than to Himself allied
       Dwelt hesitating, half of Dust
       And half of Day the Bride.

816   I could not drink it, Sweet,
       Till You had tasted first,
       Though cooler than the Water was
       The Thoughtfulness of Thirst.

817   This Consciousness that is aware
       Of Neighbors and the Sun
       Will be the one aware of Death
       And that itself alone

       Is traversing the interval   5
       Experience between
       And most profound experiment
       Appointed unto Men -

       How adequate unto itself
       It's properties shall be   10

Itself unto itself and None
Shall make discovery -

Adventure most unto itself
The Soul condemned to be -
Attended by a single Hound   15
It's own identity.

818   Given in Marriage unto Thee
Oh thou Celestial Host -
Bride of the Father and the Son
Bride of the Holy Ghost -

Other Betrothal shall dissolve -   5
Wedlock of Will, decay -
Only the Keeper of this Ring
Conquer Mortality -

819   The Luxury to apprehend
The Luxury 'twould be
To look at thee a single time
An Epicure of me
In whatsoever presence makes   5
Till for a further food
I scarcely recollect to starve
So first am I supplied.

The Luxury to meditate
The Luxury it was   10
To banquet on thy Countenance
A sumptuousness supplies
To plainer Days whose Table, far
As Certainty can see
Is laden with a single Crumb -   15
The Consciousness of thee -

820   The only news I know
       Is Bulletins all Day
       From Immortality.

       The only Shows I see -
       Tomorrow and Today -   5
       Perchance Eternity -

       The only one I meet
       Is God - The only Street -
       Existence - This traversed

       If other news there be -   10
       Or admirabler show -
       I'll tell it You -

821   Wert Thou but ill   that I might show thee
       How long a Day I could endure
       Though thine attention stop not on me
       Nor the least signal, Me assure -

       Wert Thou but stranger in ungracious country -   5
       And Mine - the Door
       Thou paused at, for a passing bounty -
       No More -

       Accused - wert Thou - and Myself - Tribunal -
       Convicted - sentenced - Ermine - not to Me   10
       Half the Condition, thy Reverse - to follow -
       Just to partake - the infamy -

       The Tenant of the narrow Cottage, wert Thou -
       Permit to be
       The Housewife in thy low attendance   15
       Contenteth Me -

       No Service hast Thou, I would not achieve it -
       To die - or live -
       The first - Sweet, proved I, ere I saw thee -
       For Life - be Love -   20

822   Midsummer, was it, when They died -
A full, and perfect time -
The Summer closed opon itself
In Consummated Bloom -

The Corn, her furthest Kernel filled   5
Before the coming Flail -
When These - leaned into Perfectness -
Through Haze of Burial -

823   The first Day that I was a Life
I recollect it - How still -
The last Day that I was a Life
I recollect it - as well -

'Twas stiller - though the first   5
Was still -
'Twas empty - but the first
Was full -

This - was my finallest Occasion -
But then   10
My tenderer Experiment
Toward Men -

"Which choose I"?
That - I cannot say -
"Which choose They"?   15
Question Memory!

824   A nearness to Tremendousness -
An Agony procures -
Affliction ranges Boundlessness -
Vicinity to Laws

Contentment's quiet Suburb -   5
Affliction cannot stay
In Acres - It's Location
Is Illocality -

825   "Unto Me"? I do not know you -
Where may be your House?

"I am Jesus - Late of Judea -
Now - of Paradise" -

Wagons - have you - to convey me?   5
This is far from Thence -

"Arms of Mine - sufficient Phaeton -
Trust Omnipotence" -

I am spotted - "I am Pardon" -
I am small - "The Least   10
Is esteemed in Heaven the Chiefest -
Occupy my House" -

826   Denial - is the only fact
Perceived by the Denied -
Whose Will - a numb significance -
The Day the Heaven died -

And all the Earth strove common round -   5
Without Delight, or Beam -
What comfort was it Wisdom - was -
The spoiler of Our Home?

827   All forgot for recollecting
Just a paltry One -
All forsook, for just a Stranger's
New Accompanying -

Grace of Wealth, and Grace of Station   5
Less accounted than
An unknown Esteem possessing -
Estimate - Who can -

Home effaced - Her faces dwindled -
Nature - altered small -   10
Sun - if shone - or Storm - if shattered -
Overlooked I all -

□

Dropped - my fate - a timid Pebble -
In thy bolder Sea -
Prove - me - Sweet - if I regret it -   15
Prove Myself - of Thee -

828   Had I not This, or This, I said,
        Appealing to Myself,
        In moment of prosperity -
        Inadequate - were Life -

        "Thou hast not Me, nor Me" - it said,   5
        In moment of Reverse -
        "And yet Thou art industrious -
        No need - had'st Thou - of us -"?

        My need - was all I had - I said
        The need did not reduce -   10
        Because the food - exterminate -
        The hunger - does not cease -

        But diligence - is sharper -
        Proportioned to the chance -
        To feed opon the Retrogade -   15
        Enfeebles - the Advance -

829   Between My Country - and the Others -
        There is a Sea -
        But Flowers - negotiate between us -
        As Ministry.

830   The Admirations - and Contempts - of time -
        Show justest - through an Open Tomb -
        The Dying - as it were a Hight
        Reorganizes Estimate
        And what We saw not   5
        We distinguish clear -
        And mostly - see not
        What We saw before -

                                                               □

'Tis Compound Vision -
Light - enabling Light -   10
The Finite - furnished
With the Infinite -
Convex - and Concave Witness -
Back - toward Time -
And forward -   15
Toward the God of Him -

831   Till Death - is narrow Loving -
The scantest Heart extant
Will hold you till your privilege
Of Finiteness - be spent -

But He whose loss procures you   5
Such Destitution that
Your Life too abject for itself
Thenceforward imitate -

Until - Resemblance perfect -
Yourself, for His pursuit   10
Delight of Nature - abdicate -
Exhibit Love - somewhat -

832   'Tis Sunrise - little Maid - Hast Thou
No Station in the Day?
'Twas not thy wont, to hinder so -
Retrieve thine industry -

'Tis Noon - My little Maid -   5
Alas - and art thou sleeping yet?
The Lily - waiting to be Wed -
The Bee - Hast thou forgot?

My little Maid - 'Tis Night - Alas
That Night should be to thee   10
Instead of Morning - Had'st thou broached
Thy little Plan to Die -
Dissuade thee, if I c'd not, Sweet,
I might have aided - thee -

833   Pain - expands the Time -
        Ages coil within
        The minute Circumference
        Of a single Brain -

        Pain contracts - the Time -   5
        Occupied with Shot
        Gammuts of Eternities
        Are as they were not -

834   Fitter to see Him, I may be
        For the long Hindrance - Grace - to Me -
        With Summers, and with Winters, grow,
        Some passing Year - a trait bestow

        To make Me fairest of the Earth -   5
        The Waiting - then - will seem so worth
        I shall impute with half a pain
        The blame that I was chosen - then -

        Time to anticipate His Gaze -
        It's first - Delight - and then - Surprise -   10
        The turning o'er and o'er my face
        For Evidence it be the Grace -

        He left behind One Day - So less
        He seek conviction, That - be This -

        I only must not grow so new   15
        That He'll mistake - and ask for me
        Of me - when first unto the Door
        I go - to Elsewhere go no more

        I only must not change so fair
        He'll sigh - "The Other - She - is Where"?   20
        The Love, tho', will array me right
        I shall be perfect - in His sight -

        If He perceive the other Truth -
        Opon an Excellenter Youth -

        How sweet I shall not lack in Vain -   25
        But gain - thro' loss - Through Grief - obtain -

The Beauty that reward Him most -
The Beauty of Demand - at Rest -

835   He who in Himself believes -
       Fraud cannot presume -
       Faith is Constancy's Result -
       And assumes - from Home -

       Cannot perish, though it fail   5
       Every second time -
       But defaced Vicariously -
       For Some Other Shame.

836   Color - Caste - Denomination -
       These - are Time's Affair -
       Death's diviner Classifying
       Does not know they are -

       As in sleep - all Hue forgotten -   5
       Tenets - put behind -
       Death's large - Democratic fingers
       Rub away the Brand -

       If Circassian - He is careless -
       If He put away   10
       Chrysalis of Blonde - or Umber -
       Equal Butterfly -

       They emerge from His Obscuring -
       What Death - knows so well -
       Our minuter intuitions -   15
       Deem unplausible

837   I make His Crescent fill or lack -
       His Nature is at Full
       Or Quarter - as I signify -
       His Tides - do I control -

                                                        □

He holds superior in the Sky
Or gropes, at my Command
Behind inferior Clouds - or round
A Mist's slow Colonnade -

But since We hold a Mutual Disc -
And front a Mutual Day -
Which is the Despot, neither knows -
Nor Whose - the Tyranny -

5

10

838   Robbed by Death - but that was easy -
       To the failing Eye
       I could hold the latest Glowing -
       Robbed by Liberty

       For Her Jugular Defences -
       This, too, I endured -
       Hint of Glory - it afforded -
       For the Brave Beloved -

       Fraud of Distance - Fraud of Danger,
       Fraud of Death - to bear -
       It is Bounty - to Suspense's
       Vague Calamity -

       Staking our entire Possession
       On a Hair's result -
       Then - Seesawing - coolly - on it -
       Trying if it split -

5

10

15

839   Unfulfilled to Observation -
       Incomplete - to Eye -
       But to Faith - a Revolution
       In Locality -

       Unto Us - the Suns extinguish -
       To our Opposite -
       New Horizons - they embellish -
       Fronting Us - with Night.

5

840   Love - is that later Thing than Death -
       More previous - than Life -
       Confirms it at it's entrance - And
       Usurps it - of itself -

       Tastes Death - the first - to hand the sting   5
       The Second - to it's friend -
       Disarms the little interval -
       Deposits Him with God -

       Then hovers - an inferior Guard -
       Lest this Beloved Charge   10
       Need - once in an Eternity -
       A smaller than the Large -

841   Struck, was I, nor yet by Lightning -
       Lightning - lets away
       Power to perceive His Process
       With Vitality -

       Maimed - was I - yet not by Venture -   5
       Stone of Stolid Boy -
       Nor a Sportsman's Peradventure -
       Who mine Enemy?

       Robbed - was I - intact to Bandit -
       All my Mansion torn -   10
       Sun - withdrawn to Recognition -
       Furthest shining - done -

       Yet was not the foe - of any -
       Not the smallest Bird
       In the nearest Orchard dwelling -   15
       Be of Me - afraid -

       Most - I love the Cause that slew Me -
       Often as I die
       It's beloved Recognition
       Holds a Sun on Me -   20

       Best - at Setting - as is Nature's -
       Neither witnessed Rise

Till the infinite Aurora
In the Other's Eyes -

842   Patience - has a quiet Outer -
Patience - Look within -
Is an Insect's futile forces
Infinites - between -

'Scaping One - against the Other   5
Fruitlesser to fling -
Patience - is the Smile's exertion
Through the quivering -

843   It bloomed and dropt, a Single Noon -
The Flower - distinct and Red -
I, passing, thought another Noon
Another in it's stead

Will equal glow, and thought no more   5
But came another Day
To find the Species disappeared -
The Same Locality -

The Sun in place - no other fraud
On Nature's perfect Sum -   10
Had I but lingered Yesterday -
Was my retrieveless blame -

Much Flowers of this and further Zones
Have perished in my Hands
For seeking it's Resemblance -   15
But unapproached it stands -

The single Flower of the Earth
That I, in passing by
Unconscious was - Great Nature's Face
Passed infinite by Me -   20

844

This Merit hath the Worst -
It cannot be again -
When Fate hath taunted last
And thrown Her furthest Stone -

The Maimed may pause, and breathe,   5
And glance securely round -
The Deer attracts no further
Than it resists - the Hound -

845

We can but follow to the Sun -
As oft as He go down
He leave Ourselves a Sphere behind -
'Tis mostly - following -

We go no further with the Dust   5
Than to the Earthen Door -
And then the Panels are reversed -
And we behold - no more

846

A Drop fell on the Apple Tree -
Another - on the Roof -
A Half a Dozen kissed the Eaves -
And made the Gables laugh -

A few went out to help the Brook   5
That went to help the Sea -
Myself Conjectured were they Pearls -
What Necklaces could be -

The Dust replaced, in Hoisted Roads -
The Birds jocoser sung -   10
The Sunshine threw his Hat away -
The Bushes - spangles flung -

The Breezes brought dejected Lutes -
And bathed them in the Glee -
Then Orient showed a single Flag,   15
And signed the Fete away -

847   Her final Summer was it -
And yet We guessed it not -
If tenderer industriousness
Pervaded Her, We thought

A further force of life   5
Developed from within -
When Death lit all the shortness up
It made the hurry plain -

We wondered at our blindness
When nothing was to see   10
But Her Carrara Guide post -
At Our Stupidity -

When duller than our dullness
The Busy Darling lay -
So busy was she - finishing -   15
So leisurely - were We -

848   Who Giants know, with lesser Men
Are incomplete, and shy -
For Greatness, that is ill at ease
In minor Company -

A Smaller, could not be perturbed -   5
The Summer Gnat displays -
Unconscious that his single Fleet
Do not comprise the skies -

849   By my Window have I for Scenery
Just a Sea - with a Stem -
If the Bird and the Farmer - deem it a "Pine" -
The Opinion will do - for them -

It has no Port, nor a "Line" - but the Jays -   5
That split their route to the Sky -
Or a Squirrel, whose giddy Peninsula
May be easier reached - this way -

□

For Inlands - the Earth is the under side -
And the upper side - is the Sun -
And it's Commerce - if Commerce it have -
Of Spice - I infer from the Odors borne -

Of it's Voice - to affirm - when the Wind is within -
Can the Dumb - define the Divine?
The Definition of Melody - is -
That Definition is none -

It - suggests to our Faith -
They - suggest to our Sight -
When the latter - is put away
I shall meet with Conviction I somewhere met
That Immortality -

Was the Pine at my Window a "Fellow
Of the Royal" Infinity?
Apprehensions - are God's introductions -
To be hallowed - accordingly -

10

15

20

25

850 Defrauded I a Butterfly -
The lawful Heir - for Thee -

851 "I want" - it pleaded - All it's life -
I want - was chief it said
When Skill entreated it - the last -
And when so newly dead -

I could not deem it late - to hear 5
That single - steadfast sigh -
The lips had placed as with a "Please"
Toward Eternity -

852 It was a Grave, yet bore no Stone
Enclosed 'twas not of Rail
A Consciousness it's Acre, and
It held a Human Soul -

Entombed by whom, for what offence
If Home or Foreign born -
Had I the curiosity
'Twere not appeased of men

Till Resurrection, I must guess
Denied the small desire
A Rose opon it's Ridge to sow
Or take away a Briar -

853   She staked Her Feathers - Gained an Arc -
Debated - Rose again -
This time - beyond the estimate
Of Envy, or of Men -

And now, among Circumference -
Her steady Boat be seen -
At home - among the Billows - As
The Bough where she was born -

854   Despair's advantage is achieved
By suffering - Despair -
To be assisted of Reverse
One must Reverse have bore -

The Worthiness of Suffering like
The Worthiness of Death
Is ascertained by tasting -

As can no other Mouth

Of Savors - make us conscious -
As did ourselves partake -
Affliction feels impalpable
Until Ourselves are struck -

855   Two - were immortal twice -
The privilege of few -

Eternity - obtained - in Time -
Reversed Divinity -

That our ignoble Eyes   5
The quality perceive
Of Paradise superlative -
Through their Comparative.

856   I play at Riches - to appease
       The Clamoring for Gold -
       It kept me from a Thief, I think,
       For often, overbold

       With Want, and Opportunity -   5
       I could have done a Sin
       And been Myself that easy Thing
       An independent Man -

       But often as my lot displays
       Too hungry to be borne   10
       I deem Myself what I would be -
       And novel Comforting

       My Poverty and I derive -
       We question if the Man -
       Who own - Esteem the Opulence -   15
       As we - Who never Can -

       Should ever these exploring Hands
       Chance Sovreign on a Mine -
       Or in the long - uneven term
       To win, become their turn -   20

       How fitter they will be - for Want -
       Enlightening so well -
       I know not which, Desire, or Grant -
       Be wholly beautiful -

857   She rose to His Requirement - dropt
       The Playthings of Her Life

To take the honorable Work
Of Woman, and of Wife -

If ought She missed in Her new Day,   5
Of Amplitude, or Awe -
Or first Prospective - or the Gold
In using, wear away,

It lay unmentioned - as the Sea
Develope Pearl, and Weed,   10
But only to Himself - be known
The Fathoms they abide -

858   Time feels so vast that were it not
       For an Eternity -
       I fear me this Circumference
       Engross my Finity -

       To His exclusion, who prepare   5
       By Processes of Size
       For the Stupendous Vision
       Of His Diameters -

859   Who Court obtain within Himself
       Sees every Man a King -
       And Poverty of Monarchy
       Is an interior thing -

       No Man depose   5
       Whom Fate Ordain -
       And Who can add a Crown
       To Him who doth continual
       Conspire against His Own

860   No Notice gave She, but a Change -
       No Message, but a sigh -
       For Whom, the Time did not suffice
       That she should specify.

                                                    □

She was not warm, though Summer shone   5
Nor scrupulous of cold
Though Rime by Rime, the steady Frost
Opon Her Bosom piled -

Of shrinking ways - she did not fright
Though all the Village looked -   10
But held Her gravity aloft -
And met the gaze - direct -

And when adjusted like a seed
In careful fitted Ground
Unto the Everlasting Spring   15
And hindered but a Mound

Her Warm return, if so she chose -
And We - imploring drew -
Removed our invitation by
As Some She never knew -   20

861   They say that "Time assuages" -
Time never did assuage -
An actual suffering strengthens
As Sinews do, with Age -

Time is a Test of Trouble -   5
But not a Remedy -
If such it prove, it prove too
There was no Malady -

862   On the Bleakness of my Lot
Bloom I strove to raise -
Late - my Garden of a Rock
Yielded Grape - and Maise -

Soil of Flint, if steady tilled   5
Will refund the Hand -
Seed of Palm, by Lybian Sun
Fructified in Sand -

863   This Bauble was preferred of Bees -
       By Butterflies admired
       At Heavenly - Hopeless Distances -
       Was justified of Bird -

       Did Noon - enamel - in Herself   5
       Was Summer to a Score
       Who only knew of Universe -
       It had created Her -

864   A Plated Life - diversified
       With Gold and Silver Pain
       To prove the presence of the Ore
       In Particles - 'tis when

       A Value struggle - it exist -   5
       A Power - will proclaim
       Although Annihilation pile
       Whole Chaoses on Him -

865   Expectation - is Contentment -
       Gain - Satiety -
       But Satiety - Conviction
       Of Nescessity

       Of an Austere trait in Pleasure -   5
       Good, without alarm
       Is a too established Fortune -
       Danger - deepens Sum -

866   This Dust, and it's Feature -
       Accredited - Today -
       Will in a second Future -
       Cease to identify -

       This Mind, and it's measure -   5
       A too minute Area
       For it's enlarged inspection's
       Comparison - appear -

       □

This World, and it's species
A too concluded show   10
For it's absorbed Attention's
Remotest scrutiny -

867   I felt a Cleaving in my Mind -
As if my Brain had split -
I tried to match it - Seam by Seam -
But could not make them fit -

The thought behind, I strove to join   5
Unto the thought before -
But Sequence ravelled out of Sound -
Like Balls - opon a Floor -

868   Fairer through Fading - as the Day
Into the Darkness dips away -
Half Her Complexion of the Sun -
Hindering - Haunting - Perishing -

Rallies Her Glow, like a dying Friend -   5
Teazing, with glittering Amend -
Only to aggravate the Dark
Through an expiring - perfect - look -

869   What I see not, I better see -
Through Faith - My Hazel Eye
Has periods of shutting -
But, No lid has Memory -

For frequent, all my sense obscured   5
I equally behold
As some one held a light unto
The Features so beloved -
And I arise - and in my Dream -
Do Thee distinguished Grace -   10
Till jealous Daylight interrupt -
And mar thy perfectness -

870   None can experience stint
       Who Bounty - have not known -
       The fact of Famine - could not be
       Except for Fact of Corn -

       Want - is a meagre Art   5
       Acquired by Reverse -
       The Poverty that was not Wealth -
       Cannot be Indigence -

871   The hallowing of Pain
       Like hallowing of Heaven,
       Obtains at a corporeal cost -
       The Summit is not given -

       To Him who strives severe   5
       At middle of the Hill -
       But He who has achieved the Top -
       All - is the price of All -

872   Deprived of other Banquet,
       I entertained Myself -
       At first - a scant nutrition -
       An insufficient Loaf -

       But grown by slender addings   5
       To so esteemed a size
       'Tis sumptuous enough for me -
       And almost to suffice

       A Robin's famine - able -
       Red Pilgrim, He and I -   10
       A Berry from our table
       Reserve - for Charity -

873   It is a lonesome Glee -
       Yet sanctifies the Mind -
       With fair association -
       Afar opon the Wind

                                                        □

A Bird to overhear -   5
Delight without a Cause -
Arrestless as invisible -
A Matter of the Skies.

874   If Blame be my side - forfeit Me -
        But doom me not to forfeit Thee -
        To forfeit Thee? The very name
        Is sentence from Belief - and Home -

875   Purple -

        The Color of a Queen, is this -
        The Color of a Sun
        At setting - this and Amber -
        Beryl - and this, at Noon -

        And when at night - Auroran widths   5
        Fling suddenly on Men -
        'Tis this - and Witchcraft - nature keeps
        A Rank - for Iodine -

876   To be alive - is Power -
        Existence - in itself -
        Without a further function -
        Omnipotence - Enough -

        To be alive - and will! -   5
        'Tis able as a God -
        The Maker - of Ourselves - be what -
        Such being Finitude!

877   The Loneliness One dare not sound -
        And would as soon surmise
        As in it's Grave go plumbing
        To ascertain the size -

The Loneliness whose worst alarm   5
Is lest itself should see -
And perish from before itself
For just a scrutiny -

The Horror not to be surveyed -
But skirted in the Dark -   10
With Consciousness suspended -
And Being under Lock -

I fear me this - is Loneliness -
The Maker of the soul
It's Caverns and it's Corridors   15
Illuminate - or seal -

878   Least Bee that brew - a Honey's Weight
        The Summer multiply -
        Content Her smallest fraction help
        The Amber Quantity -

879   This that would greet - an hour ago -
        Is quaintest Distance - now -
        Had it a Guest from Paradise -
        Nor glow, would it, nor bow -

        Had it a notice from the Noon   5
        Nor beam, would it - nor Warm -
        Match me the Silver Reticence -
        Match me the Solid Calm -

880   The Service without Hope -
        Is tenderest, I think -
        Because 'tis unsustained
        By stint - Rewarded Work -

        Has impetus of Gain -   5
        And impetus of Goal -
        There is no Diligence like that
        That knows not an Until -

881   I meant to find Her when I Came -
        Death - had the same design -
        But the Success - was His - it seems -
        And the Discomfit - Mine -

        I meant to tell Her how I longed   5
        For this specific time -
        But Death had told Her so the first -
        And she had fled, with Him -

        To wander - now - is my Abode -
        To rest - To rest would be   10
        A privilege of Hurricane
        To Memory - and Me -

882   The Truth - is stirless -
        Other force - may be presumed to move -
        This - then - is best for confidence -
        When oldest Cedars swerve -

        And Oaks untwist their fists -   5
        And Mountains - feeble - lean -
        How excellent a Body, that
        Stands without a Bone -

        How vigorous a Force
        That holds without a Prop -   10
        Truth stays Herself - and every man
        That trusts Her - boldly up -

883   A South Wind - has a pathos
        Of individual Voice -
        As One detect on Landings
        An Emigrant's address -

        A Hint of Ports - and Peoples -   5
        And much not understood -
        The fairer - for the farness -
        And for the foreignhood -

884   To wait an Hour - is long -
       If Love be just beyond -
       To wait Eternity - is short -
       If Love reward the end -

885   There is an arid Pleasure -
       As different from Joy -
       As Frost is different from Dew -
       Like Element - are they -

       Yet one - rejoices Flowers -   5
       And one - the Flowers abhor -
       The finest Honey - curdled -
       Is worthless - to the Bee -

886   Bereaved of all, I went abroad -
       No less bereaved was I
       Opon a New Peninsula -
       The Grave preceded me -

       Obtained my Lodgings, ere myself -   5
       And when I sought my Bed -
       The Grave it was reposed opon
       The Pillow for my Head -

       I waked, to find it first awake -
       I rose - It followed me -   10
       I tried to drop it in the Crowd -
       To lose it in the Sea -

       In Cups of artificial Drowse
       To steep it's shape away -
       The Grave - was finished - but the Spade   15
       Remained in Memory -

887   Severer Service of myself
       I hastened to demand
       To fill the awful Vacuum
       Your life had left behind -

                                                       □

I worried Nature with my Wheels   5
When Her's had ceased to run -
When she had put away Her Work
My own had just begun -

I strove to weary Brain and Bone -
To harass to fatigue   10
The glittering Retinue of nerves -
Vitality to clog

To some dull comfort Those obtain
Who put a Head away
They knew the Hair to -   15
And forget the color of the Day -

Affliction would not be appeased -
The Darkness braced as firm
As all my strategem had been
The Midnight to confirm -   20

No Drug for Consciousness - can be -
Alternative to die
Is Nature's only Pharmacy
For Being's Malady -

888   'Twould ease - a Butterfly -
       Elate - a Bee -
       Thou'rt neither -
       Neither - thy capacity -

       But, Blossom, were I,   5
       I would rather be
       Thy moment
       Than a Bee's Eternity -

       Content of fading
       Is enough for me -   10
       Fade I unto Divinity -

       And Dying - Lifetime -
       Ample as the Eye -
       Her least attention raise on me -

889 Such is the Force of Happiness -
The Least - can lift a ton
Assisted by it's stimulus -

Who Misery - sustain -
No Sinew can afford - 5
The Cargo of Themselves -
Too infinite for Consciousness'
Slow capabilities -

890 A Coffin - is a small Domain,
Yet able to contain
A Citizen of Paradise
In it's diminished Plane -

A Grave - is a restricted Breadth - 5
Yet ampler than the Sun -
And all the Seas He populates -
And Lands He looks opon

To Him who on it's small Repose
Bestows a single Friend - 10
Circumference without Relief -
Or Estimate - or End -

891 I learned - at least - what Home could be -
How ignorant I had been
Of pretty ways of Covenant -
How awkward at the Hymn

Round our new Fireside - but for this - 5
This pattern - of the way -
Whose Memory drowns me, like the Dip
Of a Celestial Sea -

What Mornings in our Garden - guessed -
What Bees - for us - to hum - 10
With only Birds to interrupt
The Ripple of our Theme -

 □

And Task for Both - When Play be done -
Your Problem - of the Brain -
And mine - some foolisher effect -   15
A Ruffle - or a Tune -

The Afternoons - together spent -
And Twilight - in the Lanes -
Some ministry to poorer lives -
Seen poorest - thro' our gains -   20

And then away to You to pass -
A new - diviner - Care -
Till Sunrise take us back to Scene -
Transmuted - Vivider -

This seems a Home - And Home is not -   25
But what that Place could be -
Afflicts me - as a Setting Sun -
Where Dawn - knows how to be -

892   Fame's Boys and Girls, who never die
And are too seldom born -

893   Her sovreign People
Nature knows as well
And is as fond of signifying
As if fallible -

894   The Overtakelessness of Those
Who have accomplished Death -
Majestic is to me beyond
The Majesties of Earth -
The Soul her "Not at Home"   5
Inscribes opon the Flesh,
And takes a fine aerial gait
Beyond the Writ of Touch.

895   Further in Summer than the Birds -
Pathetic from the Grass -
A minor Nation celebrates
It's unobtrusive Mass.

No Ordinance be seen -   5
So gradual the Grace
A gentle Custom it becomes -
Enlarging Loneliness -

Antiquest felt at Noon -
When August burning low   10
Arise this spectral Canticle
Repose to typify -

Remit as yet no Grace -
No furrow on the Glow,

But a Druidic Difference
Enhances Nature now -

896   Purple - is fashionable twice -
This season of the year,
And when a soul perceives itself
To be an Emperor.

897   She sped as Petals from a Rose -
Offended by the Wind -
A frail Aristocrat of Time
Indemnity to find -
Leaving on Nature a Default   5
As Cricket, or as Bee,
But Andes - in the Bosoms where
She had begun to lie.

898   An Hour is a Sea
Between a few, and me -
With them would Harbor be -

899   Experience is the Angled Road
Preferred against the Mind
By - Paradox - the Mind itself -
Presuming it to lead

Quite Opposite - How complicate   5
The Discipline of Man -
Compelling Him to choose Himself
His Preappointed Pain -

900   'Twas awkward, but it fitted me -
An Ancient fashioned Heart -
It's only lore - it's Steadfastness -
In Change - unerudite -

□

It only moved as do the Suns -   5
For merit of Return -
Or Birds - confirmed perpetual
By Alternating Zone -

I only have it not Tonight
In it's established place -   10
For technicality of Death -
Omitted in the Lease -

901   The Soul's distinct connection
        With immortality
        Is best disclosed by Danger
        Or quick Calamity -

        As Lightning on a Landscape   5
        Exhibits Sheets of Place -
        Not yet suspected - but for Flash -
        And Click - and Suddenness.

902   Too little way the House must lie
        From every Human Heart
        That holds in undisputed Lease
        A white inhabitant -

        Too narrow is the Right between -   5
        Too imminent the chance -
        Each Consciousness must emigrate
        And lose it's neighbor once -

903   A Doubt if it be Us
        Assists the staggering Mind
        In an extremer Anguish
        Until it footing find -

        An Unreality is lent,   5
        A merciful Mirage
        That makes the living possible
        While it suspends the lives.

904   Absence disembodies - so does Death
       Hiding individuals from the Earth
       Superstition helps, as well as love -
       Tenderness decreases as we prove -

905   Split the Lark - and you'll find the Music -
       Bulb after Bulb, in Silver rolled -
       Scantily dealt to the Summer Morning
       Saved for your Ear, when Lutes be old -

       Loose the Flood - you shall find it patent -   5
       Gush after Gush, reserved for you -
       Scarlet Experiment! Sceptic Thomas!
       Now, do you doubt that your Bird was true?

906   That Distance was between Us
       That is not of Mile or Main -
       The Will it is that situates -
       Equator - never can -

907   That is solemn we have ended
       Be it but a Play
       Or a Glee among the Garret
       Or a Holiday

       Or a leaving Home, or later,   5
       Parting with a World
       We have understood for better
       Still to be explained -

908   They ask but our Delight -
       The Darlings of the Soil
       And grant us all their Countenance
       For a penurious smile -

909 Because the Bee may blameless hum
    For Thee a Bee do I become
    List even unto Me -

    Because the Flowers unafraid
    May lift a look on thine, a Maid   5
    Alway a Flower would be -

    Nor Robins, Robins need not hide
    When Thou opon their Crypts intrude
    So Wings bestow on Me
    Or Petals, or a Dower of Buzz   10
    That Bee to ride - or Flower of Furze
    I that way worship Thee -

910 Finding is the first Act
    The second, loss,
    Third, Expedition for the "Golden Fleece"

    Fourth, no Discovery -
    Fifth, no Crew -   5
    Finally, no Golden Fleece -
    Jason, sham, too -

911 As Frost is best conceived
    By force of it's Result -
    Affliction is inferred
    By subsequent effect -

    If when the Sun reveal,   5
    The Garden keep the Gash -
    If as the Days resume
    The wilted countenance

    Cannot correct the crease
    Or counteract the stain -   10
    Presumption is Vitality
    Was somewhere put in twain -

912   To my quick ear the Leaves - conferred -
The Bushes - they were Bells -
I could not find a Privacy
From Nature's sentinels -

In Cave if I presumed to hide   5
The Walls - begun to tell -
Creation seemed a mighty Crack -
To make me visible -

913   A Man may make a Remark -
In itself - a quiet thing
That may furnish the Fuse unto a Spark
In dormant nature - lain -

Let us divide - with skill -   5
Let us discourse - with care -
Powder exists in Charcoal -
Before it exists in Fire -

914   A Door just opened on a street -
I - lost - was passing by -
An instant's Width of Warmth disclosed -
And Wealth - and Company -

The Door as instant shut - And I -   5
I - lost - was passing by -
Lost doubly - but by contrast - most -
Informing - Misery -

915   What shall I do when the Summer troubles -
What, when the Rose is ripe -
What when the Eggs fly off in Music
From the Maple Keep?

What shall I do when the Skies a'chirrup   5
Drop a Tune on Me -
When the Bee hangs all Noon in the Buttercup
What will become of Me?

□

Oh, when the Squirrel fills His Pockets
And the Berries stare   10
How can I bear their jocund Faces
Thou from Here, so far?

'Twould'nt afflict a Robin -
All His Goods have Wings -
I - do not fly, so Wherefore   15
My Perennial Things?

916   Drab Habitation of Whom?
        Tabernacle or Tomb -
        Or Dome of Worm -
        Or Porch of Gnome -
        Or some Elf's Catacomb?   5

917   As One does Sickness over
        In convalescent Mind,
        His scrutiny of Chances
        By blessed Health obscured -

        As One rewalks a Precipice   5
        And whittles at the Twig
        That held Him from Perdition
        Sown sidewise in the Crag

        A Custom of the Soul
        Far after suffering   10
        Identity to question
        For evidence 'thas been -

918   We met as Sparks - Diverging Flints
        Sent various - scattered ways -
        We parted as the Central Flint
        Were cloven with an Adze -
        Subsisting on the Light We bore   5
        Before We felt the Dark -

We knew by change between itself
And that etherial Spark.

919   Be Mine the Doom
        Sufficient Fame
        To perish in Her Hand.

920   Each Scar I'll keep for Him
        Instead I'll say of Gem
        In His long Absence worn
        A Costlier One

        But every Tear I bore   5
        Were He to count them o'er
        His own would fall so more
        I'll missum them -

921   Snow beneath whose chilly softness
        Some that never lay
        Make their first Repose this Winter
        I admonish Thee

        Blanket Wealthier the Neighbor   5
        We so new bestow
        Than thine Acclimated Creature
        Wilt Thou, Austere Snow?

922   The Sun is gay or stark
        According to Our Deed -
        If merry, He is merrier -
        If eager for the Dead

        Or an expended Day   5
        He helped to make too bright
        His mighty pleasure suits Us not
        It magnifies Our Freight

923   They wont frown always - some sweet Day
When I forget to teaze -
They'll recollect how cold I looked
And how I just said "Please".

Then They will hasten to the Door   5
To call the little Girl
Who cannot thank Them for the Ice
That filled the lisping full.

924   On that dear Frame the Years had worn
Yet precious as the House
In which We first experienced Light
The Witnessing, to Us -

Precious! It was conceiveless fair   5
As Hands the Grave had grimed
Should softly place within our own
Denying that they died.

925   The Lady feeds Her little Bird
At rarer intervals -
The little Bird would not dissent
But meekly recognize

The Gulf between the Hand and Her   5
And crumbless and afar
And fainting, on Her yellow Knee
Fall softly, and adore -

926   I stepped from Plank to Plank
A slow and cautious way
The Stars about my Head I felt
About my Feet the Sea -

I knew not but the next   5
Would be my final inch -
This gave me that precarious Gait
Some call Experience -

927   Each Second is the last
Perhaps, recalls the Man
Just measuring unconsciousness
The Sea and Spar between -

To fail within a chance -   5
How terribler a thing
Than perish from the chance's list
Before the Perishing!

928   The Bird must sing to earn the Crumb
What merit have the Tune
No Breakfast if it guaranty

The Rose, content may bloom
To gain renown of Lady's Drawer   5
But if the Lady come
But once a Century, the Rose
Superfluous become -

929   I've none to tell me to but Thee
So when Thou failest, nobody -
It was a little tie -
It just held Two, nor those it held
Since Somewhere thy sweet Face has spilled   5
Beyond my Boundary -

If things were opposite - and Me
And Me it were, that ebbed from Thee
On some unanswering Shore -
Would'st Thou seek so - just say   10
That I the Answer may pursue
Unto the lips it eddied through -
So - overtaking Thee -

930   The Poets light but Lamps -
Themselves - go out -

The Wicks they stimulate
If vital Light

Inhere as do the Suns -   5
Each Age a Lens
Disseminating their
Circumference -

931   An Everywhere of Silver
        With Ropes of Sand
        To keep it from effacing
        The Track called Land -

932   Our little Kinsmen - after Rain
        In plenty may be seen,
        A Pink and Pulpy multitude
        The tepid Ground opon.

        A needless life, it seemed to me   5
        Until a little Bird
        As to a Hospitality
        Advanced and breakfasted -

        As I of He, so God of Me
        I pondered, may have judged,   10
        And left the little Angle Worm
        With Modesties enlarged.

933   Of Tolling Bell I ask the cause?
        "A Soul has gone to Heaven"
        I'm answered in a lonesome tone -
        Is Heaven then a Prison?

        That Bells should ring till all should know   5
        A Soul had gone to Heaven
        Would seem to me - the more the way
        A Good News should be given -

934   These tested Our Horizon -
Then disappeared
As Birds before achieving
A Latitude.

Our Retrospection of Them   5
A fixed Delight,
But Our Anticipation
A Dice - a Doubt -

935   As imperceptibly as Grief
The Summer lapsed away -
Too imperceptible at last
To seem like Perfidy -
A Quietness distilled   5
As Twilight long begun,
Or Nature spending with herself
Sequestered Afternoon -
The Dusk drew earlier in -
The Morning foreign shone -   10
A courteous, yet harrowing Grace,
As Guest, that would be gone -
And thus, without a Wing
Or service of a Keel
Our Summer made her light escape   15
Into the Beautiful -

936   As Willing lid o'er Weary Eye
The Evening on the Day leans
Till of all our Nature's House
Remains but Balcony

937   Not all die early, dying young -
Maturity of Fate
Is consummated equally
In Ages, or a Night -

□

A Hoary Boy, I've known to drop   5
Whole statured - by the side
Of Junior of Fourscore - 'twas Act
Not Period - that died.

938   Those who have been in the Grave the longest -
        Those who begin Today -
        Equally perish from our Practise -
        Death is the other way -

        Foot of the Bold did least attempt it -   5
        It is the White Exploit -
        Once to achieve, annuls the power
        Once to communicate -

939   Impossibility, like Wine
        Exhilirates the Man
        Who tastes it; Possibility
        Is flavorless - Combine

        A Chance's faintest tincture   5
        And in the former Dram
        Enchantment makes ingredient
        As certainly as Doom -

940   So set it's Sun in Thee
        What Day be dark to me
        What Distance far
        So I the Ships may see
        That touch how seldomly   5
        Thy Shore?

941   How the Waters closed above Him
        We shall never know -
        How He stretched His anguish to us
        That - is covered too -

                                                    □

Spreads the Pond Her Base of Lilies 5
Bold above the Boy
Whose unclaimed Hat and Jacket
Sum the History -

942   Always Mine!
No more Vacation!
Term of Light, this Day begun!
Failless as the fair rotation
Of the Seasons and the Sun - 5

Old the Grace, but new the Subjects -
Old, indeed, the East,
Yet opon His Purple Programme
Every Dawn, is first.

943   I cannot buy it - 'tis not sold -
There is no other in the World -
Mine was the only one

I was so happy I forgot
To shut the Door And it went out 5
And I am all alone -

If I could find it Anywhere
I would not mind the journey there
Though it took all my store

But just to look it in the Eye - 10
"Did'st thou"? "Thou did'st not mean", to say,
Then, turn my Face away.

944   A Moth the hue of this
Haunts Candles in Brazil -
Nature's Experience would make
Our Reddest Second pale -

Nature is fond, I sometimes think, 5
Of Trinkets, as a Girl.

945   Good to hide, and hear 'em hunt!
           Better, to be found,
           If one care to, that is,
           The Fox fits the Hound -

           Good to know, and not tell -   5
           Best, to know and tell,
           Can one find the rare Ear
           Not too dull -

946   Dying! To be afraid of thee
           One must to thine Artillery
           Have left exposed a Friend -
           Than thine old Arrow is a Shot
           Delivered straighter to the Heart   5
           The leaving Love behind -

           Not for itself, the Dust is shy,
           But, enemy, Beloved be
           Thy Batteries divorce.
           Fight sternly in a Dying eye   10
           Two Armies, Love and Certainty
           And Love and the Reverse -

947   I made slow Riches but my Gain
           Was steady as the Sun
           And every Night, it numbered more
           Than the preceding One

           All Days, I did not earn the same   5
           But my perceiveless Gain
           Inferred the less by Growing than
           The Sum that it had grown.

948   Spring is the Period
           Express from God -
           Among the other seasons
           Himself abide

But during March and April
None stir abroad
Without a cordial interview
With God -

5

949   Before He comes We weigh the Time,
'Tis Heavy and 'tis Light.
When He depart, an Emptiness
Is the prevailing Freight -

950   Twice had Summer her fair Verdure
Proffered to the Plain -
Twice - a Winter's Silver Fracture
On the Rivers been -

Two full Autumns for the Squirrel
Bounteous prepared -
Nature, Had'st thou not a Berry
For thy wandering Bird?

5

951   Unable are the Loved to die
For Love is Immortality,
Nay, it is Deity -

Unable they that love - to die
For Love reforms Vitality
Into Divinity.

5

952   Finite - to fail, but infinite - to Venture -
For the one ship that struts the shore
Many's the gallant - overwhelmed Creature
Nodding in Navies Nevermore -

953   Just as He spoke it from his Hands
This Edifice remain -

A Turret more, a Turret less
Dishonor his Design -

According as his skill prefer   5
It perish, or endure -
Content, soe'er, it ornament
His Absent Character.

954   The good Will of a Flower
        The Man who would possess
        Must first present Certificate
        Of minted Holiness.

955   I sing to use the Waiting,
        My Bonnet but to tie
        And shut the Door unto my House
        No more to do have I

        Till His best step approaching   5
        We journey to the Day
        And tell each other how We sung
        To keep the Dark away.

956   Her Grace is all she has -
        And that, so least displays -
        One Art to recognize, must be,
        Another Art, to praise -

957   When the Astronomer stops seeking
        For his Pleiad's Face -
        When the lone British Lady
        Forsakes the Arctic Race

        When to his Covenant Needle   5
        The Sailor doubting turns -
        It will be amply early
        To ask what treason means -

958   Absent Place - an April Day -
       Daffodils a'blow
       Homesick curiosity
       To the Souls that snow -

       Drift may block within it   5
       Deeper than without -
       Daffodil delight but
       Him it duplicate -

959   Apology for Her
       Be rendered by the Bee -
       Herself, without a Parliament
       Apology for Me -

960   The Heart has narrow Banks
       It measures like the Sea
       In mighty - unremitting Bass
       And Blue monotony

       Till Hurricane bisect   5
       And as itself discerns
       It's insufficient Area
       The Heart convulsive learns

       That Calm is but a Wall
       Of Unattempted Gauze   10
       An instant's Push demolishes
       A Questioning - dissolves.

961   When One has given up One's life
       The parting with the rest
       Feels easy, as when Day lets go
       Entirely the West

       The Peaks, that lingered last   5
       Remain in Her regret
       As scarcely as the Iodine
       Opon the Cataract -

962   A Light exists in Spring
Not present on the Year
At any other period -
When March is scarcely here
A Color stands abroad   5
On Solitary Fields
That Science cannot overtake
But Human Nature feels.

It waits opon the Lawn,
It shows the furthest Tree   10
Opon the furthest Slope you know
It almost speaks to you.

Then as Horizons step
Or Noons report away
Without the Formula of sound   15
It passes and we stay -

A quality of loss
Affecting our Content
As Trade had suddenly encroached
Opon a Sacrament -   20

963   Banish Air from Air -
Divide Light if you dare -
They'll meet
While Cubes in a Drop
Or Pellets of Shape   5
Fit -
Films cannot annul
Odors return whole
Force Flame
And with a Blonde push   10
Over your impotence
Flits Steam.

964   Like Men and Women Shadows walk
Opon the Hills Today

With here and there a mighty Bow
Or trailing Courtesy

To Neighbors doubtless of their own   5
Not quickened to perceive
Minuter Landscape as Ourselves
And Boroughs where We live

965   How far is it to Heaven?
As far as Death this way -
Of River or of Ridge beyond
Was no discovery.

How far is it to Hell?   5
As far as Death this way -
How far left hand the Sepulchre
Defies Topography.

966   A Death blow is a Life blow to Some
Who till they died, did not alive become -
Who had they lived - had died but when
They died, Vitality begun -

967   Two Travellers perishing in Snow
The Forests as they froze
Together heard them strengthening
Each other with the words

That Heaven if Heaven, must contain   5
What Either left behind
And then the cheer too solemn grew
For language, and the Wind

Long steps across the features took
That Love had touched that Morn   10
With reverential Hyacinth -
The taleless Days went on

□

Till Mystery impatient drew
And those They left behind
Led absent, were procured of Heaven   15

As Those first furnished, said -

968   Fame is the tint that Scholars leave
       Opon their Setting Names -
       The Iris not of Occident
       That disappears as comes -

969   Escaping backward to perceive
       The Sea opon our place -
       Escaping forward, to confront
       His glittering Embrace -

       Retreating up, a Billow's hight   5
       Retreating blinded down
       Our undermining feet to meet
       Instructs to the Divine.

970   The Mountain sat opon the Plain
       In his tremendous Chair.
       His observation omnifold,
       His inquest, everywhere -

       The Seasons played around his knees   5
       Like Children round a Sire -
       Grandfather of the Days is He
       Of Dawn, the Ancestor -

971   Peace is a fiction of our Faith -
       The Bells a Winter Night
       Bearing the Neighbor out of Sound
       That never did alight.

972   Not what We did, shall be the test
           When Act and Will are done
           But what Our Lord infers We would
           Had We diviner been -

973   Death is a Dialogue between
           The Spirit and the Dust.
           "Dissolve" says Death,
           The Spirit "Sir
           I have another Trust" -   5

           Death doubts it -
           Argues from the Ground -
           The Spirit turns away
           Just laying off for evidence
           An Overcoat of Clay.   10

974   The largest Fire ever known
           Occurs each Afternoon -
           Discovered is without surprise
           Proceeds without concern -
           Consumes and no report to men   5
           An Occidental Town,
           Rebuilt another morning
           To be burned down again

975   And this, of all my Hopes
           This, is the silent end
           Bountiful colored, My Morning rose
           Early and sere, it's end

           Never Bud from a stem   5
           Stepped with so gay a Foot
           Never a Worm so confident
           Bored at so brave a Root

976   Besides this May
       We know
       There is Another -
       How fair
       Our speculations of the Foreigner!   5

       Some know Him whom We knew -
       Sweet Wonder -
       A Nature be
       Where Saints, and our plain going Neighbor
       Keep May!   10

977   I cannot be ashamed
       Because I cannot see
       The love you offer -
       Magnitude
       Reverses Modesty   5

       And I cannot be proud
       Because a Hight so high
       Involves Alpine
       Requirements
       And services of Snow -   10

978   Faith - is the Pierless Bridge
       Supporting what We see
       Unto the Scene that We do not -
       Too slender for the eye

       It bears the Soul as bold   5
       As it were rocked in Steel
       With Arms of steel at either side -
       It joins - behind the Vail

       To what, could We presume
       The Bridge would cease to be   10
       To Our far, vascillating Feet
       A first Nescessity.

979   His Feet are shod with Gauze -
His Helmet, is of Gold,
His Breast, a single Onyx
With Chrysophras, inlaid -

His Labor is a Chant -   5
His Idleness - a Tune -
Oh, for a Bee's experience
Of Clovers, and of Noon!

980   Love - is anterior to Life -
Posterior - to Death -
Initial of Creation, and
The Exponent of Earth -

981   Only a Shrine, but Mine -
I made the Taper shine -
Madonna dim, to whom all Feet may come,
Regard a Nun -

Thou knowest every Wo -   5
Needless to tell thee - so -
But can'st thou do
The Grace next to it - heal?
That looks a harder skill to us -
Still - just as easy, if it be thy Will   10
To thee - Grant Me -
Thou knowest, though, so Why tell thee?

982   If I can stop one Heart from breaking
I shall not live in vain
If I can ease one Life the Aching
Or cool one Pain

Or help one fainting Robin   5
Unto his Nest again
I shall not live in vain.

983   Bee! I'm expecting you!
Was saying Yesterday
To Somebody you know
That you were due -

The Frogs got Home last Week -   5
Are settled, and at work -
Birds mostly back -
The Clover warm and thick -

You'll get my Letter by
The Seventeenth; Reply   10
Or better, be with me -
Your's, Fly.

984   Satisfaction - is the Agent
Of Satiety -
Want - a quiet Comissary
For Infinity -

To possess, is past the instant   5
We achieve the Joy -
Immortality contented
Were Anomaly -

985   Here, where the Daisies fit my Head
'Tis easiest to lie
And every Grass that plays outside
Is sorry, some, for Me -

986   Where I am not afraid to go
I may confide my Flower -
Who was not Enemy of Me
Will gentle be, to Her -

Nor separate, Herself and Me   5
By Distances become -
A single Bloom we constitute
Departed, or at Home -

987 Her little Parasol to lift
    And once to let it down
    Her whole Responsibility -
    To imitate, be Mine -

    A Summer further I must wear,   5
    Content if Nature's Drawer
    Present Me from sepulchral Crease
    As blemishless, as Her -

988 Said Death to Passion
    "Give of thine an Acre unto me".
    Said Passion, through contracting Breaths
    "A Thousand Times Thee Nay".

    Bore Death from Passion   5
    All His East
    He - sovreign as the Sun
    Resituated in the West
    And the Debate was done

989 Air has no Residence, no Neighbor,
    No Ear, no Door,
    No Apprehension of Another
    Oh, Happy Air!

    Etherial Guest at e'en an Outcast's Pillow -   5
    Essential Host, in Life's faint, wailing Inn,
    Later than Light thy Consciousness accost Me
    Till it depart, persuading Mine -

990 His Bill an Augur is
    His Head, a Cap and Frill
    He laboreth at every Tree
    A Worm, His utmost Goal -

991   To undertake is to achieve
        Be Undertaking blent
        With fortitude of obstacle
        And toward encouragement

        That fine suspicion, Natures must   5
        Permitted to revere
        Departed Standards and the few
        Criterion sources here

992   Three Weeks passed since I had seen Her -
        Some Disease had vext
        'Twas with Text and Village Singing
        I beheld Her next

        And a Company - Our pleasure   5
        To discourse alone
        Gracious now to me as any -
        Gracious unto none -

        Borne without dissent of Either
        To the Parish night -   10
        Of the Separated Parties
        Which be out of sight?

993   A Sickness of this World it most occasions
        When Best Men die.
        A Wishfulness their far Condition
        To occupy.

        A Chief indifference, as Foreign   5
        A World must be
        Themselves forsake - contented -
        For Deity

994   He scanned it - Staggered -
        Dropped the Loop
        To Past or Period -

Caught helpless at a sense as if
His Mind were going blind -   5

Groped up, to see if God were there -
Groped backward at Himself
Caressed a Trigger absently
And wandered out of Life -

995   The missing All, prevented Me
        From missing minor Things.
        If nothing larger than a World's
        Departure from a Hinge
        Or Sun's Extinction, be observed   5
        'Twas not so large that I
        Could lift my Forehead from my work
        For Curiosity.

996   I heard, as if I had no Ear
        Until a Vital Word
        Came all the way from Life to me
        And then I knew I heard -

        I saw, as if my Eye were on   5
        Another, till a Thing
        And now I know 'twas Light, because
        It fitted them, came in.

        I dwelt, as if Myself were out,
        My Body but within   10
        Until a Might detected me
        And set my Kernel in -

        And Spirit turned unto the Dust
        "Old Friend, thou knowest Me",
        And Time went out to tell the News   15
        And met Eternity

997   Not so the infinite Relations - Below
        Division is Adhesion's forfeit - On High

415   ∾   1865

Affliction but a speculation - And Wo
A Fallacy, a Figment, We knew -

998   Somewhat, to hope for,
Be it ne'er so far
Is Capital against Despair -

Somewhat, to suffer,
Be it ne'er so keen -   5
If terminable, may be borne -

999   Spring comes on the World -
I sight the Aprils -
Hueless to me, until thou come
As, till the Bee
Blossoms stand negative,   5
Touched to Conditions
By a Hum -

1000   Lest this be Heaven indeed
An Obstacle is given
That always guages a Degree
Between Ourself and Heaven.

1001   The Stimulus, beyond the Grave
His Countenance to see
Supports me like imperial Drams
Afforded Day by Day.

1002   Aurora is the effort
Of the Celestial Face
Unconsciousness of Perfectness
To simulate, to Us.

1003   Dying at my music!
              Bubble! Bubble!
              Hold me till the Octave's run!
              Quick! Burst the Windows!
              Ritardando!   5
              Phials left, and the Sun!

1004   There is no Silence in the Earth - so silent
              As that endured
              Which uttered, would discourage Nature
              And haunt the World -

1005   Bind me - I still can sing -
              Banish - my mandolin
              Strikes true, within -

              Slay - and my Soul shall rise
              Chanting to Paradise -   5
              Still thine -

1006   The first We knew of Him was Death -
              The second, was Renown -
              Except the first had justified
              The second had not been -

1007   Falsehood of Thee, could I suppose
              'Twould undermine the Sill
              To which my Faith pinned Block by Block
              Her Cedar Citadel -

1008   How still the Bells in Steeples stand
              Till swollen with the Sky
              They leap opon their silver Feet
              In frantic Melody!

"You're soon", the Town replied,   5
"My Faces are asleep
But swear, and I will let you by
You will not wake them up".

The easy Guest complied
But once within the Town   10
The transport of His Countenance
Awakened Maid and Man

The Neighbor in the Pool
Opon His Hip elate
Made loud obeisance and the Gnat   15
Held up His Cup for Light.

1016   Ideals are the Fairy Oil
        With which We help the Wheel
        But when the Vital Axle turns
        The Eye rejects the Oil.

1017   The Soul should always stand ajar
        That if the Heaven inquire
        He will not be obliged to wait
        Or shy of troubling Her

        Depart, before the Host have slid   5
        The Bolt unto the Door
        To search for the accomplished Guest,
        Her Visitor, no more -

1018   Up Life's Hill with my little Bundle
        If I prove it steep -
        If a Discouragement withold me -
        If my newest step

        Older feel than the Hope that prompted -   5
        Spotless be from blame
        Heart that proposed as Heart that accepted
        Homelessness, for Home -

1019   She rose as high as His Occasion
        Then sought the Dust -
        And lower lay in low Westminster
        For Her brief Crest -

1020   There is a Zone whose even Years
        No Solstice interrupt -
        Whose Sun constructs perpetual Noon
        Whose perfect Seasons wait -

        Whose Summer set in Summer, till   5
        The Centuries of June
        And Centuries of August cease
        And Consciousness - is Noon -

1021   Which is best? Heaven -
        Or only Heaven to come
        With that old Codicil of Doubt?
        I cannot help esteem

        The "Bird within the Hand"   5
        Superior to the one
        The "Bush" may yield me
        Or may not -
        Too late to choose again.

1022   A prompt - executive Bird is the Jay -
        Bold as a Bailiff's Hymn -
        Brittle and Brief in quality -
        Warrant in every Line -
        Sitting a Bough like a Brigadier   5
        Confident and straight -
        Good is the look of him in March
        As a Benefit.

Guides the Little One predestined
To the Native Land -

1033   I knew that I had gained
        And yet I knew not how
        By Diminution it was not
        But Discipline unto

        A Rigor unrelieved   5
        Except by the Content
        Another bear it's Duplicate
        In other Continent.

1034   It rises - passes - on our South
        Inscribes a simple Noon -
        Cajoles a Moment with the Spires
        And infinite is gone -

1035   So large my Will
        The little that I may
        Embarrasses
        Like gentle infamy -

        Affront to Him   5
        For whom the Whole were small
        Affront to me
        Who know His meed of all.

        Earth at the best
        Is but a scanty Toy -   10
        Bought, carried Home
        To Immortality

        It looks so small
        We chiefly wonder then
        At our Conceit   15
        In purchasing.

1036 The Products of my Farm are these
    Sufficient for my Own
    And here and there a Benefit
    Unto a Neighbor's Bin.

    With Us, 'tis Harvest all the Year   5
    For when the Frosts begin
    We just reverse the Zodiac
    And fetch the Acres in -

1037 The Dying need but little, Dear,
    A Glass of Water's all,
    A Flower's unobtrusive Face
    To punctuate the Wall,

    A Fan, perhaps, a Friend's Regret   5
    And Certainty that one
    No color in the Rainbow
    Perceive, when you are gone -

1038 Bloom - is Result - to meet a Flower
    And casually glance
    Would cause one scarcely to suspect
    The minor Circumstance

    Assisting in the Bright Affair   5
    So intricately done
    Then offered as a Butterfly
    To the Meridian -

    To pack the Bud - oppose the Worm -
    Obtain it's right of Dew -   10
    Adjust the Heat - elude the Wind -
    Escape the prowling Bee -

    Great Nature not to disappoint
    Awaiting Her that Day -
    To be a Flower, is profound   15
    Responsibility -

1039   My Heart opon a little Plate
        Her Palate to delight
        A Berry or a Bun, would be,
        Might it an Apricot!

1040   'Twas my one Glory -
        Let it be
        Remembered
        I was owned of Thee -

1041   Nor Mountain hinder Me
        Nor Sea -
        Who's Baltic
        Who's Cordillera?

1042   When they come back - if Blossoms do -
        I always feel a doubt
        If Blossoms can be born again
        When once the Art is out -

        When they begin, if Robins may,   5
        I always had a fear
        I did not tell, it was their last Experiment
        Last Year,

        When it is May, if May return,
        Had nobody a pang   10
        Lest in a Face so beautiful
        He might not look again?

        If I am there - One does not know
        What Party - One may be
        Tomorrow, but if I am there   15
        I take back all I say -

1043   Superiority to Fate
        Is difficult to gain

'Tis not conferred of any
But possible to earn

A pittance at a time   5
Until to Her surprise
The Soul with strict economy
Subsist till Paradise.

1044   Revolution is the Pod
Systems rattle from
When the Winds of Will are stirred
Excellent is Bloom

But except it's Russet Base   5
Every Summer be
The entomber of itself,
So of Liberty -

Left inactive on the Stalk
All it's Purple fled   10
Revolution shakes it for
Test if it be dead -

1045   We learn in the Retreating
How vast an one
Was recently among us -
A Perished Sun

Endear in the departure   5
How doubly more
Than all the Golden presence
It was - before -

1046   What Twigs We held by -
Oh the View
When Life's swift River striven through
We pause before a further plunge
To take Momentum -   5
As the Fringe

□

Opon a former Garment shows
The Garment cast,
Our Props disclose
So scant, so eminently small   10
Of Might to help, so pitiful
To sink, if We had labored, fond
The diligence were not more blind

How scant, by everlasting Light
The Discs that satisfied our sight -   15
How dimmer than a Saturn's Bar
The Things esteemed, for Things that are!

1047 We miss a Kinsman more
When warranted to see
Than when witheld of Oceans
From possibility

A Furlong than a League   5
Inflicts a pricklier pain,
Till We, who smiled at Pyrrhenees -
Of Parishes, complain.

1048 Ended, ere it begun -
The Title was scarcely told
When the Preface perished from Consciousness
The story, unrevealed -

Had it been mine, to print!   5
Had it been your's, to read!
That it was not our privilege
The interdict of God -

1049 Myself can read the Telegrams
A Letter chief to me
The Stock's advance and retrogade
And what the Markets say

□

The Weather - how the Rains
In Counties have begun.
'Tis News as null as nothing,
But sweeter so, than none.

1050   I am afraid to own a Body -
        I am afraid to own a Soul -
        Profound - precarious Property -
        Possession, not optional -

        Double Estate, entailed at pleasure   5
        Opon an unsuspecting Heir -
        Duke in a moment of Deathlessness
        And God, for a Frontier.

1051   The Well opon the Brook
        Were foolish to depend -
        Let Brooks - renew of Brooks -
        But Wells - of failless Ground!

1052   It was not Saint - it was too large -
        Nor Snow - it was too small -
        It only held itself aloof
        Like something spiritual -

1053   Because 'twas Riches I could own,
        Myself had earned it - Me,
        I knew the Dollars by their names -
        It feels like Poverty

        An Earldom out of sight, to hold,   5
        An Income in the Air,
        Possession - has a sweeter chink
        Unto a Miser's Ear -

1054   Themself are all I have -
         Myself a freckled - be -
         I thought you'd choose
         A Velvet Cheek
         Or one of Ivory -   5
         Would you - instead of Me?

1055   To Whom the Mornings stand for Nights,
         What must the Midnights - be!

1056   Could I but ride indefinite
         As doth the Meadow Bee
         And visit only where I liked
         And no one visit me

         And flirt all Day with Buttercups   5
         And marry whom I may
         And dwell a little everywhere
         Or better, run away

         With no Police to follow
         Or chase Him if He do   10
         Till He should jump Peninsulas
         To get away from me -

         I said "But just to be a Bee"
         Opon a Raft of Air
         And row in Nowhere all Day long   15
         And anchor "off the Bar"

         What Liberty! So Captives deem
         Who tight in Dungeons are.

1057   Embarrassment of one another
         And God
         Is Revelation's limit,
         Aloud
         Is nothing that is chief,   5

But still,
Divinity dwells under Seal -

1058 To One denied to drink
To tell what Water is
Would be acuter, would it not
Than letting Him surmise?

To lead Him to the Well   5
And let Him hear it drip
Remind Him, would it not, somewhat
Of His condemned lip?

1059 Uncertain lease - developes lustre
On Time -
Uncertain Grasp, appreciation
Of Sum -

The shorter Fate - is oftener the chiefest 5
Because
Inheritors opon a tenure
Prize -

1060 Noon - is the Hinge of Day -
Evening - the Tissue Door -
Morning - the East compelling the Sill
Till all the World is ajar -

1061 This Chasm, Sweet, opon my life
I mention it to you,
When Sunrise through a fissure drop
The Day must follow too.

If we demur, it's gaping sides   5
Disclose as 'twere a Tomb
Ourself am lying straight wherein
The Favorite of Doom -

□

When it has just contained a Life
Then, Darling, it will close   10
And yet so bolder every Day
So turbulent it grows

I'm tempted half to stitch it up
With a remaining Breath
I should not miss in yielding, though   15
To Him, it would be Death -

And so I bear it big about
My Burial - before
A Life quite ready to depart
Can harass me no more -   20

1062   My best Acquaintances are those
        With Whom I spoke no Word -
        The Stars that stated come to Town
        Esteemed Me never rude
        Although to their Celestial Call   5
        I failed to make reply -
        My constant - reverential Face
        Sufficient Courtesy -

1063   The Sun and Moon must make their haste -
        The Stars express around
        For in the Zones of Paradise
        The Lord alone is burned -

        His Eye, it is the East and West -   5
        The North and South when He
        Do concentrate His Countenance
        Like Glow Worms, flee away -

        Oh Poor and Far -
        Oh Hindered Eye   10
        That hunted for the Day -
        The Lord a Candle entertains
        Entirely for Thee -

1064 As the Starved Maelstrom laps the Navies
   As the Vulture teazed
   Forces the Broods in lonely Valleys
   As the Tiger eased

   By but a Crumb of Blood, fasts Scarlet   5
   Till he meet a Man
   Dainty adorned with Veins and Tissues
   And partakes - his Tongue

   Cooled by the Morsel for a moment
   Grows a fiercer thing   10
   Till he esteem his Dates and Cocoa
   A Nutrition mean

   I, of a finer Famine
   Deem my Supper dry
   For but a Berry of Domingo   15
   And a Torrid Eye -

1065 Ribbons of the Year -
   Multitude Brocade -
   Worn to Nature's Party once

   Then, as flung aside
   As a faded Bead   5
   Or a Wrinkled Pearl -
   Who shall charge the Vanity
   Of the Maker's Girl?

1066 Death leaves Us homesick, who behind,
   Except that it is gone
   Are ignorant of it's Concern
   As if it were not born.

   Through all their former Places, we   5
   Like Individuals go
   Who something lost, the seeking for
   Is all that's left them, now -

1067   Crisis is a Hair
Toward which forces creep
Past which - forces retrogade
If it come in sleep

To suspend the Breath   5
Is the most we can
Ignorant is it Life or Death
Nicely balancing -

Let an instant push
Or an Atom press   10
Or a Circle hesitate
In Circumference

It may jolt the Hand
That adjusts the Hair
That secures Eternity   15
From presenting - Here -

1068   Under the Light, yet under,
Under the Grass and the Dirt,
Under the Beetle's Cellar
Under the Clover's Root,

Further than Arm could stretch   5
Were it Giant long,
Further than Sunshine could
Were the Day Year long,

Over the Light, yet over,
Over the Arc of the Bird -   10
Over the Comet's chimney -
Over the Cubit's Head,

Further than Guess can gallop
Further than Riddle ride -
Oh for a Disc to the Distance   15
Between Ourselves and the Dead!

1069   Who occupies this House?
A Stranger I must judge
Since No one knows His Circumstance -
'Tis well the name and age

Are writ opon the Door   5
Or I should fear to pause
Where not so much as Honest Dog
Approach encourages -

It seems a Curious Town -
Some Houses very old,   10
Some - newly raised this Afternoon,
Were I compelled to build

It should not be among
Inhabitants so still
But where the Birds assemble   15
And Boys were possible

Before Myself was born
'Twas settled, so they say,
A Territory for the Ghosts
And Squirrels, formerly.   20

Until a Pioneer, as
Settlers often do
Liking the quiet of the Place
Attracted more unto -

And from a Settlement   25
A Capitol has grown
Distinguished for the gravity
Of every Citizen -

The Owner of this House
A Stranger He must be -   30
Eternity's Acquaintances
Are mostly so - to me -

1070   The Chemical conviction
That Nought be lost

Enable in Disaster
My fractured Trust -

The Faces of the Atoms 5
If I shall see
How more the Finished Creatures
Departed Me!

1071   The Hollows round His eager Eyes
Were Pages where to read
Pathetic Histories - although
Himself had not complained.
Biography to All who passed 5
Of Unobtrusive Pain
Except for the italic Face
Endured, unhelped - unknown -

1072   A loss of something ever felt I -
The first that I could recollect
Bereft I was - of what I knew not
Too young that any should suspect

A Mourner walked among the children 5
I notwithstanding went about
As one bemoaning a Dominion
Itself the only Prince cast out -

Elder, Today, A session wiser,
And fainter, too, as Wiseness is 10
I find Myself still softly searching
For my Delinquent Palaces -

And a Suspicion, like a Finger
Touches my Forehead now and then
That I am looking oppositely 15
For the Site of the Kingdom of Heaven -

1073   Herein a Blossom lies -
A Sepulchre, between -

Cross it, and overcome the Bee -
Remain - 'tis but a Rind -

1074   What did They do since I saw Them?
        Were They industrious?
        So many questions to put Them
        Have I the Eagerness

        That could I snatch Their Faces   5
        That could Their lips reply
        Not till the last was answered
        Should They start for the Sky -

        Not if the Just suspect Me
        And offer a Reward   10
        Would I restore my Booty
        To that Bold Person, God,

        Not if Their Party were waiting,
        Not if to talk with Me
        Were to Them now, Homesickness   15
        After Eternity -

1075   As plan for Noon and plan for Night
        So differ Life and Death
        In positive Prospective -
        The Foot opon the Earth

        At Distance, and Achievement, strains,   5
        The Foot opon the Grave
        Makes effort at Conclusion
        Assisted faint, of Love -

1076   Of Consciousness, her awful mate
        The Soul cannot be rid -
        As easy the secreting her
        Behind the eyes of God -

                                                                  □

The deepest hid is sighted first 5
And scant to Him the Crowd -
What triple Lenses burn opon
The Escapade from God -

1077   A Cloud withdrew from the Sky
        Superior Glory be
        But that Cloud and it's Auxiliaries
        Are forever lost to me

        Had I but further scanned 5
        Had I secured the Glow
        In an Hermetic Memory
        It had availed me now -

        Never to pass the Angel
        With a glance and a Bow 10
        Till I am firm in Heaven
        Is my intention, now -

1078   Of Silken Speech and Specious Shoe
        A Traitor is the Bee
        His service to the newest Grace
        Present continually

        His Suit a chance 5
        His Troth a Term
        Protracted as the Breeze
        Continual Ban propoundeth He
        Continual Divorce.

1079   How fortunate the Grave -
        All Prizes to obtain,
        Successful certain, if at last,
        First Suitor not in vain.

1080 How happy I was if I could forget
   To remember how sad I am
   Would be an easy adversity
   But the recollecting of Bloom

   Keeps making November difficult   5
   Till I who was almost bold
   Lose my way like a little Child
   And perish of the cold.

1081 Experiment to me
   Is every one I meet
   If it contain a Kernel?
   The Figure of a nut

   Presents opon a Tree   5
   Equally plausibly
   But meat within is requisite
   To Squirrels and to me

1082 That Such have died enable Us
   The tranquiller to die -
   That Such have lived,
   Certificate for Immortality.

1083 Sang from the Heart, Sire,
   Dipped my Beak in it,
   If the Tune drip too much
   Have a tint too Red

   Pardon the Cochineal -   5
   Suffer the Vermillion -
   Death is the Wealth
   Of the Poorest Bird.

   Bear with the Ballad -
   Awkward - faltering -   10
   Death twists the strings -
   'Twas'nt my blame -

               □

Pause in your Liturgies -
Wait your Chorals -
While I repeat your   15
Hallowed Name -

1084   Fate slew Him, but He did not drop -
        She felled - He did not fall -
        Impaled Him on Her fiercest stakes -
        He neutralized them all -

        She stung Him - sapped His firm Advance -   5
        But when Her Worst was done
        And He - unmoved regarded Her -
        Acknowledged Him a Man -

1085   Who is the East?
        The Yellow Man
        Who may be Purple if He can
        That carries in the Sun.

        Who is the West?   5
        The Purple Man
        Who may be Yellow if He can
        That lets Him out again.

1086   Nature rarer uses Yellow
        Than another Hue -
        Saves she all of that for Sunsets
        Prodigal of Blue

        Spending Scarlet, like a Woman   5
        Yellow she affords
        Only scantly and selectly
        Like a Lover's Words -

1087   To help our Bleaker Parts
        Salubrious Hours are given

Which if they do not fit for Earth -
Drill silently for Heaven -

1088   I've dropped my Brain - My Soul is numb -
The Veins that used to run
Stop palsied - 'tis Paralysis
Done perfecter in stone -

Vitality is Carved and cool -   5
My nerve in marble lies -
A Breathing Woman
Yesterday - endowed with Paradise.

Not dumb - I had a sort that moved -
A Sense that smote and stirred -   10
Instincts for Dance - a caper part -
An Aptitude for Bird -

Who wrought Carrara in me
And chiselled all my tune
Were it a witchcraft - were it Death -   15
I've still a chance to strain

To Being, somewhere - Motion - Breath -
Though Centuries beyond,
And every limit a Decade -
I'll shiver, satisfied.   20

1089   The Opening and the Close
Of Being, are alike
Or differ, if they do,
As Bloom opon a Stalk -

That from an equal Seed   5
Unto an equal Bud
Go parallel, perfected
In that they have decayed -

1090   This quiet Dust was Gentlemen and Ladies
And Lads and Girls -
Was laughter and ability and Sighing
And Frocks and Curls.

This Passive Place a Summer's nimble mansion   5
Where Bloom and Bees
Exist an Oriental Circuit
Then cease, like these -

1091   To own the Art within the Soul
The Soul to entertain
With Silence as a Company
And Festival maintain

In an unfurnished Circumstance   5
Possession is to One
As an Estate perpetual
Or a reduceless Mine.

1092   There is a finished feeling
Experienced at Graves -
A leisure of the Future -
A Wilderness of Size.

By Death's bold Exhibition   5
Preciser what we are
And the Eternal function
Enabled to infer.

1093   'Twas Crisis - All the length had passed -
That dull - benumbing time
There is in Fever or Event -
And now the Chance had come -

The instant holding in it's Claw   5
The privilege to live
Or Warrant to report the Soul
The other side the Grave.

□

The Muscles grappled as with leads
That would not let the Will -   10
The Spirit shook the Adamant -
But could not make it feel -

The Second poised - debated - shot -
Another, had begun -
And simultaneously, a Soul   15
Escaped the House unseen -

1094   We outgrow love, like other things
        And put it in the Drawer -
        Till it an Antique fashion shows -
        Like Costumes Grandsires wore.

1095   When I have seen the Sun emerge
        From His amazing House -
        And leave a Day at every Door
        A Deed, in every place -

        Without the incident of Fame   5
        Or accident of Noise -
        The Earth has seemed to me a Drum,
        Pursued of little Boys

1096   A narrow Fellow in the Grass
        Occasionally rides -
        You may have met him? Did you not
        His notice instant is -

        The Grass divides as with a Comb -   5
        A spotted Shaft is seen,
        And then it closes at your Feet
        And opens further on -

        He likes a Boggy Acre -
        A Floor too cool for Corn -   10
        But when a Boy and Barefoot
        I more than once at Noon

                                                          □

Have passed I thought a Whip Lash
Unbraiding in the Sun
When stooping to secure it   15
It wrinkled And was gone -

Several of Nature's People
I know and they know me
I feel for them a transport
Of Cordiality   20

But never met this Fellow
Attended or alone
Without a tighter Breathing
And Zero at the Bone.

1097   Ashes denote that Fire was -
        Revere the Grayest Pile
        For the Departed Creature's sake
        That hovered there awhile -

        Fire exists the first in light   5
        And then consolidates
        Only the Chemist can disclose
        Into what Carbonates -

1098   The Leaves like Women, interchange
        Sagacious Confidence -
        Somewhat of Nods and somewhat
        Portentous inference -

        The Parties in both cases   5
        Enjoining secrecy -
        Inviolable compact
        To notoriety.

1099   At Half past Three
        A Single Bird
        Unto a silent sky

Propounded but a single term
Of cautious Melody.   5

At Half past Four
Experiment had subjugated test
And lo, her silver principle
Supplanted all the rest.

At Half past Seven   10
Element nor implement be seen
And Place was where the Presence was
Circumference between

1100   The last Night that She lived
       It was a Common Night
       Except the Dying - this to Us
       Made Nature different

       We noticed smallest things -   5
       Things overlooked before
       By this great light opon our minds
       Italicized - as 'twere.

       As We went out and in
       Between Her final Room   10
       And Rooms where Those to be alive
       Tomorrow, were, a Blame

       That others could exist
       While She must finish quite
       A Jealousy for Her arose   15
       So nearly infinite -

       We waited while She passed -
       It was a narrow time -
       Too jostled were Our Souls to speak
       At length the notice came.   20

       She mentioned, and forgot -
       Then lightly as a Reed
       Bent to the Water, struggled scarce -
       Consented, and was dead -

                                                         □

And We - We placed the Hair -
And drew the Head erect -
And then an awful leisure was
Belief to regulate -   25

1101   If Nature smiles - the Mother must
        I'm sure, at many a whim
        Of Her eccentric Family -
        Is She so much to blame?

1102   Dew - is the Freshet in the Grass -
        'Tis many a tiny Mill
        Turns unperceived beneath - our feet
        And Artisan lies still -

        We spy the Forests and the Hills   5
        The Tents to Nature's Show
        Mistake the Outside for the in
        And mention what we saw.

        Could Commentators on the Sign
        Of Nature's Caravan   10
        Obtain "admission" as a Child
        Some Wednesday Afternoon.

1103   Perception of an Object costs
        Precise the Object's loss -
        Perception in itself a Gain
        Replying to it's price -

        The Object absolute, is nought -   5
        Perception sets it fair
        And then upbraids a Perfectness
        That situates so far -

1104   The Crickets sang
        And set the Sun

And Workmen finished one by one
Their Seam the Day opon -

The low Grass loaded with the Dew   5
The Twilight stood, as Strangers do
With Hat in Hand, polite and new
To stay as if, or go -

A Vastness, as a Neighbor, came,
A Wisdom, without Face, or Name,   10
A Peace, as Hemispheres at Home
And so the Night became -

1105   Of the Heart that goes in, and closes the Door
        Shall the Playfellow Heart complain
        Though the Ring is unwhole, and the Company broke
        Can never be fitted again?

1106   These are the Signs to Nature's Inns -
        Her invitation broad
        To Whosoever famishing
        To taste her mystic Bread -

        These are the rites of Nature's House -   5
        The Hospitality
        That opens with an equal width
        To Beggar and to Bee

        For Sureties of her staunch Estate
        Her undecaying Cheer   10
        The Purple in the East is set
        And in the North, the Star -

1107   My Cocoon tightens - Colors teaze -
        I'm feeling for the Air -
        A dim capacity for Wings
        Demeans the Dress I wear -

                                                     □

A power of Butterfly must be -　　　　　　　　　5
The Aptitude to fly
Meadows of Majesty concedes
And easy Sweeps of Sky -

So I must baffle at the Hint
And cipher at the Sign　　　　　　　　　　　10
And make much blunder, if at last
I take the clue divine -

1108　　The Bustle in a House
　　　　The Morning after Death
　　　　Is solemnest of industries
　　　　Enacted opon Earth -

　　　　The Sweeping up the Heart　　　　　　　5
　　　　And putting Love away
　　　　We shall not want to use again
　　　　Until Eternity -

1109　　The Sun went down - no Man looked on -
　　　　The Earth and I, alone,
　　　　Were present at the Majesty -
　　　　He triumphed, and went on -

　　　　The Sun went up - no Man looked on -　　5
　　　　The Earth and I and One
　　　　A nameless Bird - a Stranger
　　　　Were Witness for the Crown -

1110　　One Day is there of the series
　　　　Termed "Thanksgiving Day"
　　　　Celebrated part at table
　　　　Part in memory -
　　　　Neither Ancestor nor Urchin　　　　　　5
　　　　I review the Play -
　　　　Seems it to my Hooded thinking
　　　　Reflex Holiday -

　　　　　　　　　　　　　　　　　　　□

Had There been no sharp subtraction
From the early Sum -   10
Not an Acre or a Caption
Where was once a Room
Not a mention whose small Pebble
Wrinkled any Sea,
Unto such, were such Assembly   15
'Twere "Thanksgiving Day" -

1111   He outstripped Time with but a Bout,
       He outstripped Stars and Sun
       And then, unjaded, challenged God
       In presence of the Throne -

       And He and He in mighty List   5
       Unto this present, run,
       The larger Glory for the less
       A just sufficient Ring.

1112   This is a Blossom of the Brain -
       A small - italic Seed
       Lodged by Design or Happening
       The Spirit fructified -

       Shy as the Wind of his Chambers   5
       Swift as a Freshet's Tongue
       So of the Flower of the Soul
       It's process is unknown -

       When it is found, a few rejoice
       The Wise convey it Home   10
       Carefully cherishing the spot
       If other Flower become -

       When it is lost, that Day shall be
       The Funeral of God,
       Opon his Breast, a closing Soul   15
       The Flower of Our Lord -

1113   All Circumstances are the Frame
        In which His Face is set -
        All Latitudes exist for His
        Sufficient Continent -

        The Light His Action, and the Dark   5
        The Leisure of His Will -
        In Him Existence serve or set
        A Force illegible.

1114   A Shade opon the mind there passes
        As when on Noon
        A Cloud the mighty Sun encloses
        Remembering

        That some there be too numb to notice   5
        Oh God
        Why give if Thou must take away
        The Loved?

1115   It is an honorable Thought
        And makes One lift One's Hat
        As One met sudden Gentlefolk
        Opon a daily Street

        That We've immortal Place   5
        Though Pyramids decay
        And Kingdoms, like the Orchard
        Flit Russetly away

1116   The Sunset stopped on Cottages
        Where Sunset hence must be
        For treason not of His, but Life's,
        Gone Westerly, Today -

        The Sunset stopped on Cottages   5
        Where Morning just begun -
        What difference, after all, Thou mak'st
        Thou Supercilious Sun?

1117 Let down the Bars, Oh Death -
The tired Flocks come in
Whose bleating ceases to repeat
Whose wandering is done -

Thine is the stillest night 5
Thine the securest Fold
Too near Thou art for seeking Thee
Too tender, to be told -

1118 Reportless Subjects, to the Quick
Continual addressed -
But foreign as the Dialect
Of Danes, unto the rest.

Reportless Measures, to the Ear 5
Susceptive - stimulus -
But like an Oriental Tale
To others, fabulous -

1119 Pain has but one Acquaintance
And that is Death -
Each one unto the other
Society enough -

Pain is the Junior Party 5
By just a Second's right -
Death tenderly assists Him
And then absconds from Sight -

1120 Gratitude - is not the mention
Of a Tenderness,
But it's still appreciation
Out of Plumb of Speech -

When the Sea return no Answer 5
By the Line and Lead
Proves it there's no Sea, or rather
A remoter Bed?

1121 The Sky is low - the Clouds are mean.
  A Travelling Flake of Snow
  Across a Barn or through a Rut
  Debates if it will go -
  A Narrow Wind complains all Day   5
  How some one treated him
  Nature, like Us is sometimes caught
  Without her Diadem -

1122 I cannot meet the Spring - unmoved -
  I feel the old desire -
  A Hurry with a lingering, mixed,
  A Warrant to be fair -

  A Competition in my sense   5
  With something, hid in Her -
  And as she vanishes, Remorse
  I saw no more of Her -

1123 Between the form of Life and Life
  The difference is as big
  As Liquor at the Lip between
  And liquor in the Jug
  The latter - excellent to keep -   5
  But for extatic need
  The corkless is superior -
  I know for I have tried

1124 Count not that far that can be had
  Though sunset lie between
  Nor that adjacent that beside
  Is further than the sun.

1125   Paradise is of the Option -
          Whosoever will
          Own in Eden notwithstanding
          Adam, and Repeal.

1126   His Bill is locked - his Eye estranged
          His Feathers wilted low -
          The Claws that clung, like lifeless Gloves
          Indifferent hanging now -
          The Joy that in his happy Throat   5
          Was waiting to be poured
          Gored through and through with Death, to be
          Assassin of a Bird
          Resembles to my outraged mind
          The firing in Heaven,   10
          On Angels - squandering for you
          Their Miracles of Tune -

1127   After the Sun comes out
          How it alters the World -
          Wagons like messengers hurry about
          Yesterday is old -

          All men meet as if   5
          Each foreclosed a news -
          Fresh as a Cargo from Balize
          Nature's qualities -

1128   Distance - is not the Realm of Fox
          Nor by Relay of Bird
          Abated - Distance is
          Until thyself, Beloved.

1129   I fit for them - I seek the Dark
          Till I am thorough fit.

The labor is a sober one
With the austerer sweet -

That abstinence of mine produce   5
A purer food for them, if I succeed,
If not I had
The transport of the Aim -

1130   The Frost of Death was on the Pane -
        "Secure your Flower" said he.
        Like Sailors fighting with a Leak
        We fought Mortality -

        Our passive Flower we held to Sea -   5
        To mountain - to the Sun -
        Yet even on his Scarlet shelf
        To crawl the Frost begun -

        We pried him back
        Ourselves we wedged   10
        Himself and her between -
        Yet easy as the narrow Snake
        He forked his way along

        Till all her helpless beauty bent
        And then our wrath begun -   15
        We hunted him to his Ravine
        We chased him to his Den -

        We hated Death and hated Life
        And nowhere was to go -
        Than Sea and continent there is   20
        A larger - it is Woe

1131   A Diamond on the Hand
To Custom Common grown
Subsides from it's significance
The Gem were best unknown -
Within a Seller's shrine   5
How many sight and sigh
And cannot, but are mad with fear
That any other buy -

1132   Some Wretched creature, savior take
Who would exult to die
And leave for thy sweet mercy's sake
Another Hour to me

1133   There is a strength in proving that it can be borne
Although it tear -
What are the sinews of such cordage for
Except to bear
The ship might be of satin had it not to fight -   5
To walk on seas requires cedar Feet

1134   The Merchant of the Picturesque
A Counter has and sales
But is within or negative
Precisely as the calls -
To Children he is small in price   5
And large in courtesy -
It suits him better than a check
Their artless currency -
Of Counterfeits he is so shy
Do one advance so near   10
As to behold his ample flight -

1135   None who saw it ever told it
              'Tis as hid as Death
              Had for that specific treasure
              A departing breath -
              Surfaces may be invested   5
              Did the Diamond grow
              General as the Dandelion
              Would you serve it so?

1136   Soul, take thy risk,
              With Death to be
              Were better than be not with thee

1137   Too cold is this
              To warm with Sun -
              Too stiff to bended be.
              To joint this Agate were a work -
              Outstaring Masonry -   5

              How went the Agile Kernel out
              Contusion of the Husk
              Nor Rip, nor wrinkle indicate
              But just an Asterisk.

1138   There is another Loneliness
              That many die without -
              Not want of friend occasions it
              Or circumstance of Lot

              But nature, sometimes, sometimes thought   5
              And whoso it befall
              Is richer than could be revealed
              By mortal numeral -

1139   We do not know the time we lose -
              The awful moment is

And takes it's fundamental place
Among the certainties -

A firm appearance still inflates   5
The card - the chance - the friend -
The spectre of solidities
Whose substances are sand -

1140   The Lightning is a yellow Fork
From Tables in the Sky
By inadvertent fingers dropt
The awful Cutlery

Of mansions never quite disclosed   5
And never quite concealed
The Apparatus of the Dark
To ignorance revealed -

1141   A full fed Rose on meals of Tint
A Dinner for a Bee
In process of the Noon became -
Each bright mortality
The Forfeit is of Creature fair   5
Itself, adored before
Submitting for our unknown sake
To be esteemed no more

1142   The murmuring of Bees, has ceased
But murmuring of some
Posterior, prophetic,
Has simultaneous come.
The lower metres of the Year   5
When Nature's laugh is done
The Revelations of the Book
Whose Genesis was June.
Appropriate Creatures to her change
The Typic Mother sends   10
As Accent fades to interval

With separating Friends
Till what we speculate, has been
And thoughts we will not show
More intimate with us become 15
Than Persons, that we know.

1143   The smouldering embers blush -
Oh Heart within the Coal
Hast thou survived so many years?
The smouldering embers smile -

Soft stirs the news of Light   5
The stolid seconds glow
One requisite has Fire that lasts
Prometheus never knew -

1144   Paradise is that old mansion
Many owned before -
Occupied by each an instant
Then reversed the Door -
Bliss is frugal of her Leases   5
Adam taught her Thrift
Bankrupt once through his excesses -

1145   In thy long Paradise of Light
No moment will there be
When I shall long for Earthly Play
And mortal Company -

1146   Soft as the massacre of Suns
By Evening's sabres slain

1147   The Bird did prance - the Bee did play -
The Sun ran miles away
So blind with joy he could not choose
Between his Holiday -

The morn was up - the meadows out   5
The Fences all but ran -

Republic of Delight, I thought
Where each is Citizen -

From Heavy laden Lands to thee
Were seas to cross to come   10
A Caspian were crowded -
Too near thou art for Fame -

1148   Tell as a Marksman - were forgotten
       Tell - this Day endures
       Ruddy as that Coeval Apple
       The Tradition bears -

       Fresh as Mankind that humble story   5
       Though a statelier Tale
       Grown in the Repetition hoary
       Scarcely would prevail -

       Tell had a son - The ones that knew it
       Need not linger here -   10
       Those who did not to Human nature
       Will subscribe a Tear -

       Tell would not bare his Head
       In Presence
       Of the Ducal Hat -   15
       Threatened for that with Death - by Gessler -
       Tyranny bethought

       Make of his only Boy a Target
       That surpasses Death -
       Stolid to Love's supreme entreaty   20
       Not forsook of Faith -

       Mercy of the Almighty begging -
       Tell his Arrow sent -
       God it is said replies in Person
       When the Cry is meant   25

1149   After a hundred years
       Nobody knows the Place

Agony that enacted there
Motionless as Peace

Weeds triumphant ranged   5
Strangers strolled and spelled
At the lone Orthography
Of the Elder Dead

Winds of Summer Fields
Recollect the way -   10
Instinct picking up the Key
Dropped by memory -

1150   These are the Nights that Beetles love -
        From Eminence remote
        Drives ponderous perpendicular
        His figure intimate -
        The terror of the Children   5
        The merriment of men
        Depositing his Thunder
        He hoists abroad again -
        A Bomb opon the Ceiling
        Is an improving thing -   10
        It keeps the nerves progressive
        Conjecture flourishing -
        Too dear the Summer evening
        Without discreet alarm -
        Supplied by Entomology   15
        With it's remaining charm

1151   'Tis my first night beneath the Sun
        If I should spend it here -
        Above him is too low a hight
        For his Barometer
        Who Airs of expectation breathes   5
        And takes the Wind at prime -
        But Distance his Delights confides
        To those who visit him

1152   The Wind took up the Northern Things
And piled them in the South -
Then gave the East unto the West
And opening his mouth
The Four Divisions of the Earth   5
Did make as to devour
While everything to corners slunk
Behind the awful power -

The Wind unto his Chamber went
And nature ventured out -   10
Her subjects scattered into place
Her systems ranged about

Again the smoke from Dwellings rose
The Day abroad was heard
How intimate, a Tempest past   15
The Transport of the Bird -

1153   The longest day that God appoints
Will finish with the sun.
Anguish can travel to it's stake,
And then it must return.

1154 I noticed People disappeared
When but a little child -
Supposed they visited remote
Or settled Regions wild -
Now know I - They both visited   5
And settled Regions wild -
But did because they died
A Fact witheld the little child -

1155 The Snow that never drifts -
The transient, fragrant snow
That comes a single time a Year
Is softly driving now -

So thorough in the Tree   5
At night beneath the star
That it was Febuary's Foot
Experience would swear -

Like Winter as a Face
We stern and former knew   10
Repaired of all but Loneliness
By Nature's Alibi -

Were every Storm so spice
The Value could not be -
We buy with contrast - Pang is good   15
As near as memory -

1156 That odd old man is dead a year -
We miss his stated Hat -
'Twas such an evening bright and stiff
His faded lamp went out -

Who miss his antiquated Wick -   5
Are any hoar for him?

Waits any indurated mate
His wrinkled coming Home?

Oh Life, begun in fluent Blood
And consummated dull -   10
Achievement, contemplating thee -
Feels transitive and cool.

1157   Exhiliration is the Breeze
        That lifts us from the Ground
        And leaves us in another place
        Whose statement is not found -

        Returns us not, but after time   5
        We soberly descend
        A little newer for the term
        Opon Enchanted Ground -

1158   Best Witchcraft is Geometry
        To the magician's mind -
        His ordinary acts are feats
        To thinking of mankind -

1159   The Work of Her that went,
        The Toil of Fellows done -
        In Ovens green our Mother bakes,
        By Fires of the Sun -

1160   The duties of the Wind are few -
        To cast the ships, at Sea,
        Establish March, the Floods escort,
        And usher Liberty.

        The pleasures of the Wind are broad,   5
        To dwell Extent among,
        Remain, or wander,
        Speculate, or Forests entertain -

        □

The kinsmen of the Wind, are Peaks
Azof - the Equinox,   10
Also with Bird and Asteroid
A bowing intercourse -

The limitations of the Wind
Do he exist, or die,
Too wise he seems for Wakelessness,   15
However, know not I -

1161   When Etna basks and purrs
        Naples is more afraid
        Than when she shows her Garnet Tooth -
        Security is loud -

1162   A Mine there is no Man would own
        But must it be conferred,
        Demeaning by exclusive wealth
        A Universe beside -

        Potosi never to be spent   5
        But hoarded in the mind
        What Misers wring their hands tonight
        For Indies in the Ground!

1163   A Spider sewed at Night
        Without a Light
        Opon an Arc of White -

        If Ruff it was of Dame
        Or Shroud of Gnome   5
        Himself himself inform -

        Of Immortality
        His strategy
        Was physiognomy -

1164   The Day grew small, surrounded tight
By early, stooping Night -
The Afternoon in Evening deep
It's Yellow shortness dropt -
The Winds went out their martial ways   5
The Leaves obtained excuse -
November hung his Granite Hat
Opon a nail of Plush -

1165   Were it to be the last
        How infinite would be
        What we did not suspect was marked
        Our final interview.

1166   Great Streets of silence led away
        To Neighborhoods of Pause -
        Here was no Notice - no Dissent
        No Universe - no Laws -

        By Clocks, 'Twas Morning, and for Night   5
        The Bells at Distance called -
        But Epoch had no basis here
        For Period exhaled.

1167   I bet with every Wind that blew
        Till Nature in chagrin
        Employed a Fact to visit me
        And scuttle my Balloon -

1168   My God - He sees thee -
        Shine thy best -
        Fling up thy Balls of Gold
        Till every Cubit play with thee
        And every Crescent hold -   5
        Elate the Acre at his feet -
        Opon his Atom swim -
        Oh Sun - but just a Second's right
        In thy long Race with him!

1169   Some Days retired from the rest
        In soft distinction lie

The Day that a Companion came
Or was obliged to die -

1170   Of Nature I shall have enough
When I have entered these
Entitled to a Bumble bee's
Familiarities -

1171   The Suburbs of a Secret
A Strategist should keep -
Better than on a Dream intrude
To scrutinize the Sleep -

1172   The incidents of Love
Are more than it's Events -
Investment's best expositor
Is the minute Per Cents -

1173   He is alive, this morning -
He is alive - and awake -
Birds are resuming for Him -
Blossoms - dress for His sake -
Bees - to their Loaves of Honey   5
Add an Amber Crumb
Him - to regale - Me - Only -
Motion, and am dumb.

1174   Alone and in a Circumstance
Reluctant to be told
A spider on my reticence
Assiduously crawled

And so much more at Home than I   5
Immediately grew

I felt myself a visitor
And hurriedly withdrew -

Revisiting my late abode
With articles of claim   10
I found it quietly assumed
As a Gymnasium
Where Tax asleep and Title off
The inmates of the Air
Perpetual presumption took   15
As each were special Heir -
If any strike me on the street
I can return the Blow -
If any take my property
According to the Law   20
The Statute is my Learned friend
But what redress can be
For an offence nor here nor there
So not in Equity -
That Larceny of time and mind   25
The marrow of the Day
By spider, or forbid it Lord
That I should specify -

1175   Contained in this short Life
        Are magical extents
        The soul returning soft at night
        To steal securer thence
        As Children strictest kept   5
        Turn soonest to the sea
        Whose nameless Fathoms slink away
        Beside infinity

1176   Nature affects to be sedate
        Opon Occasion, grand
        But let our observation halt
        Her practises extend
        To Necromancy and the Trades   5

Remote to understand
Behold our spacious Citizen
Unto a Juggler turned -

1177   Trust adjusts her "Peradventure" -
        Phantoms entered "and not you."

1178   The Life we have is very great.
        The Life that we shall see
        Surpasses it, we know, because
        It is Infinity.
        But when all space has been beheld   5
        And all Dominion shown
        The smallest Human Heart's extent
        Reduces it to none.

1179   Where every Bird is bold to go
        And Bees abashless play
        The Foreigner before he knocks
        Must thrust the Tears away -

1180   The Riddle we can guess
        We speedily despise -
        Not anything is stale so long
        As Yesterday's surprise -

1181   Experiment escorts us last -
        His pungent company
        Will not allow an Axiom
        An Opportunity -

1182   Too happy Time dissolves itself
        And leaves no remnant by -

'Tis Anguish not a Feather hath
Or too much weight to fly -

1183   Because He loves Her
We will pry and see if she is fair
What difference is on her Face
From Features others wear.

It will not harm her magic pace   5
That we so far behind -
Her Distances propitiate
As Forests touch the Wind

Not hoping for his notice vast
But nearer to adore   10
'Tis Glory's overtakelessness
That makes our running poor.

1184   We introduce ourselves
To Planets and to Flowers
But with ourselves
Have etiquettes
Embarrassments   5
And awes

1185   Had we known the Ton she bore
We had helped the terror
But she straighter walked for Freight
So be her's the error -

1186   Oh Sumptuous moment
Slower go
That I may gloat on thee -
'Twill never be the same to starve
Now I abundance see -   5
Which was to famish, then or now -

The difference of Day
Ask him unto the Gallows led -
With morning in the sky

1187   A great Hope fell
        You heard no noise
        The Ruin was within
        Oh cunning Wreck
        That told no Tale   5
        And let no Witness in

        The mind was built for mighty Freight
        For dread occasion planned
        How often foundering at Sea
        Ostensibly, on Land   10

1188   A not admitting of the wound
        Until it grew so wide
        That all my Life had entered it
        And there were troughs beside -

        A closing of the simple lid that opened to the sun   5
        Until the tender Carpenter
        Perpetual nail it down -

1189   That this should feel the need of Death
        The same as those that lived
        Is such a Feat of Irony
        As never was achieved -

        Not satisfied to ape the Great in his simplicity   5
        The small must die, the same as he -
        Oh the audacity -

1190   The Frost was never seen -
        If met, too rapid passed,

Or in too unsubstantial Team -
The Flowers notice first

A Stranger hovering round   5
A Symptom of alarm
In Villages remotely set
But search effaces him

Till some retrieveless night
Our Vigilance at waste   10
The Garden gets the only shot
That never could be traced.

Unproved is much we know -
Unknown the worst we fear -
Of Strangers is the Earth the Inn   15
Of Secrets is the Air -

To Analyze perhaps
A Philip would prefer
But Labor vaster than myself
I find it to infer.   20

1191   Lest any doubt that we are glad that they were born Today
        Whose having lived is held by us in noble holiday
        Without the date, like Consciousness or Immortality -

1192   God made no act without a cause -
        Nor heart without an aim -
        Our inference is premature,
        Our premises to blame.

1193   White as an Indian Pipe
Red as a Cardinal Flower
Fabulous as a Moon at Noon
Febuary Hour -

1194 *E* We like March - his Shoes are Purple -
He is new and high -
Makes he Mud for Dog and Peddler -
Makes he Forest dry -

Knows the Adder's Tongue his coming   5
And begets her Spot -
Stands the Sun so close and mighty
That our Minds are hot -

News is he of all the others -
Bold it were to die   10
With the Blue Birds buccaneering
On his British Sky -

1195   Society for me my misery
Since Gift of Thee -

1196   Safe Despair it is that raves -
Agony is frugal.
Puts itself severe away
For it's own perusal.

Garrisoned no Soul can be   5
In the Front of Trouble -
Love is one, not aggregate -
Nor is Dying double -

1197   We never know how high we are
        Till we are asked to rise
        And then if we are true to plan
        Our statures touch the skies -

        The Heroism we recite   5
        Would be a normal thing
        Did not ourselves the Cubits warp
        For fear to be a King -

1198   This slow Day moved along -
        I heard it's axles go
        As if they could not hoist themselves
        They hated motion so -

        I told my soul to come -   5
        It was no use to wait -
        We went and played and came again
        And it was out of sight

1199   A soft Sea washed around the House
        A Sea of Summer Air
        And rose and fell the magic Planks
        That sailed without a care -
        For Captain was the Butterfly   5
        For Helmsman was the Bee
        And an entire universe
        For the delighted Crew -

1200   Whatever it is - she has tried it -
        Awful Father of Love -
        Is not Our's the chastising -
        Do not chastise the Dove -

        Not for Ourselves, petition -   5
        Nothing is left to pray -
        When a subject is finished -
        Words are handed away -

□

Only lest she be lonely
In thy beautiful House
Give her for her Transgression
License to think of us -

10

1201 Too few the mornings be,
Too scant the nights.
No lodging can be had
For the delights
That come to earth to stay,
But no apartment find
And ride away.

5

1202 Of so divine a Loss
We enter but the Gain,
Indemnity for Loneliness
That such a Bliss has been.

1203 On the World you colored
Morning painted rose -
Idle his Vermillion
Aimless crept the Glows
Over Realms of Orchards
I the Day before
Conquered with the Robin -
Misery - how fair
Till your wrinkled Finger
Shoved the Sun away
Midnight's awful Pattern
In the Goods of Day -

5

10

1204 Lest they should come - is all my fear
When sweet incarcerated - here

1205   All men for Honor hardest work
But are not known to earn -
Paid after they have ceased to work
In Infamy or Urn -

1206   Of Paul and Silas it is said
They were in Prison laid
But when they went to take them out
They were not there instead.

Security the same insures   5
To our assaulted minds -
The staple must be optional
That an Immortal binds.

1207   The Voice that stands for Floods to me
Is sterile borne to some -
The Face that makes the Morning mean
Glows impotent on them -

What difference in Substance lies   5
That what is Sum to me
By other Financiers be deemed
Exclusive Poverty!

1208   "Remember Me" implored the Thief -
Oh Magnanimity!
My Visitor in Paradise
I give thee guaranty.

That Courtesy will fair remain   5
When the Delight is Dust
With which we cite this mightiest case
Of compensated Trust.

Of All, we are allowed to hope
But Affidavit stands   10
That this was due, where some, we fear,
Are unexpected friends -

1209   Somehow myself survived the Night
And entered with the Day -
That it be saved the Saved suffice
Without the Formula -

Henceforth I take my living place   5
As one commuted led -
A Candidate for Morning Chance
But dated with the Dead.

1210   Some we see no more, Tenements of Wonder
Occupy to us though perhaps to them
Simpler are the Days than the Supposition
Their removing Manners
Leave us to presume.   5

That oblique Belief which we call Conjecture
Grapples with a Theme stubborn as sublime
Able as the Dust to equip it's feature
Adequate as Drums to enlist the Tomb.

1211   It's Hour with itself
The Spirit never shows -
What Terror would enthrall the Street
Could Countenance disclose

The Subterranean Freight   5
The Cellars of the Soul -
Thank God the loudest Place he made
Is licensed to be still.

1212   My Triumph lasted till the Drums
Had left the Dead alone
And then I dropped my Victory
And chastened stole along
To where the finished Faces   5
Conclusion turned on me

And then I hated Glory
And wished myself were They.

What is to be is best descried
When it has also been -   10
Could Prospect taste of Retrospect
The Tyrannies of Men
Were Tenderer, diviner
The Transitive toward -
A Bayonet's contrition   15
Is nothing to the Dead -

1213   Like Trains of Cars on Tracks of Plush
I hear the level Bee -
A Jar across the Flowers goes
Their Velvet Masonry

Withstands until the sweet Assault   5
Their Chivalry consumes -
While He, victorious tilts away
To vanquish other Blooms.

1214   Not any higher stands the Grave
For Heroes than for Men -
Not any nearer for the Child
Than numb Three score and Ten -

This latest Leisure equal lulls   5
The Beggar and his Queen
Propitiate this Democrat
A Summer's Afternoon -

1215   The harm of Years is on him -
The infamy of Time -
Depose him like a Fashion
And give Dominion room -

Forget his Morning Forces -   5
The Glory of Decay

Is a minuter Pageant
Than least Vitality.

1216   A Wind that rose though not a Leaf
        In any Forest stirred -
        But with itself did cold commune
        Beyond the realm of Bird.

        A Wind that woke a lone Delight   5
        Like Separation's Swell -
        Restored in Arctic confidence
        To the invisible.

1217   I worked for chaff and earning Wheat
        Was haughty and betrayed.
        What right had Fields to arbitrate
        In Matters ratified?

        I tasted Wheat and hated Chaff   5
        And thanked the ample friend -
        Wisdom is more becoming viewed
        At distance than at hand.

1218   The Bone that has no Marrow,
        What Ultimate for that?
        It is not fit for Table
        For Beggar or for Cat -

        A Bone has obligations -   5
        A Being has the same -
        A Marrowless Assembly
        Is culpabler than shame -

        But how shall finished Creatures
        A function fresh obtain?   10
        Old Nicodemus' Phantom
        Confronting us again!

1219   Who goes to dine must take his Feast
Or find the Banquet mean -
The Table is not laid without
Till it is laid within.

For Pattern is the Mind bestowed   5
That imitating her
Our most ignoble services
Exhibit worthier.

1220   The Popular Heart is a Cannon first -
Subsequent a Drum -
Bells for an Auxiliary
And an Afterward of Rum -

Not a Tomorrow to know it's name   5
Nor a Past to stare -
Ditches for Realms and a Trip to Jail
For a Souvenir.

1221   It came at last but prompter Death
Had occupied the House -
His pallid Furniture arranged
And his metallic Peace -

Oh faithful Frost that kept the Date   5
Had Love as punctual been
Delight had aggrandized the Gate
And blocked the coming in.

1222   The pungent Atom in the Air
Admits of no debate -
All that is named of Summer Days
Relinquished our Estate -

For what Department of Delight   5
As positive are we
As Limit of Dominion
Or Dams - of Extasy -

1223   Immortal is an ample word
When what we need is by
But when it leaves us for a time
'Tis a nescessity.

Of Heaven above the firmest proof   5
We fundamental know
Except for it's marauding Hand
It had been Heaven below -

1224   Are Friends Delight or Pain?
Could Bounty but remain
Riches were good -

But if they only stay
Ampler to fly away   5
Riches are sad.

1225   The Mountains stood in Haze -
The Valleys stopped below
And went or waited as they liked
The River and the Sky.

At leisure was the Sun -   5
His interests of Fire
A little from remark withdrawn -
The Twilight spoke the Spire.

So soft opon the Scene
The Act of evening fell   10
We felt how neighborly a thing
Was the Invisible.

1226   Somewhere opon the general Earth
Itself exist Today -
The Magic passive but extant
That consecrated me -

□

Indifferent Seasons doubtless play   5
Where I for right to be -
Would pay each Atom that I am
But Immortality -

Reserving that but just to prove
Another Date of Thee -   10
Oh God of Width, do not for us
Curtail Eternity!

1227   Step lightly on this narrow Spot -
        The Broadest Land that grows
        Is not so ample as the Breast
        These Emerald Seams enclose -

        Step lofty for this name be told   5
        As far as cannon dwell,
        Or Flag subsist, or Fame export
        Her deathless Syllable

1228   I cannot want it more -
        I cannot want it less -
        My Human Nature's fullest force
        Expends itself on this.

        And yet it nothing is   5
        To him who easy owns -
        Is Worth itself or Distance -
        He fathoms who obtains.

1229   The Days that we can spare
        Are those a Function die
        Or Friend or Nature - stranded then
        In our Economy
        Our Estimates a Scheme   5
        Our Ultimates a Sham
        We let go all of Time without
        Arithmetic of him -

1230   'Twas fighting for his Life he was -
That sort accomplish well -
The Ordnance of Vitality
Is frugal of it's Ball.

It aims once - kills once - conquers once -   5
There is no second War
In that Campaign inscrutable
Of the Interior.

1231   Frigid and sweet Her parting Face -
Frigid and fleet my Feet -
Alien and vain whatever Clime
Acrid whatever Fate -

Given to me without the Suit   5
Riches and Name and Realm -
Who was She to withold from me
Penury and Home?

1232   An honest Tear
Is durabler than Bronze -
This Cenotaph
May each that dies -

Reared by itself -   5
No Deputy suffice -
Gratitude bears
When Obelisk decays

1233   I should not dare to be so sad
So many Years again -
A Load is first impossible
When we have put it down -

The Superhuman then withdraws   5
And we who never saw
The Giant at the other side
Begin to perish now.

1234   Remembrance has a Rear and Front.
        'Tis something like a House -
        It has a Garret also
        For Refuse and the Mouse -

        Besides the deepest Cellar   5
        That ever Mason laid -
        Look to it by it's Fathoms
        Ourselves be not pursued -

1235   Because my Brook is fluent
        I know 'tis dry -
        Because my Brook is silent
        It is the Sea -

        And startled at it's rising   5
        I try to flee
        To where the Strong assure me
        Is "no more Sea" -

1236   A little Dog that wags his tail
        And knows no other joy
        Of such a little Dog am I
        Reminded by a Boy

        Who gambols all the living Day   5
        Without an earthly cause
        Because he is a little Boy
        I honestly suppose -

        The Cat that in the Corner dwells
        Her martial Day forgot   10
        The Mouse but a Tradition now
        Of her desireless Lot

        Another class remind me
        Who neither please nor play
        But not to make a "bit of noise"   15
        Beseech each little Boy -

1237   Oh Shadow on the Grass -
           Art thou a Step or not?
           Go make thee fair my Candidate
           My nominated Heart -
           Oh Shadow on the Grass   5
           While I delay to guess
           Some other thou wilt consecrate -
           Oh Unelected Face -

1238   To make Routine a Stimulus
           Remember it can cease -
           Capacity to terminate
           Is a specific Grace -
           Of Retrospect the Arrow   5
           That power to repair
           Departed with the torment
           Become, alas, more fair -

1239   To disappear enhances -
           The Man that runs away
           Is tinctured for an instant
           With Immortality

           But yesterday a Vagrant   5
           Today in Memory lain
           With superstitious value -
           We tamper with again

           But Never - far as Honor
           Withdraws the worthless Thing   10
           And impotent to cherish
           We hasten to adorn -

           Of Death the sternest function
           That just as we discern
           The excellence defies us -   15
           Securest gathered then

           The Fruit perverse to plucking
           But leaning to the Sight

With the extatic limit
Of unobtained Delight.   20

1240   So much of Heaven has gone from Earth
         That there must be a Heaven
         If only to enclose the Saints
         To Affidavit given -

         The Missionary to the Mole   5
         Must prove there is a Sky
         Location doubtless he would plead
         But what excuse have I?

         Too much of Proof affronts Belief
         The Turtle will not try   10
         Unless you leave him - then return -
         And he has hauled away.

1241   Like Brooms of Steel
The Snow and Wind
Had swept the Winter Street -
The House was hooked
The Sun sent out   5
Faint Deputies of Heat -
Where rode the Bird
The Silence tied
His ample - plodding Steed
The Apple in the Cellar snug   10
Was all the one that played.

1242   The Stars are old, that stood for me -
The West a little worn -
Yet newer glows the only Gold
I ever cared to earn -
Presuming on that lone result   5
Her infinite disdain
But vanquished her with my defeat
'Twas Victory was slain.

1243   Shall I take thee, the Poet said
To the propounded word?
Be stationed with the Candidates
Till I have finer tried -

Let the Poet searched Philology   5
And was about to ring
For the suspended Candidate
There came unsummoned in -
That portion of the Vision
The Word applied to fill   10
Not unto nomination
The Cherubim reveal -

1244   Fly - fly - but as you fly -
Remember - the second pass you by -
The Second is pursuing the Century
The Century is chasing Eternity -
What a Responsibility -   5
No wonder that the little Second flee -
Out of it's frightened way -

1245   Like Rain it sounded till it curved
And then we knew 'twas Wind -
It walked as wet as any Wave
But swept as dry as Sand -
When it had pushed itself away   5
To some remotest Plain
A coming as of Hosts was heard
That was indeed the Rain -
It filled the Wells, it pleased the Pools
It warbled in the Road -   10
It pulled the spigot from the Hills
And let the Floods abroad -
It loosened acres, lifted seas
The sites of Centres stirred
Then like Elijah rode away   15
Opon a Wheel of Cloud -

1246   The Clouds their Backs together laid
The North begun to push
The Forests galloped till they fell
The Lightning played like mice

The Thunder crumbled like a stuff   5
How good to be in Tombs
Where nature's Temper cannot reach
Nor missile ever comes

1247   We like a Hairbreadth 'scape
It tingles in the Mind

Far after Act or Accident
Like paragraphs of Wind

If we had ventured less   5
The Breeze were not so fine
That reaches to our utmost Hair
It's Tentacles divine.

1248   The Sun and Fog contested
        The Government of Day -
        The Sun took down his Yellow Whip
        And drove the Fog away -

1249   Had I not seen the Sun
        I could have borne the shade
        But Light a newer Wilderness
        My Wilderness has made -

1250   If my Bark sink
        'Tis to another Sea -
        Mortality's Ground Floor
        Is Immortality -

1251   Look back on Time, with kindly Eyes -
        He doubtless did his best -
        How softly sinks that trembling Sun
        In Human Nature's West -

1252   It is the Meek that Valor wear
        Too mighty for the Bold.

1253   Risk is the Hair that holds the Tun
        Seductive in the Air -

That Tun is hollow - but the Tun -
With Hundred Weights - to spare -
Too ponderous to suspect the snare   5
Espies that fickle chair
And seats itself to be let go
By that perfidious Hair -

The "foolish Tun" the Critics say -
While that delusive Hair   10
Persuasive as Perdition,
Decoys it's Traveller

1254   Let my first knowing be of thee
With morning's warming Light -
And my first Fearing, lest Unknowns
Engulph thee in the night -

1255   Fortitude incarnate
Here is laid away
In the swift Partitions
Of the awful Sea -

Babble of the Happy   5
Cavil of the Bold
Hoary the Fruition
But the Sea is old

Edifice of Ocean
Thy tumultuous Rooms   10
Suit me at a venture
Better than the Tombs

1256   A Clover's simple Fame
Remembered of the Cow
Is sweeter than enamelled Realms
Of notoriety -

Renown perceives itself   5
And that defiles the power

The Daisy that has looked behind
Has forfeited the Dower -

1257   A Sparrow took a Slice of Twig
And thought it very nice
I think, because his empty Plate
Was handed Nature twice -

Invigorated, waded   5
In all the deepest Sky
Until his little Figure
Was forfeited away -

1258   A Stagnant pleasure like a Pool
That lets it's Rushes grow
Until they heedless tumble in
And make the Water slow

Impeding navigation bright   5
Of Shadows going down
Yet even this shall rouse itself
When Freshets come along -

1259   As old as Woe -
How old is that?
Some Eighteen thousand years -
As old as Bliss
How old is that   5
They are of equal years -

Together chiefest they are found
But seldom side by side -
From neither of them tho' he try
Can Human nature hide   10

1260   Is Heaven a Physician?
They say that He can heal -

But Medicine Posthumous
Is unavailable -
Is Heaven an Exchequer?   5
They speak of what we owe -
But that negotiation
I'm not a Party to -

1261   The Lilac is an ancient Shrub
        But ancienter than that
        The Firmamental Lilac
        Opon the Hill Tonight -
        The Sun subsiding on his Course   5
        Bequeathes this final plant
        To Contemplation - not to Touch -
        The Flower of Occident.

        Of one Corolla is the West -
        The Calyx is the Earth -   10
        The Capsule's burnished Seeds the Stars -
        The Scientist of Faith
        His research has but just begun -
        Above his Synthesis
        The Flora unimpeachable   15
        To Time's Analysis -
        "Eye hath not seen" may possibly
        Be current with the Blind
        But let not Revelation
        By Theses be detained -   20

1262   Until the Desert knows
        That Water grows
        His Sands suffice
        But let him once suspect
        That Caspian Fact   5
        Sahara dies

        Utmost is relative -
        Have not or Have
        Adjacent Sums

Enough - the first Abode
On the familiar Road
Galloped in Dreams -

1263   Tell all the truth but tell it slant -
Success in Circuit lies
Too bright for our infirm Delight
The Truth's superb surprise
As Lightning to the Children eased   5
With explanation kind
The Truth must dazzle gradually
Or every man be blind -

1264   Like Time's insidious wrinkle
On a beloved Face -
We clutch the Grace the tighter
Though we resent the Crease
The Frost himself so comely   5
Dishevels every prime
Asserting from his Prism
That none can punish him

1265   Through what transports of Patience
I reached the stolid Bliss
To breathe my Blank without thee
Attest me this and this -
By that bleak exultation   5
I won as near as this
Thy privilege of dying
Abbreviate me this

1266   He preached opon "Breadth" till it argued him narrow -
The Broad are too broad to define
And of "Truth" until it proclaimed him a Liar -
The Truth never flaunted a Sign -

Simplicity fled from his counterfeit presence   5
As Gold the Pyrites would shun -
What confusion would cover the innocent Jesus
To meet so enabled a Man!

1267   Our own Possessions though our own
        'Tis well to hoard anew
        Remembering the dimensions
        Of Possibility.

1268   A Word dropped careless on a Page
        May consecrate an Eye
        When folded in perpetual seam
        The Wrinkled Author lie

        Infection in the sentence breeds   5
        We may inhale Despair
        At distances of Centuries
        From the Malaria -

1269   I thought that nature was enough
        Till Human nature came
        But that the other did absorb
        As Parallax a Flame -

        Of Human nature just aware   5
        There added the Divine
        Brief struggle for capacity
        The power to contain
        Is always as the contents
        But give a Giant room   10
        And you will lodge a Giant
        And not a smaller man

1270   The Show is not the Show
        But they that go -

Menagerie to me
My Neighbor be -
Fair Play -   5
Both went to see -

1271   So I pull my Stockings off
        Wading in the Water
        For the Disobedience' Sake
        Boy that lived for "Ought to"

        Went to Heaven perhaps at Death   5
        And perhaps he did'nt
        Moses was'nt fairly used -
        Ananias was'nt -

1272   What we see we know somewhat
        Be it but a little -
        What we dont surmise we do
        Though it shows so fickle

        I shall vote for Lands with Locks   5
        Granted I can pick 'em -
        Transport's doubtful Dividend
        Patented by Adam.

1273   The Past is such a curious Creature
        To look her in the Face
        A Transport may receipt us
        Or a Disgrace -

        Unarmed if any meet her   5
        I charge him fly
        Her faded Ammunition
        Might yet reply.

1274   Now I knew I lost her -
        Not that she was gone -

But Remoteness travelled
On her Face and Tongue.

Alien, though adjoining   5
As a Foreign Race -
Traversed she though pausing
Latitudeless Place.

Elements Unaltered -
Universe the same   10
But Love's transmigration -
Somehow this had come -

Henceforth to remember
Nature took the Day
I had paid so much for -   15
His is Penury
Not who toils for Freedom
Or for Family
But the Restitution
Of Idolatry.   20

1275   The Sea said "Come" to the Brook -
        The Brook said "Let me grow" -
        The Sea said "then you will be a Sea -
        I want a Brook - Come now"!

        The Sea said "Go" to the Sea -   5
        The Sea said "I am he
        You cherished" - "Learned Waters -
        Wisdom is stale - to Me" -

1276   I cannot see my soul, but know 'tis there -
Nor ever saw his house, nor furniture -
Who has invited me with him to dwell;
But a confiding guest, consult as well,
What raiment honor him the most,   5
That I be adequately dressed -
For he insures to none
Lest men specifical adorn -
Procuring him perpetual drest
By dating it a sudden feast.   10

1277   "Was Not" was all the statement.
The Unpretension stuns -
Perhaps - the Comprehension -
They wore no Lexicons -

But lest our Speculation   5
In inanition die
Because "God took him" mention -
That was Philology -

1278   So proud she was to die
It made us all ashamed
That what we cherished, so unknown
To her desire seemed -
So satisfied to go   5
Where none of us should be
Immediately - that Anguish stooped
Almost to Jealousy -

1279   The things we thought that we should do
We other things have done
But those peculiar industries
Have never been begun.

□

The Lands we thought that we should seek   5
When large enough to run
By Speculation ceded
To Speculation's Son -

The Heaven, in which we hoped to pause
When Discipline was done   10
Untenable to Logic
But possibly the one -

1280   Who were "the Father and the Son"
We pondered when a child -
And what had they to do with us
And when portentous told

With inference appalling   5
By Distance fortified
We thought, at least they are no worse
Than they have been described.

Who are "the Father and the Son"
Did we demand Today   10
"The Father and the Son" himself
Would doubtless specify -

But had they the felicity
When we desired to know,
We better Friends had been, perhaps,   15
Than time ensue to be -

We start - to learn that we believe
But once - entirely -
Belief, it does not fit so well
When altered frequently -   20

We blush - that Heaven if we achieve -
Event ineffable -
We shall have shunned until ashamed
To own the Miracle -

1281   Had this one Day not been,
           Or could it cease to be
           How smitten, how superfluous,
           Were every other Day!

           Lest Love should value less   5
           What Loss would value more
           Had it the stricken privilege,
           It cherishes before.

1282   Could Hope inspect her Basis
           Her Craft were done -
           Has a fictitious Charter
           Or it is none -

           Balked in the vastest instance   5
           But to renew -
           Felled by but one assassin -
           Prosperity -

1283   I know Suspense - it steps so terse
           And turns so weak away -
           Besides - Suspense is neighborly
           When I am riding by -

           Is always at the Window   5
           Though lately I descry
           And mention to my Horses
           The need is not of me -

1284   This is the place they hoped before,
           Where I am hoping now
            The seed of disappointment grew
           Within a capsule gay
           Too distant to arrest the feet   5
           That walk this plank of balm,
           Before them lies escapeless sea
           The way is closed they came.

1285   The most triumphant Bird I ever knew or met
        Embarked opon a Twig Today
        And till Dominion set
        I famish to behold so eminent a sight
        And sang for nothing scrutable   5
        But intimate Delight.
        Retired, and resumed his transitive Estate -
        To what delicious Accident
        Does finest Glory fit!

1286   There is no Frigate like a Book
        To take us Lands away
        Nor any Coursers like a Page
        Of prancing Poetry -
        This Traverse may the poorest take   5
        Without oppress of Toll -
        How frugal is the Chariot
        That bears the Human Soul -

1287   Power is a familiar growth -
        Not foreign - not to be -
        Beside us like a bland Abyss
        In every company -
        Escape it - there is but a chance -   5
        When consciousness and clay
        Lean forward for a final glance
        Disprove that, and you may -

1288   Elijah's Wagon knew no thill
        Was innocent of Wheel
        Elijah's horses as unique
        As was his vehicle -

        Elijah's journey to portray   5
        Expire with him the skill
        Who justified Elijah
        In feats inscrutable -

1289 Left in immortal Youth
   On that low Plain
   That hath nor Retrospection
   Nor Again -
   Ransomed from years -   5
   Sequestered from Decay
   Canceled like Dawn
   In comprehensive Day -

1290 Yesterday is History,
   'Tis so far away -
   Yesterday is Poetry - 'tis Philosophy -
   Yesterday is mystery -
   Where it is Today   5
   While we shrewdly speculate
   Flutter both away

1291 The Beggar at the Door for Fame
   Were easily supplied
   But Bread is that Diviner thing
   Disclosed to be denied

1292 In this short Life that only lasts an hour
   How much - how little - is within our power

1293 The Face we choose to miss -
   Be it but for a Day
   As absent as a Hundred Years,
   When it has rode away -

1294 A Deed knocks first at Thought
   And then - it knocks at Will -
   That is the manufactoring spot
   And Will at Home and well

□

It then goes out an Act   5
Or is entombed so still
That only to the Ear of God
It's Doom is audible -

1295   I think that the Root of the Wind is Water -
        It would not sound so deep
        Were it a Firmamental Product -
        Airs no Oceans keep -
        Mediterranean intonations -   5
        To a Current's Ear -
        There is a maritime conviction
        In the Atmosphere -

1296   Not one by Heaven defrauded stay -
        Although he seem to steal
        He restitutes in some sweet way
        Secreted in his will -

1297   A Single Clover Plank
        Was all that saved a Bee
        A Bee I personally knew
        From sinking in the sky -

        Twixt Firmament above   5
        And Firmament below
        The Billows of Circumference
        Were sweeping him away -

        The idly swaying Plank
        Responsible to nought   10
        A sudden Freight of Wind assumed
        And Bumble Bee was not -

        This harrowing event
        Transpiring in the Grass
        Did not so much as wring from him   15
        A wandering "Alas" -

1298   Longing is like the Seed
That wrestles in the Ground,
Believing if it intercede
It shall at length be found -

The Hour, and the Zone,   5
Each Circumstance unknown -
What Constancy must be achieved
Before it see the Sun!

1299   Dominion lasts until obtained -
Possession just as long -
But these - endowing as they flit
Eternally belong.

How everlasting are the Lips   5
Known only to the Dew -
These are the Brides of permanence -
Supplanting me and you.

1300   Silence is all we dread.
There's Ransom in a Voice -
But Silence is Infinity.
Himself have not a face.

1301   When Memory is full
Put on the perfect Lid -
This Morning's finest syllable
Presumptuous Evening said -

1302   The Day She goes
Or Day she stays
Are equally supreme -
Existence has a stated width
Departed, or at Home -   5

1303   Confirming All who analyze
In the Opinion fair
That Eloquence is when the Heart
Has not a Voice to spare -

1304   I saw that the Flake was on it
But plotted with Time to dispute -
"Unchanged" I urged with a candor
That cost me my honest Heart -

But "you" - she returned with valor   5
Sagacious of my mistake
"Have altered - Accept the pillage
For the progress' sake" -

1305   The Butterfly in honored Dust
Assuredly will lie
But none will pass the Catacomb
So chastened as the Fly -

1306   Recollect the Face of me
When in thy Felicity,
Due in Paradise today
Guest of mine assuredly -

Other Courtesies have been -   5
Other Courtesy may be -
We commend ourselves to thee
Paragon of Chivalry -

1307   Warm in her Hand these accents lie
While faithful and afar
The Grace so awkward for her sake
It's fond subjection wear -

1308   To break so vast a Heart
Required a Blow as vast -
No Zephyr felled this Cedar straight -
'Twas undeserved Blast -

1309   Lain in Nature - so suffice us
The enchantless Pod
When we advertise existence
For the missing Seed -

Maddest Heart that God created   5
Cannot move a sod
Pasted by the simple summer
On the Longed for Dead -

1310   Had we our senses
But perhaps 'tis well they're not at Home
So intimate with Madness
He's liable with them

Had we the eyes within our Head -   5
How well that we are Blind -
We could not look opon the Earth -
So utterly unmoved -

1311   Art thou the thing I wanted?
Begone - my Tooth has grown -
Affront a minor palate
Thou could'st not goad so long -

I tell thee while I waited -   5

The mystery of Food
Increased till I abjured it
Subsisting now like God -

1312 'Twas later when the summer went
    Than when the Cricket came -
    And yet we knew that gentle Clock
    Meant nought but Going Home -
    'Twas sooner when the Cricket went   5
    Than when the Winter came
    Yet that pathetic Pendulum
    Keeps Esoteric Time.

1313 September's Baccalaureate
    A combination is
    Of Crickets - Crows - and Retrospects
    And a dissembling Breeze

    That hints without assuming -   5
    An Innuendo sear
    That makes the Heart put up it's Fun -
    And turn Philosopher.

1314   Because that you are going
       And never coming back
       And I, however absolute
       May overlook your Track -

       Because that Death is final,   5
       However first it be
       This instant be suspended
       Above Mortality.

       Significance that each has lived
       The other to detect   10
       Discovery not God himself
       Could now annihilate

       Eternity, Presumption
       The instant I perceive
       That you, who were Existence   15
       Yourself forgot to live -

       The "Life that is" will then have been
       A Thing I never knew -
       As Paradise fictitious
       Until the Realm of you -   20

       The "Life that is to be," to me,
       A Residence too plain
       Unless in my Redeemer's Face
       I recognize your own.

       Of Immortality who doubts   25
       He may exchange with me
       Curtailed by your obscuring Face
       Of Everything but He -

       Of Heaven and Hell I also yield
       The Right to reprehend   30
       To whoso would commute this Face
       For his less priceless Friend.

□

If "God is Love" as he admits
We think that he must be
Because he is a "jealous God"   35
He tells us certainly

If "All is possible with" him
As he besides concedes
He will refund us finally
Our confiscated Gods -   40

1315   Death's Waylaying not the sharpest
       Of the Thefts of Time -
       There marauds a sorer Robber -
       Silence - is his name -
       No Assault, nor any menace   5
       Doth betoken him.
       But from Life's consummate Cluster,
       He supplants the Balm.

1316   There's the Battle of Burgoyne -
       Over, every Day,
       By the Time that Man and Beast
       Put their work away -
       "Sunset" sounds majestic -   5
       But that solemn War
       Could you comprehend it
       You would chastened stare -

1317   While we were fearing it, it came -
       But came with less of fear
       Because that fearing it so long
       Had almost made it fair -

       There is a Fitting - a Dismay -   5
       A Fitting - a Despair -
       'Tis harder knowing it is Due
       Than knowing it is Here.

                                         □

The Trying on the Utmost
The Morning it is New 10
Is terribler than wearing it
A whole existence through -

1318   Our little secrets slink away -
Beside God's shall not tell -
He kept his word a Trillion years
And might we not as well -
But for the niggardly delight 5
To make each other stare
Is there no sweet beneath the sun
With this that may compare -

1319   The Notice that is called the Spring
Is but a month from here -
Put up my Heart thy Hoary work
And take a Rosy Chair -

Not any House the Flowers keep - 5
The Birds enamor Care -
Our salary the longest Day
Is nothing but a Bier -

1320   Dear March - Come in -
How glad I am -
I hoped for you before -
Put down your Hat -
You must have walked - 5
How out of Breath you are -
Dear March, how are you, and the Rest -
Did you leave Nature well -
Oh March, Come right up stairs with me -
I have so much to tell - 10

I got your Letter, and the Birds -
The Maples never knew that you were coming -
I declare - how Red their Faces grew -

But March, forgive me -
All those Hills you left for me to Hue -
There was no Purple suitable -
You took it all with you -

Who knocks? That April -
Lock the Door -
I will not be pursued -
He stayed away a Year to call
When I am occupied -
But trifles look so trivial
As soon as you have come

That Blame is just as dear as Praise
And Praise as mere as Blame -

1321   When Continents expire
The Giants they discarded - are
Promoted to endure -

1322   Go slow, my soul to feed thyself
Opon his rare approach -
Go rapid, lest competing death
Prevail opon the coach,
Go timid, should his testing eye
Determine thee amiss
Go boldly for thou paid'st the price,
Redemption for a kiss.

1323   The vastest earthly Day
Is shrunken small
By one Defaulting Face
Behind a Pall -

1324   Surprise is like a thrilling - pungent -
Opon a tasteless meat.

Alone - too acrid - but combined
An edible Delight -

1325 I never hear that one is dead
Without the chance of Life
Afresh annihilating me
That mightiest Belief,

Too mighty for the Daily mind   5
That tilling it's abyss,
Had Madness, had it once or, Twice
The yawning Consciousness,

Beliefs are Bandaged, like the Tongue
When Terror were it told   10
In any Tone commensurate
Would strike us instant Dead -

I do not know the man so bold
He dare in lonely Place
That awful stranger - Consciousness   15
Deliberately face -

1326 How many schemes may die
In one short Afternoon
Entirely unknown
To those they most concern -
The man that was not lost   5
Because by accident
He varied by a Ribbon's width
From his accustomed route -
The Love that would not try
Because beside the Door   10
Some unsuspecting Horse was tied
Surveying his Despair

1327   Of Life to own -
From Life to draw -
But never touch the Reservoir -

1328   The Symptom of the Gale -
The Second of Dismay -
Between it's Rumor and it's Face -
Is almost Revelry -

The Houses firmer root -   5
The Heavens cannot be found -
The Upper Surfaces of things
Take covert in the Ground -

The Mem'ry of the Sun
Not Any can recall -   10
Although by Nature's sterling Watch
So scant an interval -

And when the Noise is caught
And Nature looks around -
"We dreamed it"? she interrogates -   15
"Good Morning" - we propound?

1329   The Butterfly's Assumption Gown
In Chrysoprase Apartments hung
This Afternoon put on -

How condescending to descend
And be of Buttercups the friend   5
In a New England Town -

1330   When a Lover is a Beggar
Abject is his Knee -
When a Lover is an Owner
Different is he -

What he begged is then the Beggar -   5
Oh disparity -

Bread of Heaven resents bestowal
Like an obloquy

1331   My Heart ran so to thee
    It would not wait for me
    And I affronted grew
    And drew away
    For whatsoe'er my pace   5
    He first achieve thy Face -
    How general a Grace
    Allotted two -

    Not in malignity
    Mentioned I this to thee -   10
    Had he obliquity
    Soonest to share
    But for the Greed of him -
    Boasting my Premium -
    Basking in Bethleem   15
    Ere I be there -

1332   Abraham to kill him
    Was distinctly told -
    Isaac was an Urchin -
    Abraham was old -

    Not a hesitation -   5
    Abraham complied -
    Flattered by Obeisance
    Tyranny demurred -

    Isaac - to his Children
    Lived to tell the tale -   10
    Moral - with a Mastiff
    Manners may prevail.

1333   Knock with tremor -
    These are Caesars -

Should they be at Home
Flee as if you trod unthinking
On the Foot of Doom -   5

These seceded from your summons
Centuries ago -
Should they rend you with "How are you"
What have you to show?

1334   Whether they have forgotten
        Or are forgetting now
        Or never remembered -
        Safer not to know -

        Miseries of conjecture   5
        Are a softer wo
        Than a Fact of Iron
        Hardened with I know -

1335   Floss wont save you from an Abyss
        But a Rope will -
        Notwithstanding a Rope for a Souvenir
        Is not beautiful -

        But I tell you every step is a Trough -   5
        And every stop a well -
        Now will you have the Rope or the Floss?
        Prices reasonable -

1336   Elisabeth told Essex
        That she could not forgive
        The clemency of Deity
        However - might survive -
        That secondary succor   5
        We trust that she partook
        When suing - like her Essex
        For a reprieving Look -

1337   The Pile of Years is not so high
          As when you came before
          But it is rising every Day
          From recollection's Floor
          And while by standing on my Heart   5
          I still can reach the top
          Efface the mountain with your face
          And catch me ere I drop

1338   Time does go on -
          I tell it gay to those who suffer now -
          They shall survive -
          There is a Sun -
          They dont believe it now -   5

1339   From his slim Palace in the Dust
          He relegates the Realm,
          More loyal for the exody
          That has befallen him.

1340   Without a smile - Without a throe
          A Summer's soft assemblies go
          To their entrancing end
          Unknown - for all the times we met -
          Estranged, however intimate -   5
          What a dissembling Friend -

1341   As Summer into Autumn slips
          And yet we sooner say
          The Summer than the Autumn - lest
          We turn the Sun away

          And count it almost an Affront   5
          The Presence to concede
          Of one however lovely - not
          The one that we have loved

□

So we evade the Charge of Years
On one attempting shy
The Circumvention of the shaft
Of Life's Declivity -

10

1342   No man saw awe, nor to his house
Admitted he a man
Though by his awful residence
Has human nature been.

Not deeming of his dread abode
Till laboring to flee
A grasp on comprehension laid
Detained vitality.

5

Returning is a different route
The Spirit could not show
For breathing is the only work
To be enacted now.

10

"Am not consumed," old Moses wrote,
"Yet saw Him face to face" -
That very physiognomy
I am convinced was this

15

1343   To flee from memory
Had we the Wings
Many would fly
Inured to slower things
Birds with surprise
Would scan the cowering Van
Of men escaping
From the mind of man

5

1344   The Infinite a sudden Guest
Has been assumed to be -
But how can that stupendous come
Which never went away?

1345   The most pathetic thing I do
Is play I hear from you -
I make believe until my Heart
Almost believes it too
But when I break it with the news   5
You knew it was not true
I wish I had not broken it -
Goliah - so would you -

1346   I send you a decrepit flower
That nature sent to me
At parting - she was going south
And I designed to stay -

Her motive for the souvenir   5
If sentiment for me
Or circumstance prudential
Witheld invincibly -

1347   Wonder - is not precisely knowing
And not precisely knowing not -
A beautiful but bleak condition
He has not lived who has not felt -

Suspense - is his maturer Sister -   5
Whether Adult Delight is Pain
Or of itself a new misgiving -
This is the Gnat that mangles men -

1348   The Way to know the Bobolink
From every other Bird
Precisely as the Joy of him -
Obliged to be inferred.

Of impudent Habiliment   5
Attired to defy,
Impertinence subordinate
At times to Majesty -

□

Of Sentiments seditious
Amenable to Law -   10
As Heresies of Transport
Or Puck's Apostacy -

Extrinsic to Attention
Too intimate with Joy -
He compliments Existence   15
Until allured away

By Seasons or his Children -
Adult and urgent grown -
Or unforeseen Aggrandizement
Or, happily, Renown -   20

By Contrast certifying
The Bird of Birds is gone -
How nullified the Meadow -
Her Sorcerer withdrawn!

1349   Not with a Club, the Heart is broken
        Nor with a Stone -
        A Whip so small you could not see it
        I've known

        To lash the Magic Creature   5
        Till it fell,
        Yet that Whip's Name
        Too noble then to tell.

        Magnanimous as Bird
        By Boy descried -   10
        Singing unto the Stone
        Of which it died -

        Shame need not crouch
        In such an Earth as Our's -
        Shame - stand erect -   15
        The Universe is your's.

1350   The Mushroom is the Elf of Plants -
At Evening, it is not
At Morning, in a Truffled Hut
It stop opon a Spot

As if it tarried always   5
And yet it's whole Career
Is shorter than a Snake's Delay -
And fleeter than a Tare -

'Tis Vegetation's Juggler -
The Germ of Alibi -   10
Doth like a Bubble antedate
And like a Bubble, hie -

I feel as if the Grass was pleased
To have it intermit -
This surreptitious Scion   15
Of Summer's circumspect.

Had Nature any supple Face
Or could she one contemn -
Had Nature an Apostate -
That Mushroom - it is Him!   20

1351   A Bee his Burnished Carriage
Drove boldly to a Rose -
Combinedly alighting -
Himself - his Carriage was.

The Rose received his Visit   5
With frank tranquility,
Witholding not a Crescent
To his cupidity.

Their Moment consummated
Remained for him - to flee -   10
Remained for her, of Rapture
But the Humility.

1352   How soft this Prison is
        How sweet these sullen bars
        No Despot but the King of Down
        Invented this repose

        Of Fate if this is all   5
        Has he no added Realm
        A Dungeon but a Kinsman is
        Incarceration - Home.

1353   To pile like Thunder to it's close
        Then crumble grand away
        While everything created hid
        This - would be Poetry -

        Or Love - the two coeval come -   5
        We both and neither prove -
        Experience either and consume -
        For none see God and live -

1354   Two Lengths has every Day -
        It's absolute extent
        And Area superior
        By Hope or Horror lent -

        Eternity will be   5
        Velocity or Pause
        At Fundamental Signals
        From Fundamental Laws.

        To die is not to go -
        On Doom's consummate Chart   10
        No Territory new is staked -
        Remain thou as thou Art.

1355 His Mansion in the Pool
 The Frog forsakes -
 He rises on a Log
 And statements makes -
 His Auditors two Worlds   5
 Deducting me -
 The Orator of April
 Is hoarse Today -
 His Mittens at his Feet
 No Hand hath he -   10
 His eloquence a Bubble
 As Fame should be -
 Applaud him to discover
 To your chagrin
 Demosthenes has vanished   15
 In Waters Green -

1356 A little Madness in the Spring
 Is wholesome even for the King,
 But God be with the Clown -
 Who ponders this tremendous scene -
 This whole Experiment of Green -   5
 As if it were his own!

1357 Pink - small - and punctual -
 Aromatic - low -
 Covert in April -
 Candid in May -

 Dear to the Moss -   5
 Known to the Knoll -
 Next to the Robin
 In every human Soul -

 Bold little Beauty -
 Bedecked with thee   10
 Nature forswears -
 Antiquity -

1358   What tenements of Clover
        Are fitting for the Bee
        What edifices azure
        For Butterflies and me
        What residences nimble   5
        Arise and evanesce
        Without a rhythmic rumor
        Or an assaulting guess.

1359   You Cannot take itself
        From any Human soul -
        That indestructible estate
        Enable him to dwell -
        Impregnable as Light   5
        That every man behold
        But take away as difficult
        As undiscovered Gold -

1360   Luck is not chance -
        It's Toil -
        Fortune's expensive smile
        Is earned -
        The Father of the Mine   5
        Is that old fashioned Coin
        We spurned -

1361   Let me not mar that perfect Dream
        By an Auroral stain
        But so adjust my daily Night
        That it will come again.

        Not when we know, the Power accosts -   5
        The Garment of Surprise
        Was all our timid Mother wore
        At Home - in Paradise.

1362   Lift it - with the Feathers
Not alone we fly -
Launch it - the aquatic
Not the only sea -
Advocate the Azure   5
To the lower Eyes -
He has obligation
Who has Paradise -

1363   That short - potential stir
That each can make but once -
That Bustle so illustrious
'Tis almost Consequence -

Is the eclat of Death -   5
Oh - thou unknown Renown
That not a Beggar would accept
Had he the power to spurn -

1364   Escape is such a thankful Word
I often in the Night
Consider it unto myself
No spectacle in sight

Escape - it is the Basket   5
In which the Heart is caught
When down some awful Battlement
The rest of Life is dropt -

'Tis not to sight the savior -
It is to be the saved -   10
And that is why I lay my Head
Opon this trusty word -

1365   Crisis is sweet and yet the Heart
Opon the hither side
Has Dowers of Prospective
To Denizen denied -

Inquire of the closing Rose   5
Which rapture - she preferred
And she will point you sighing -
To her rescinded Bud -

1366   I'd rather recollect a Setting
Than own a rising Sun
Though one is beautiful forgetting
And true the other one.

Because in going is a Drama   5
Staying cannot confer -
To die divinely once a twilight -
Than wane is easier -

1367   An antiquated Grace
Becomes that cherished Face
Better than prime
Enjoining us to part
We and our pouting Heart   5
Good friends with time

1368   Opon a Lilac Sea
To toss incessantly
His Plush Alarm
Who fleeing from the Spring
The Spring avenging fling   5
To Dooms of Balm -

1369   The Rat is the concisest Tenant.
He pays no Rent.
Repudiates the Obligation -
On schemes intent

Balking our Wit   5
To sound or circumvent -

Hate cannot harm
A Foe so reticent -

Neither Decree prohibit him -
Lawful as Equilibrium.   10

1370   Unto the Whole - how add?
        Has "All" a further Realm -
        Or Utmost an Ulterior?
        Oh, Subsidy of Balm!

1371   Nature assigns the Sun -
        That - is Astronomy -
        Nature cannot enact a Friend -
        That - is Astrology.

1372   A Dew sufficed itself -
        And satisfied a Leaf
        And felt "How vast a Destiny" -
        "How trivial is Life"!

        The Sun went out to work -   5
        The Day went out to play
        And not again that Dew be seen
        By Physiognomy -

        Whether by Day Abducted
        Or emptied by the Sun   10
        Into the Sea, in passing
        Eternally unknown -

        Attested to this Day
        That awful Tragedy
        By Transport's instability   15
        And Doom's celerity.

1373   The Spider as an Artist
Has never been employed -
Though his surpassing Merit
Is freely certified

By every Broom and Bridget   5
Throughout a Christian Land -
Neglected Son of Genius
I take thee by the Hand -

1374   Winter is good - his Hoar Delights
Italic flavor yield -
To Intellects inebriate
With Summer, or the World -

Generic as a Quarry   5
And hearty - as a Rose -
Invited with asperity
But welcome when he goes.

1375   Delight's Despair at setting
Is that Delight is less
Than the sufficing Longing
That so impoverish.

Enchantment's Perihelion   5
Mistaken oft has been
For the Authentic orbit
Of it's Anterior Sun.

1376   Which is the best - the Moon or the Crescent?
Neither - said the Moon -
That is best which is not - Achieve it -
You efface the Sheen -

Not of detention is Fruition -   5
Shudder to attain.
Transport's decomposition follows -
He is Prism born.

1377   A Rat surrendered here
A brief career of Cheer
And Fraud and Fear.

Of Ignominy's due
Let all addicted to   5
Beware -

The most obliging Trap
It's tendency to snap
Cannot resist -

Temptation is the Friend   10
Repugnantly resigned
At last.

1378   This dirty - little - Heart
Is freely mine -
I won it with a Bun -
A Freckled shrine -

But eligibly fair   5
To him who sees
The Visage of the Soul
And not the knees.

1379   How News must feel when travelling
If News have any Heart
Alighting at the Dwelling
'Twill enter like a Dart!

What News must think when pondering   5
If News have any Thought
Concerning the stupendousness
Of it's perceiveless freight!

What News will do when every Man
Shall comprehend as one   10
And not in all the Universe
A thing to tell remain?

1380   The last of Summer is Delight -
       Deterred by Retrospect.
       'Tis Ecstasy's revealed Review -
       Enchantment's Syndicate.

       To meet it - nameless as it is -   5
       Without celestial Mail -
       Audacious as without a knock
       To walk within the Vail.

1381   The Heart is the Capital of the Mind
       The Mind is a single State -
       The Heart and the Mind together make
       A single Continent -

       One - is the Population -   5
       Numerous enough -
       This ecstatic Nation
       Seek - it is Yourself.

1382   Not any more to be lacked -
       Not any more to be known -
       Denizen of Significance
       For a span so worn -

       Even Nature herself   5
       Has forgot it is there -
       Sedulous of her Multitudes
       Notwithstanding Despair -

       Of the Ones that pursued it
       Suing it not to go   10
       Some have solaced the longing
       To accompany -

       Some - rescinded the Wrench -
       Others - Shall I say
       Plated the residue of Adz   15
       With Monotony.

1383   After all Birds have been investigated and laid aside -
Nature imparts the little Blue Bird - assured
Her conscientious Voice will soar unmoved
Above ostensible Vicissitude.

First at the March - competing with the Wind -   5
Her panting note exalts us - like a friend -
Last to adhere when Summer cleaves away -
Elegy of Integrity.

1384   The Mind lives on the Heart
Like any Parasite -
If that is full of Meat
The Mind is fat -

But if the Heart omit   5
Emaciate the Wit -
The Aliment of it
So absolute.

1385   That sacred Closet when you sweep -
Entitled "Memory" -
Select a reverential Broom -
And do it silently -

'Twill be a Labor of surprise -   5
Besides Identity
Of other Interlocutors
A probability -

August the Dust of that Domain -
Unchallenged - let it lie -   10
You cannot supersede itself,
But it can silence you.

1386   "Faithful to the end" amended
From the Heavenly clause -
Constancy with a Proviso
Constancy abhors -

"Crowns of Life" are servile Prizes   5
To the stately Heart,
Given for the Giving, solely,
No Emolument.

1387   To his simplicity
To die - was little Fate -
If Duty live - contented
But her Confederate.

1388   The Treason of an accent
Might Ecstasy transfer -
Of her effacing Fathom
Is no Recoverer -

1389   I suppose the time will come
Aid it in the coming
When the Bird will crowd the Tree
And the Bee be booming -

I suppose the time will come   5
Hinder it a little
When the Corn in Silk will dress
And in Chintz the Apple

I believe the Day will be
When the Jay will giggle   10
At his new white House the Earth
That, too, halt a little -

1390   Take all away -
        The only thing worth larceny
        Is left - the Immortality -

1391   I sued the News - yet feared - the News
        That such a Realm could be -
        "The House not made with Hands" it was -
        Thrown open wide - to me -

1392   Love's stricken "why"
        Is all that love can speak -
        Built of but just a syllable,
        The hugest hearts that break.

1393   Those Cattle smaller than a Bee
        That herd opon the Eye -
        Whose tillage is the passing Crumb -
        Those Cattle are the Fly -
        Of Barns for Winter - blameless -   5
        Extemporaneous stalls
        They found to our objection -
        On Eligible Walls -
        Reserving the presumption
        To suddenly descend   10
        And gallop on the Furniture -
        Or odiouser offend -
        Of their peculiar calling
        Unqualified to judge
        To Nature we remand them   15
        To justify or scourge -

1394   The long sigh of the Frog
        Opon a Summer's Day
        Enacts intoxication
        Opon the Revery -

But his receding Swell   5
Substantiates a Peace
That makes the Ear inordinate
For corporal release -

1395   The Butterfly's Numidian Gown
With spots of Burnish - roasted on
Is proof against the Sun -
But prone to shut it's spotted Fan
And panting on a Clover lean   5
As if it were undone -

1396   Of his peculiar light
We keep one ray -
To clarify the sight
To seek him by -

1397   How firm eternity must look
To crumbling men like me -
The only adamant Estate
In all Identity -

How mighty to the insecure -   5
Thy Physiognomy
To whom not any Face cohere -
Unless concealed in thee.

1398   Gathered into the Earth,
And out of story -
Gathered to that strange Fame -
That lonesome Glory
That hath no omen here - but Awe -   5

1399   The Sun is one - and on the Tare
He doth as punctual call

As on the conscientious Flower
And estimates them all -

1400   The worthlessness of Earthly things
        The Ditty is that Nature Sings -
        And then - enforces their delight
        Till Synods are inordinate -

1401   Dreams are the subtle Dower
        That make us rich an Hour -
        Then fling us poor
        Out of the Purple Door
        Into the Precinct raw   5
        Possessed before -

1402   His Heart was darker than the starless night
        For that there is a morn
        But in this black Receptacle
        Can be no Bode of Dawn

1403   Touch lightly Nature's sweet Guitar
        Unless thou know'st the Tune
        Or every Bird will point at thee
        Because a Bard too soon -

1404   In many and reportless places
        We feel a Joy -
        Reportless, also, but sincere as Nature
        Or Deity -

        It comes, without a consternation -   5
        Dissolves - the same -
        But leaves a sumptuous Destitution -
        Without a Name -

                                                                 □

Profane it by a search - we cannot -
It has no home -   10
Nor we who having once waylaid it -
Thereafter roam.

1405   Long Years apart - can make no
        Breach a second cannot fill -
        The absence of the Witch does not
        Invalidate the spell -

        The embers of a Thousand Years   5
        Uncovered by the Hand
        That fondled them when they were Fire
        Will stir and understand

1406   Praise it - 'tis dead -
        It cannot glow -
        Warm this inclement Ear
        With the encomium it earned
        Since it was gathered here -   5
        Invest this alabaster Zest
        In the Delights of Dust -
        Remitted - since it flitted it
        In recusance august.

1407   A Saucer holds a Cup
        In sordid human Life
        But in a Squirrel's estimate
        A Saucer holds a Loaf -

        A Table of a Tree   5
        Demands the little King
        And every Breeze that run along
        His Dining Room do swing -

        His Cutlery - he keeps
        Within his Russet Lips -   10

To see it flashing when he dines
Do Birmingham eclipse -

Convicted - could we be
Of our Minutiae
The smallest Citizen that flies 15
Is heartier than we -

1408   The Bat is dun, with wrinkled Wings -
Like fallow Article -
And not a song pervade his Lips -
Or none perceptible.

His small Umbrella quaintly halved 5
Describing in the Air
An Arc alike inscrutable
Elate Philosopher.

Deputed from what Firmament -
Of what Astute Abode - 10
Empowered with what malignity
Auspiciously withheld -

To his adroit Creator
Ascribe no less the praise -
Beneficent, believe me, 15
His eccentricities -

1409   Death warrants are supposed to be
An enginery of Equity
A merciful mistake
A pencil in an Idol's Hand
A Devotee has oft consigned 5
To Crucifix or Block

1410   The Flake the Wind exasperate
More eloquently lie
Than if escorted to it's Down
By Arm of Chivalry.

1411   Summer laid her simple Hat
On it's subtle Shelf -
Unobserved a Ribin dropt -
Covet it yourself!

Summer laid her supple Glove   5
In it's sylvan Drawer -
Wheresoe'er, or was she -
The demand of Awe?

1412   How know it from a Summer's Day?
It's Fervors are as firm -
And nothing in the Countenance
But scintillates the same -
Yet Birds examine it and flee -   5
And Vans without a name
Inspect the Admonition
And sunder as they came -

1413   Summer - we all have seen -
A few of us - believed -
A few - the more aspiring
Unquestionably loved -

But Summer does not care -   5
She goes her spacious way
As eligible as the Moon
To the Temerity -

Deputed to adore -
The Doom to be adored   10
Unknown as to an Ecstasy
The Embryo endowed -

1414   How fits his Umber Coat
The Tailor of the Nut?
Combined without a seam
Like Raiment of a Dream -

□

Who spun the Auburn Cloth?   5
Computed how the girth?
The Chestnut aged grows
In those primeval Clothes -

We know that we are wise -
Accomplished in Surprise -   10
Yet by this Countryman -
This nature - how undone!

1415   Trusty as the stars
Who quit their shining working
Prompt as when I lit them
In Genesis' new house,
Durable as dawn   5
Whose antiquated blossom
Makes a world's suspense
Perish and rejoice.

1416   These held their Wick above the west -
Till when the Red declined -
Or how the Amber aided it -
Defied to be defined -

Then waned without disparagement   5
In a dissembling Hue
That would not let the Eye decide
Did it abide or no -

1417   "Tomorrow" - whose location
        The Wise deceives
        Though it's hallucination
        Is last that leaves -
        Tomorrow, thou Retriever   5
        Of every tare -
        Of Alibi art thou
        Or ownest where?

1418   A wild Blue sky abreast of Winds
        That threatened it - did run
        And crouched behind his Yellow Door
        Was the defiant sun -
        Some conflict with those upper friends   5
        So genial in the main
        That we deplore peculiarly
        Their arrogant Campaign -

1419   A - Field of Stubble, lying sere
        Beneath the second Sun -
        It's Toils to Brindled People thrust -
        It's Triumphs - to the Bin -
        Accosted by a timid Bird   5
        Irresolute of Alms -
        Is often seen - but seldom felt,
        On our New England Farms -

1420   How much the present moment means
        To those who've nothing more -
        The Fop - the Carp - the Atheist -
        Stake an entire store
        Upon a moment's shallow Rim   5
        While their commuted Feet

The Torrents of Eternity
Do all but inundate -

1421   Of Paradise' existence
        All we know
        Is the uncertain certainty -
        But it's vicinity, infer,
        By it's Bisecting Messenger -   5

1422   March is the Month of Expectation.
        The things we do not know -
        The Persons of prognostication
        Are coming now -
        We try to show becoming firmness -   5
        But pompous Joy
        Betrays us, as his first Betrothal
        Betrays a Boy.

1423   The inundation of the Spring
        Enlarges every Soul -
        It sweeps the - tenement - away
        But leaves the Water whole -

        In which the Soul at first estranged -   5
        Seeks faintly for it's shore -
        But acclimated - pines no more
        For that Peninsula -

1424   Hope is a strange invention -
        A Patent of the Heart -
        In unremitting action
        Yet never wearing out -

        Of this electric adjunct   5
        Not anything is known

But it's unique momentum
Embellish all we own -

1425   They might not need me - yet they might.
I'll let my Heart be just in sight -
A smile so small as mine might be
Precisely their necessity -

1426   Bees are Black - with Gilt Surcingles -
Buccaneers of Buzz -
Ride abroad in ostentation
And subsist on Fuzz -

Fuzz ordained - not Fuzz contingent -   5
Marrows of the Hill.
Jugs - a Universe's fracture
Could not jar or spill.

1427   Whose Pink career may have a close
Portentous as our own, who knows?
To imitate these neighbors fleet
In Awe and innocence, were meet.

1428   Lay this Laurel on the one
Triumphed and remained unknown -
Laurel - fell your futile Tree -
Such a Victor could not be -
Lay this Laurel on the one   5
Too intrinsic for Renown -
Laurel - vail your deathless Tree -
Him you chasten - that is he -

1429   I shall not murmur if at last
The ones I loved below
Permission have to understand

For what I shunned them so -
Divulging it would rest my Heart
But it would ravage their's -
Why, Katie, Treason has a Voice -
But mine - dispels - in Tears.

5

1430 We shun because we prize her Face
Lest sight's ineffable disgrace
Our Adoration stain

1431 Such are the inlets of the mind -
His outlets - would you see
Ascend with me the eminence
Of Immortality -

1432 I have no Life but this -
To lead it here -
Nor any Death - but lest
Dispelled from there -
Nor tie to Earths to come,
Nor Action new
Except through this Extent
The love of you.

5

1433 What mystery pervades a well!
The water lives so far -
A neighbor from another world
Residing in a jar

Whose limit none have ever seen,
But just his lid of glass -
Like looking every time you please
In an abyss's face!

5

The grass does not appear afraid,
I often wonder he

10

Can stand so close and look so bold
At what is awe to me.

Related somehow they may be,
The sedge stands next the sea
Where he is floorless   15
And does no timidity betray -

But nature is a stranger yet;
The ones that cite her most
Have never passed her haunted house,
Nor simplified her ghost.   20

To pity those that know her not
Is helped by the regret
That those who know her, know her less
The nearer her they get.

1434   To the stanch Dust
         We safe commit thee -
         Tongue if it hath,
         Inviolate to thee -
         Silence - denote -   5
         And Sanctity - enforce thee -
         Passenger - of Infinity -

1435   The Fact that Earth is Heaven -
         Whether Heaven is Heaven or not
         If not an Affidavit
         Of that specific Spot
         Not only must confirm us   5
         That it is not for us
         But that it would affront us
         To dwell in such a place -

1436   To own a Susan of my own
         Is of itself a Bliss -

Whatever Realm I forfeit, Lord,
Continue me in this!

1437   Shame is the shawl of Pink
In which we wrap the Soul
To keep it from infesting Eyes -
The elemental Veil
Which helpless Nature drops   5
When pushed opon a scene
Repugnant to her probity -
Shame is the tint divine -

1438   Sweet skepticism of the Heart -
That knows - and does not know -
And tosses like a Fleet of Balm -
Affronted by the snow -
Invites and then retards the truth   5
Lest Certainty be sere
Compared with the delicious throe
Of transport thrilled with Fear -

1439   Unworthy of her Breast
Though by that scathing test
What Soul survive?
By her exacting light
How counterfeit the white   5
We chiefly have!

1440   How Human Nature dotes
On what it cant detect -
The moment that a Plot is plumbed
Prospective is extinct -

Prospective is the friend   5
Reserved for us to know

When Constancy is clarified
Of Curiosity -

Of subjects that resist
Redoubtablest is this   10
Where go we -
Go we anywhere
Creation after this?

1441   How lonesome the Wind must feel Nights -
        When People have put out the Lights
        And everything that has an Inn
        Closes the shutter and goes in -
        How pompous the Wind must feel Noons   5
        Stepping to incorporeal Tunes
        Correcting errors of the sky
        And clarifying scenery
        How mighty the Wind must feel Morns
        Encamping on a thousand Dawns -   10
        Espousing one and spurning all
        Then soaring to his Temple Tall -

1442   It was a quiet seeming Day -
        There was no harm in earth or sky -
        Till with the closing sun
        There strayed an accidental Red
        A strolling Hue, one would have said   5
        To westward of the Town -

        But when the Earth begun to jar
        And Houses vanished with a roar
        And Human Nature hid
        We comprehended by the Awe   10
        As those that Dissolution saw
        The Poppy in the Cloud -

1443   The fairest Home I ever knew
        Was founded in an Hour

By Parties also that I knew
A spider and a Flower -
A manse of mechlin and of Floss -   5

1444   The pretty Rain from those sweet Eaves
Her unintending Eyes -
Took her own Heart, including our's,
By innocent Surprise -

The wrestle in her simple throat   5
To hold the feeling down
That vanquished her - defeated Feat -
Was Fervor's sudden Crown -

1445   To earn it by disdaining it
Is Fame's consummate Fee -
He loves what spurns him -
Look behind - He is pursuing thee -

So let us gather - every Day -   5
The Aggregate of Life's Bouquet
Be Honor and not shame -

1446   Water makes many Beds
For those averse to sleep -
It's awful chamber open stands -
It's Curtains blandly sweep -
Abhorrent is the Rest   5
In undulating Rooms
Whose Amplitude no end invades -
Whose Axis never comes

1447   Who never wanted - maddest Joy
Remains to him unknown -
The Banquet of Abstemiousness
Defaces that of Wine -

□

Within it's reach, though yet ungrasped   5
Desire's perfect Goal -
No nearer - lest the Actual -
Should disenthrall thy soul -

1448   With Pinions of Disdain
The soul can farther fly
Than any feather specified
In - Ornithology -
It wafts this sordid Flesh   5
Beyond it's dull - control
And during it's electric gale -
The Body is - a soul -
Instructing by the same -
How little work it be -   10
To put off filaments like this
For immortality -

1449   Ourselves - we do inter - with sweet derision
The channel of the Dust - who once achieves -
Invalidates the Balm of that Religion
That doubts - as fervently as it believes -

1450   One Joy of so much anguish
Sweet Nature has for me -
I shun it as I do Despair
Or dear iniquity -
Why Birds, a Summer morning   5
Before the Quick of Day
Should stab my ravished Spirit
With Dirks of Melody
Is part of an inquiry
That will receive reply   10
When Flesh and Spirit sunder
In Death's immediately -

1451 No Passenger was known to flee -
That lodged a Night in memory -
That wily - subterranean Inn
Contrives that none go out again -

1452 Incredible the Lodging
But limited the Guest

1453 She laid her docile Crescent down
And this subjunctive stone
Still states to Dates that have forgot
The News that she is gone -

So constant to it's stolid trust   5
The Shaft that never knew.
It shames the Constancy that fled
Before it's emblem flew.

1454 It sounded as if the Streets were running -
And then the Streets stood still -
Eclipse - was all we could see at the Window,
And Awe - was all we could feel -

By and by - the boldest stole out of his Covert 5
To see if Time was there -
Nature was in an Opal Apron,
Mixing fresher Air.

1455 Perhaps they do not go so far
As we who stay, suppose -
Perhaps come closer, for the lapse
Of their corporeal clothes -

It may be, know so certainly   5
How short we have to fear
That Comprehension antedates
And estimates us there -

1456   Could mortal Lip divine
        The undeveloped Freight
        Of a delivered Syllable -
        'Twould crumble with the weight -

        The Prey of Unknown Zones -   5
        The Pillage of the Sea
        The Tabernacles of the Minds
        That told the Truth to me -

1457   Summer has two Beginnings -
        Beginning once in June -
        Beginning in October
        Affectingly again -

        Without, perhaps, the Riot   5
        But graphicer for Grace -
        As finer is a going
        Than a remaining Face -
        Departing then - forever -
        Forever - until May -   10
        Forever is deciduous -
        Except to those who die -

1458   The Gentian has a parched Corolla -
        Like Azure dried
        'Tis Nature's buoyant juices
        Beatified -
        Without a vaunt or sheen   5
        As casual as Rain
        And as benign -

        When most is past - it comes -
        Nor isolate it seems -
        It's Bond it's Friend -   10
        To fill it's Fringed career
        And aid an aged Year
        Abundant end -

                                                       □

It's lot - were it forgot -
This truth endear -
Fidelity is gain
Creation o'er -

1459 How brittle are the Piers
On which our Faith doth tread -
No Bridge below doth totter so -
Yet none hath such a Crowd.
It is as old as God -   5
Indeed - 'twas built by him -
He sent his Son to test the Plank -
And he pronounced it firm.

1460 Than Heaven more remote,
For Heaven is the Root,
But these the flitted Seed,
More flown indeed,
Than Ones that never were,   5
Or those that hide, and are -

What madness, by their side,
A Vision to provide
Of future Days
They cannot praise -   10

My Soul - to find them - come -
They cannot call - they're dumb -
Nor prove - nor Woo -
But that they have Abode -
Is absolute as God -   15
And instant - too -

1461 Not that he goes - we love him more
Who led us while he stayed.
Beyond Earth's trafficking frontier,
For what he moved, he made.

1462   Brother of Ophir
            Bright Adieu -
            Honor, the shortest route
            To you -

1463   My Maker - let me be
            Enamored most of thee -
            But nearer this
            I more should miss -

1464   Behold this little Bane -
            The Boon of all alive -
            As common as it is unknown
            The name of it is Love -

            To lack of it is Woe -   5
            To own of it is Wound -
            Not elsewhere - if in Paradise
            It's Tantamount be found -

1465   How ruthless are the gentle -
            How cruel are the kind -
            God broke his contract to his Lamb
            To qualify the Wind -

1466   The healed Heart shows it's shallow scar
            With confidential moan -
            Not mended by Mortality
            Are Fabrics truly torn -
            To go it's convalescent way   5
            So shameless is to see
            More genuine were perfidy
            Than such Fidelity -

1467 These Fevered Days - to take them to the Forest
   Where Waters cool around the mosses crawl -
   And shade is all that devastates the stillness
   Seems it sometimes this would be all -

1468 To mend each tattered Faith
   There is a needle fair
   Though no appearance indicate -
   'Tis threaded in the Air -

   And though it do not wear   5
   As if it never Tore
   'Tis very comfortable indeed
   And specious as before -

1469 A Chilly Peace infests the Grass
   The Sun respectful lies -
   Not any Trance of industry
   These shadows scrutinize -

   Whose Allies go no more astray   5
   For service or for Glee -
   But all mankind deliver here
   From whatsoever Sea -

1470 Death is the supple Suitor
   That wins at last -
   It is a stealthy Wooing
   Conducted first
   By pallid innuendoes   5
   And dim approach
   But brave at last with Bugles
   And a bisected Coach
   It bears away in triumph
   To Troth unknown   10
   And Kinsmen as divulgeless
   As Clans of Down -

1471   His Mind like Fabrics of the East -
              Displayed to the despair
              Of everyone but here and there
              An humble Purchaser -
              For though his price was not of Gold -   5
              More arduous there is -
              That one should comprehend the worth,
              Was all the price there was -

1472   How good his Lava Bed,
              To this laborious Boy -
              Who must be up to call the World
              And dress the sleepy Day -

1473   I thought the Train would never come -
              How slow the whistle sang -
              I dont believe a peevish Bird
              So whimpered for the Spring -
              I taught my Heart a hundred times   5
              Precisely what to say -
              Provoking Lover, when you came
              It's Treatise flew away
              To hide my strategy too late
              To wiser be too soon -   10
              For miseries so halcyon
              The happiness atone -

1474   The Road was lit with Moon and star -
              The Trees were bright and still -
               Descried I - by - the gaining Light
              A traveller on a Hill -
               To magic Perpendiculars   5
              Ascending, though terrene -
              Unknown his shimmering ultimate -
              But he indorsed the sheen -

1475 Whoever disenchants
   A single Human soul
   By failure or irreverence
   Is guilty of the whole -

   As guileless as a Bird   5
   As graphic as a Star
   Till the suggestion sinister
   Things are not what they are -

1476 Your thoughts dont have words every day
   They come a single time
   Like signal esoteric sips
   Of the communion Wine
   Which while you taste so free seems 5
   So affable so to be
   You cannot comprehend it's price -
   Nor it's infrequency

1477 Oh, honey of an hour,
   I never knew thy power,
   Prohibit me
   Till my minutest dower,
   My unfrequented flower   5
   Deserving be.

1478 One note from One Bird
   Is better than a Million Word -
   A scabbard has - but one sword

1479 Go not too near a House of Rose -
   The depredation of a Breeze
   Or inundation of a Dew
   Alarm it's Walls away -
   Nor try to tie the Butterfly,   5
   Nor climb the Bars of Ecstasy -

In insecurity to lie
Is Joy's insuring quality -

1480   A little Snow was here and there
       Disseminated in her Hair -
       Since she and I had met and played
       Decade had gathered to Decade -

       But Time had added, not obtained   5
       Impregnable the Rose
       For summer too indelible -
       Too obdurate - for Snows -

1481   We knew not that we were to live -
       Nor when we are to die -
       Our ignorance our Cuirass is -
       We wear Mortality
       As lightly as an Option Gown   5
       Till asked to take it off -
       By his intrusion, God is known -
       It is the same with Life -

1482   Forbidden Fruit a flavor has
That lawful Orchards mocks -
How luscious lies within the Pod
The Pea that Duty locks -

1483   Summer is shorter than any one -
Life is shorter than Summer -
Seventy Years is spent as quick
As an only Dollar -

    Sorrow - now - is polite - and stays -   5
See how well we spurn him -
Equally to abhor Delight -
Equally retain him -

1484   Before you thought of Spring
Except as a Surmise
You see - God bless his suddenness -
A Fellow in the Skies
Of independent Hues   5
A little weather worn
Inspiriting habiliments
Of Indigo and Brown -
With Specimens of Song
As if for you to choose -   10
Discretion in the interval
With gay delays he goes
To some superior Tree
Without a single Leaf
And shouts for joy to Nobody   15
But his seraphic self -

1485   Spurn the temerity -
Rashness of Calvary -

Gay were Gethsemane
Knew we of thee -

1486   Those not live yet
         Who doubt to live again -
         "Again" is of a twice
         But this - is one -
         The Ship beneath the Draw   5
         Aground - is he?
         Death - so - the Hyphen of the Sea -
         Deep is the Schedule
         Of the Disk to be -
         Costumeless Consciousness,   10
         That is he -

1487   Belshazzar had a Letter -
         He never had but one -
         Belshazzar's Correspondent
         Concluded and begun
         In that immortal Copy   5
         The Conscience of us all
         Can read without it's Glasses
         On Revelation's Wall -

1488   One of the ones that Midas touched
         Who failed to touch us all
         Was that confiding Prodigal
         The reeling Oriole -

         So drunk he disavows it   5
         With badinage divine -
         So dazzling we mistake him
         For an alighting Mine -

         A Pleader - a Dissembler -
         An Epicure - a Thief -   10
         Betimes an Oratorio -
         An Ecstasy in chief -

         □

The Jesuit of Orchards
He cheats as he enchants
Of an entire Attar   15
For his decamping wants -

The splendor of a Burmah
The Meteor of Birds,
Departing like a Pageant
Of Ballads and of Bards -   20

I never thought that Jason sought
For any Golden Fleece
But then I am a rural Man
With thoughts that make for Peace -
But if there were a Jason,   25
Tradition bear with me
Behold his lost Aggrandizement
Opon the Apple Tree -

1489   A Route of Evanescence,
        With a revolving Wheel -
        A Resonance of Emerald
        A Rush of Cochineal -
        And every Blossom on the Bush   5
        Adjusts it's tumbled Head -
        The Mail from Tunis - probably,
        An easy Morning's Ride -

1490   It's little Ether Hood
        Doth sit opon it's Head -
        The millinery supple
        Of the sagacious God -

        Till when it slip away   5
        A nothing at a time -
        And Dandelion's Drama
        Expires in a stem.

1491 To see the Summer Sky
Is Poetry, though never in a Book it lie -
True Poems flee -

1492 Ferocious as a Bee without a wing
The Prince of Honey and the Prince of Sting
So plain a flower presents her Disk to thee

1493 Hope is a subtle Glutton -
He feeds opon the Fair -
And yet - inspected closely
What Abstinence is there -

His is the Halcyon Table -   5
That never seats but One -
And whatsoever is consumed
The same amount remain -

1494 "Secrets" is a daily word
Yet does not exist -
Muffled - it remits surmise -
Murmured - it has ceased -
Dungeoned in the Human Breast   5
Doubtless secrets lie -
But that Grate inviolate -
Comes nor goes away
Nothing with a Tongue or Ear -
Secrets stapled there   10
Will emerge but once - and dumb -
To the Sepulchre -

1495 Opinion is a flitting thing,
But Truth, outlasts the Sun -
If then we cannot own them both -
Possess the oldest one -

1496   So gay a Flower
        Bereaves the mind
        As if it were a Woe -
        Is Beauty an Affliction - then?
        Tradition ought to know -   5

1497   It stole along so stealthy
        Suspicion it was done
        Was dim as to the wealthy
        Beginning not to own -

1498   Time's wily Chargers will not wait
        At any Gate but Woe's -
        But there - so gloat to hesitate
        They will not stir for blows -

1499   His Cheek is his Biographer -
        As long as he can blush
        Perdition is Opprobrium -
        Past that, he sins in peace -

1500   "Heavenly Father" - take to thee
        The supreme iniquity
        Fashioned by thy candid Hand
        In a moment contraband -
        Though to trust us - seem to us   5
        More respectful - "We are Dust" -
        We apologize to thee
        For thine own Duplicity -

1501   A little overflowing word
        That any, hearing, had inferred
        For Ardor or for Tears,
        Though Generations pass away,

Traditions ripen and decay,   5
As eloquent appears -

1502   A winged spark doth soar about -
        I never met it near
        For Lightning it is oft mistook
        When nights are hot and sere -

        It's twinkling Travels it pursues   5
        Above the Haunts of men -
        A speck of Rapture - first perceived
        By feeling it is gone -

1503   If wrecked opon the Shoal of Thought
        How is it with the Sea?
        The only Vessel that is shunned
        Is safe - Simplicity -

1504   The Sweets of Pillage, can be known
        To no one but the Thief -
        Compassion for Integrity
        Is his divinest Grief -

1505   Their Barricade against the Sky
        The martial Trees withdraw,
        And with a Flag at every turn
        Their Armies are no more -

        What Russet Halts in Nature's March   5
        They indicate or cause,
        An inference of Mexico
        Effaces the Surmise -

        Recurrent to the After Thought
        That Massacre of Air -   10
        The Wound that was not Wound nor Scar,
        But Holidays of War -

1506   We talked with each other about each other
Though neither of us spoke -
We were listening to the Second's Races
And the Hoofs of the Clock -
Pausing in Front of our Palsied Faces   5
Time compassion took -
Arks of Reprieve he offered to us -
Ararats - we took -

1507   Fame is the one that does not stay -
It's occupant must die
Or out of sight of estimate
Ascend incessantly -
Or be that most insolvent thing   5
A Lightning in the Germ -
Electrical the embryo
But we demand the Flame

1508   His voice decrepit was with Joy -
Her words did totter so
How old the News of Love must be
To make Lips elderly
That purled a moment since with Glee -   5
Is it Delight or Woe -
Or Terror - that do decorate
This livid - interview -

1509   How destitute is he
Whose Gold is firm
Who finds it every time
The small stale Sum
When Love with but a Pence   5
Will so display
As is a disrespect
To India

1510   The Devil - had he fidelity
         Would be the best friend -
         Because he has ability -
         But Devils cannot mend -
         Perfidy is the virtue   5
         That would but he resign
         The Devil - without question
         Were thoroughly divine

1511   The fascinating chill that Music leaves
         Is Earth's corroboration
         Of Ecstasy's impediment -
         'Tis Rapture's germination
         In timid and tumultuous soil   5
         A fine - estranging creature -
         To something upper wooing us
         But not to our Creator -

1512   The way Hope builds his House
         It is not with a sill -
         Nor Rafter - has that Edifice
         But only Pinnacle -

         Abode in as supreme   5
         This superficies
         As if it were of Ledges smit
         Or mortised with the Laws -

1513   'Tis whiter than an Indian Pipe -
         'Tis dimmer than a Lace -
         No stature has it, like a Fog
         When you approach the place -
         Not any voice imply it here -   5
         Or intimate it there -
         A spirit - how doth it accost -
         What function hath the Air?
         This limitless Hyperbole

Each one of us shall be -
'Tis Drama - if Hypothesis
It be not Tragedy -

1514   A Counterfeit - a Plated Person -
        I would not be -
        Whatever Strata of Iniquity
        My Nature underlie -
        Truth is good Health - and Safety, and the Sky -   5
        How meagre, what an Exile - is a Lie,
        And Vocal - when we die -

1515   Estranged from Beauty - none can be -
        For Beauty is Infinity -
        And power to be finite ceased
        Before Identity was creased -

1516   One thing of thee I covet -
        The power to forget -
        The pathos of the Avarice
        Defrays the Dross of it -

        One thing of thee I borrow   5
        And promise to return -
        The Booty and the Sorrow
        Thy sweetness to have known -

1517   We shall find the Cube of the Rainbow -
Of that - there is no doubt -
But the Arc of a Lover's conjecture
Eludes the finding out -

1518   Glass was the Street - in Tinsel Peril
Tree and Traveller stood.
Filled was the Air with merry venture
Hearty with Boys the Road.

Shot the lithe Sleds like Shod vibrations   5
Emphacized and gone
It is the Past's supreme italic
Makes the Present mean -

1519   It came his turn to beg -
The begging for the life
Is different from another Alms
'Tis Penury in Chief -
I scanned his narrow Realm
I gave him leave to live   5
Lest Gratitude revive the snake
Though - smuggled my - Reprieve

1520   The Robin is a Gabriel
In humble circumstances -
His Dress denotes him socially,
Of Transport's Working Classes -
He has the punctuality
Of the New England Farmer -   5
The same oblique integrity,
A Vista vastly warmer -
A small but sturdy Residence,
A Self denying Household,   10

The Guests of Perspicacity
Are all that cross his Threshold -
As covert as a Fugitive,
Cajoling Consternation
By Ditties to the Enemy   15
And Silvan Punctuation -

1521   The Face in Evanescence lain
         Is more distinct than our's -
         And our's surrendered for it's sake
         As Capsules are for Flower's -
         Or is it the confiding Sheen   5
         Dissenting to be won
         Descending to enamor us
         Of Detriment divine?

1522   A Dimple in the Tomb
         Makes that ferocious Room
         A Home -

1523   How soft a Caterpillar steps -
         I find one on my Hand
         From such a Velvet world it came -
         Such plushes at command
         It's soundless travels just arrest   5
         My slow - terrestrial eye -
         Intent opon it's own career -
         What use has it for me -

1524   Could that sweet Darkness where they dwell
         Be once disclosed to us
         The clamor for their loveliness
         Would burst the Loneliness -

1525 The Road to Paradise is plain -
    And holds scarce one -
    Not that it is not firm
    But we presume
    A Dimpled Road
    Is more preferred -   5
    The Belles of Paradise are few -
    Not me - nor you -
    But unsuspected things -
    Mines have no Wings -   10

1526 Love is done when Love's begun,
    Sages say -
    But have Sages known?
    Truth adjourn your Boon
    Without Day.   5

1527 Her spirit rose to such a hight
    Her countenance it did inflate
    Like one that fed on awe.
    More prudent to assault the dawn
    Than merit the etherial scorn   5
    That effervesced from her.

1528 The Thrill came slowly like a Boon for
    Centuries delayed
    It's fitness growing like the Flood
    In sumptuous solitude -
    The desolation only missed   5
    While Rapture changed it's Dress
    And stood arrayed before the change
    In ravished Holiness -

1529 All that I do
    Is in review

To his enamored mind
I know his eye
Where e'er I ply   5
Is pushing close behind

Not any Port
Not any flight
But he doth there preside
What omnipresence lies in wait   10
For her to be a Bride

1530   Facts by our side are never sudden
Until they look around
And then they scare us like a spectre
Protruding from the Ground -

The hight of our portentous Neighbor   5
We never know -
Till summoned to his recognition
By an Adieu -
Adieu for whence the sage cannot Conjecture
The bravest die   10
As ignorant of their resumption
As you or I -

1531   I saw the wind within her -
I knew it blew for me -
But she must buy my shelter
I asked Humility

I watched the fluttering spirit   5
That would not intercede
Gibraltar could surrender
But not this little maid -
Precisely how it ended -
Redemption is the one   10
Of whom the explanation
Is hitherto unknown -

□

The saved have no remembrance
In our competing Days
'Tis still an assistance
But their's forget in praise

15

1532 More than the Grave is closed to me -
The Grave and that Eternity
To which the Grave adheres -
I cling to nowhere till I fall -
The Crash of nothing, yet of all -
How similar appears -

5

1533 Of whom so dear
The name to hear
Illumines with a Glow
As intimate - as fugitive
As Sunset on the snow -

5

1534 I do not care - why should I care
And yet I fear I'm caring
To rock a fretting truth to sleep -
Is short security
The terror it will wake
Persistent as perdition
Is harder than to face
The frank adversity -

5

1535 She could not live upon the Past
The Present did not know her
And so she sought this sweet at last
And nature gently owned her
The mother that has not a Knell
For either Duke or Robin

5

1536   You cannot make Remembrance grow
When it has lost it's Root -
The tightening the Soil around
And setting it upright
Deceives perhaps the Universe   5
But not retrieves the Plant -
Real Memory, like Cedar Feet
Is shod with Adamant -
Nor can you cut Remembrance down
When it shall once have grown -   10
It's Iron Buds will sprout anew
However overthrown -
Disperse it - slay it -
[*remaining text unknown*]

1537   "And with what Body do they come"?
Then they *do* come, Rejoice!
What Door - what Hour - Run - run - My Soul!
Illuminate the House!
"Body"! Then real - a Face - and Eyes -   5
To know that it is them! -
Paul knew the Man that knew the News -
He passed through Bethlehem -

1538   The Savior must have been
A docile Gentleman -
To come so far so cold a Day
For little Fellow men -

The Road to Bethlehem   5
Since He and I were Boys
Was leveled, but for that 'twould be
A rugged billion Miles -

1539   Mine Enemy is growing old -
I have at last Revenge -
The Palate of the Hate departs -
If any would avenge

                                       □

Let him be quick -
The Viand flits -
It is a faded Meat -
Anger as soon as fed - is dead -
'Tis Starving makes it fat -

1540   My country need not change her gown,
         Her triple suit as sweet
         As when 'twas cut at Lexington,
         And first pronounced "a fit."

         Great Britain disapproves "the stars;"
         Disparagement discreet,—
         There's something in their attitude
         That taunts her bayonet.

1541   Birthday of but a single pang
         That there are less to come -
         Afflictive is the Adjective
         But affluent the doom -

1542   Drowning is not so pitiful
         As the attempt to rise.
         Three times, 'tis said, a sinking man
         Comes up to face the skies,
         And then declines forever
         To that abhorred abode,
         Where hope and he part company -
         For he is grasped of God.
         The Maker's cordial visage,
         However good to see,
         Is shunned, we must admit it,
         Like an adversity.

1543   The Stem of a departed Flower
Has still a silent rank -
The Bearer from an Emerald Court
Of a Despatch of Pink.

1544   An Antiquated Tree
Is cherished of the Crow
Because that Junior Foliage is disrespectful now
To venerable Birds
Whose Corporation Coat   5
Would decorate Oblivion's
Remotest Consulate -

1545   A Pang is more conspicuous in Spring
In contrast with the things that sing
Not Birds entirely - but Minds -
And Winds - Minute Effulgencies
When what they sung for is undone   5
Who cares about a Blue Bird's Tune -
Why, Resurrection had to wait
Till they had moved a Stone -

1546   We never know we go when we are going -
We jest and shut the Door -
Fate - following - behind us bolts it -
And we accost no more -

1547   The Bumble Bee's Religion -

His little Hearse like Figure
Unto itself a Dirge

To a delusive Lilac
The vanity divulge
Of Industry and Morals
And every righteous thing
For the divine Perdition
Of Idleness and Spring -

5

1548   All things swept sole away
This - is immensity -

1549   A faded Boy - in sallow Clothes
Who drove a lonesome Cow
To pastures of Oblivion -
A statesman's Embryo -

The Boys that whistled are extinct -
The Cows that fed and thanked
Remanded to a Ballad's Barn
Or Clover's Retrospect -

5

1550   Oh give it motion - deck it sweet
With Artery and Vein -
Upon it's fastened Lips lay words -
Affiance it again
To that Pink stranger we call Dust -
Acquainted more with that
Than with this horizontal one
That will not lift it's Hat -

5

1551   'Tis Seasons since the Dimpled War
In which we each were Conqueror
And each of us were slain
And Centuries 'twill be and more
Another Massacre before
So modest and so vain -

5

Without a Formula we fought
Each was to each the Pink Redoubt -

1552   Above Oblivion's Tide there is a Pier
And an effaceless "Few" are lifted there -
Nay - lift themselves - Fame has no Arms -
And but one Smile - that meagres Balms -

1553   From all the Jails the Boys and Girls
Ecstatically leap -
Beloved only Afternoon
That Prison does'nt keep -

They storm the Earth And stun the Air,   5
A Mob of solid Bliss -
Alas - that Frowns should lie in wait
For such a Foe as this -

1554   On that specific Pillow
Our projects flit away -
The Night's tremendous Morrow
And whether sleep will stay
Or usher us - a stranger -   5
To situations new
The effort to comprise it
Is all the soul can do -

1555   The Life that tied too tight escapes
Will ever after run
With a prudential look behind
And spectres of the Rein -
The Horse that scents the living Grass   5
And sees the Pastures smile
Will be retaken with a shot
If he is caught at all -

1556   The Bird her punctual music brings
        And lays it in it's place -
        It's place is in the Human Heart
        And in the Heavenly Grace -
        What respite from her thrilling toil   5
        Did Beauty ever take -
        But work might be Electric Rest
        To those that Magic make -

1557   How fleet - how indiscreet an one -
        How always wrong is Love -
        The joyful little Deity
        We are not scourged to serve -

1558   The Blood is more showy than the Breath
        But cannot dance as well -

1559   The Butterfly upon the Sky
        That does'nt know it's Name
        And has'nt any Tax to pay
        And has'nt any Home
        Is just as high as you and I,   5
        And higher, I believe,
        So soar away and never sigh
        And that's the way to grieve -

1560   There comes a warning like a spy
        A shorter breath of Day
        A stealing that is not a stealth
        And Summers are away -

1561   "Go traveling with us"!
        Her Travels daily be

By routes of ecstasy
To Evening's Sea -

1562   His oriental heresies
        Exhilirate the Bee,
        And filling all the Earth and Air
        With gay apostasy

        Fatigued at last, a Clover plain   5
        Allures his jaded Eye
        That lowly Breast where Butterflies
        Have felt it meet to die -

1563   No Autumn's intercepting Chill
        Appalls that Tropic Breast -
        But African Exuberance
        And Asiatic Rest.

1564   The Things that never can come back, are several -
        Childhood - some forms of Hope - the Dead -
        Though Joys - like Men - may sometimes make a Journey -
        And still abide -
        We do not mourn for Traveler, or Sailor,   5
        Their Routes are fair -
        But think enlarged of all that they will tell us
        Returning here -
        "Here"! There are typic "Heres" -
        Foretold Locations -   10
        The Spirit does not stand -
        Himself - at whatsoever Fathom
        His Native Land -

1565   The Dandelion's pallid Tube
        Astonishes the Grass -
        And Winter instantly becomes
        An infinite Alas -

The Tube uplifts a signal Bud
And then a shouting Flower -
The Proclamation of the Suns
That sepulture is o'er -

5

1566 Not seeing, still we know -
Not knowing, guess -
Not guessing, smile and hide
And half caress -
And quake - and turn away,
Seraphic fear -
Is Eden's innuendo
"If you dare"?

5

1567 How much of Source escapes with thee -
How chief thy sessions be -
For thou hast borne a universe
Entirely away.

1568   Sweet Pirate of the Heart,
Not Pirate of the Sea -
What wrecketh thee?
Some Spice's Mutiny -
Some Attar's perfidy?   5
Confide in me -

1569   Echo has no Magistrate -
Catch a Drop of Dew
And the Sun will loose him
With a sneer at you -

Follow fine Orion till you furl your Eye -   5
Dazzlingly decamping
He is just as high -

1570   How happy is the little Stone
That rambles in the Road alone,
And does'nt care about Careers
And Exigencies never fears -
Whose Coat of elemental Brown   5
A passing Universe put on,
And independent as the sun,
Associates or glows alone,
Fulfilling absolute Decree
In casual simplicity -   10

1571   He lived the Life of Ambush
And went the way of Dusk
And now against his subtle name
There stands an Asterisk
As confident of him as we -   5
Impregnable we are -

The whole of Immortality
Secreted in a star -

1572   Come show thy Durham Breast
       To her who loves thee best
       Delicious Robin -
       And if it be not me
       At least within my Tree   5
       Do the avowing -
       Thy Nuptial so minute
       Perhaps is more astute
       Than vaster suing -
       For so to soar away   10
       Is our propensity
       The Day ensuing -

1573   Obtaining but our own extent
       In whatsoever Realm -
       'Twas Christ's own personal Expanse
       That bore him from the Tomb -

1574   The Moon upon her fluent Route
       Defiant of a Road
       The Star's Etruscan Argument
       Substantiate a God -
       How archly spared the Heaven "to come" -   5
       If such prospective be -
       By superseding Destiny
       And dwelling there Today -

1575   Now I lay thee down to Sleep -
       I pray the Lord thy Dust to keep -
       And if thou live before thou wake -
       I pray the Lord thy Soul to make -

1576   No matter where the Saints abide,
They make their Circuit fair
Behold how great a Firmament
Accompanies a Star.

1577   The Bible is an antique Volume -
Written by faded Men
At the suggestion of Holy Spectres -
Subjects - Bethlehem -
Eden - the ancient Homestead -   5
Satan - the Brigadier -
Judas - the Great Defaulter -
David - the Troubadour -
Sin - a distinguished Precipice
Others must resist -   10
Boys that "believe" are very lonesome -
Other Boys are "lost" -
Had but the Tale a warbling Teller -
All the Boys would come -
Orpheu's Sermon captivated -   15
It did not condemn -

1578   Meeting by Accident,
We hovered by design -
As often as a Century
An error so divine
Is ratified by Destiny,   5
But Destiny is old
And economical of Bliss
As Midas is of Gold -

1579   My Wars are laid away in Books -
I have one Battle more -
A Foe whom I have never seen
But oft has scanned me o'er -
And hesitated me between   5
And others at my side,

But chose the best - Neglecting me - till
All the rest have died -
How sweet if I am not forgot
By Chums that passed away -
Since Playmates at threescore and ten
Are such a scarcity -

10

1580 The pattern of the sun
Can fit but him alone
For sheen must have a Disk
To be a sun -

1581 Those - dying then,
Knew where they went -
They went to God's Right Hand -
That Hand is amputated now
And God cannot be found -

5

The abdication of Belief
Makes the Behavior small -
Better an ignis fatuus
Than no illume at all -

1582 Within thy Grave!
Oh no, but on some other flight -
Thou only camest to mankind
To rend it with Good night -

1583 Bliss is the sceptre of the child
The lever of the man
The sacred stealth of boy and girl -
Indict it, if we can.

1584 "Go tell it" - What a Message -
To whom - is specified -

Not murmur - not endearment -
But simply - we obeyed -
Obeyed - a Lure - a Longing? 5
Oh Nature - none of this -
To Law - said Sweet Thermopylae
I give my dying Kiss -

1585   I groped for him before I knew
With solemn nameless need
All other bounty sudden chaff
For this foreshadowed Food
Which others taste and spurn and sneer - 5
Though I within suppose
That consecrated it could be
The only Food that grows

1586   Image of Light, Adieu -
Thanks for the interview -
So long - so short -
Preceptor of the whole -
Coeval Cardinal - 5
Impart - Depart -

1587   Lives he in any other world
My faith cannot reply
Before it was imperative
'Twas all distinct to me -

1588   Of Death I try to think like this,
The Well in which they lay us
Is but the Likeness of the Brook
That menaced not to slay us,
But to invite by that Dismay 5
Which is the Zest of sweetness

To the same Flower Hesperian,
Decoying but to greet us -

I do remember when a Child
With bolder Playmates straying   10
To where a Brook that seemed a Sea
Withheld us by it's roaring
From just a Purple Flower beyond
Until constrained to clutch it
If Doom itself were the result,   15
The boldest leaped, and clutched it -

1589   Tried always and Condemned by thee
Permit me this reprieve
That dying I may earn the look
For which I cease to live -

1590   Elysium is as far as to
The very nearest Room
If in that Room a Friend await
Felicity or Doom -

What fortitude the Soul contains,   5
That it can so endure
The accent of a coming Foot -
The opening of a Door -

1591   If I should see a single bird
[*remaining text unknown*]

1592   Cosmopolites without a plea
Alight in every Land
The Compliments of Paradise
From those within my Hand
Their dappled Journey - to themselves   5
A compensation fair -

Knock and it shall be opened
Is their Theology

1593   He ate and drank the precious Words -
His Spirit grew robust -
He knew no more that he was poor,
Nor that his frame was Dust -
He danced along the dingy Days   5
And this Bequest of Wings
Was but a Book - What Liberty
A loosened Spirit brings -

1594   Pompless no Life can pass away -
The lowliest career
To the same Pageant wends it's way
As that exalted here -

How cordial is the mystery!   5
The hospitable Pall
A "this way" beckons spaciously -
A Miracle for all!

1595 We shun it ere it comes,
   Afraid of Joy,
   Then sue it to delay
   And lest it fly,
   Beguile it more and more,   5
   May not this be
   Old Suitor Heaven,
   Like our dismay at thee?

1596 No Brigadier throughout the Year
   So civic as the Jay -
   A Neighbor and a Warrior too
   With shrill felicity
   Pursuing Winds that censure us   5
   A Febuary Day,
   The Brother of the Universe
   Was never blown away -
   The Snow and he are intimate -
   I've often seen them play   10
   When Heaven looked upon us all
   With such severity
   I felt apology were due
   To an insulted sky
   Whose pompous frown was Nutriment 15
   To their temerity -
   The Pillow of this daring Head
   Is pungent Evergreens -
   His Larder - terse and Militant -
   Unknown - refreshing things -   20
   His Character - a Tonic -
   His Future - a Dispute -
   Unfair an Immortality
   That leaves this Neighbor out -

1597   To see her is a Picture -
            To hear her is a Tune -
            To know her, a disparagement of every other Boon -
            To know her not, Affliction -
            To own her for a Friend   5
            A warmth as near as if the Sun
            Were shining in your Hand -

1598   The Clock strikes One
            That just struck Two -
            Some Schism in the Sum -
            A Sorcerer from Genesis
            Has wrecked the Pendulum -   5

1599   A Sloop of Amber slips away
            Upon an Ether Sea,
            And wrecks in Peace a Purple Tar,
            The Son of Ecstasy -

1600   Forever honored be the Tree
            Whose Apple Winterworn
            Enticed to Breakfast from the Sky
            Two Gabriels Yestermorn -
            They registered in Nature's Book   5
            As Robins - Sire and Son -
            But Angels have that modest way
            To screen them from Renown -

1601   To be forgot by thee
            Surpasses Memory
            Of other minds
            The Heart cannot forget
            Unless it contemplate   5
            What it declines
            I was regarded then

Raised from oblivion
A single time
To be remembered what -   10
Worthy to be forgot
Is my renown

1602   His Losses made our Gains ashamed -
        He bore Life's empty Pack
        As gallantly as if the East
        Were swinging at his Back -
        Life's empty Pack is heaviest   5
        As every Porter knows -
        In vain to punish Honey -
        It only sweeter grows -

1603   To the bright east she flies,
        Brothers of Paradise
        Remit her home
        Without a change of wings
        Or Love's convenient things   5
        Enticed to come.

        Fashioning what she is,
        Fathoming what she was,
        We deem we dream -
        And that dissolves the days   10
        Through which existence strays
        Homeless at home.

1604   Not at Home to Callers
        Says the Naked Tree -
        Jacket due in April -
        Wishing you Good Day -

1605   No ladder needs the bird but skies
        To situate it's wings,

Nor any leader's grim baton
Arraigns it as it sings.
The implements of bliss are few -   5
As Jesus says of *Him,*
'Come unto me' the moiety
That wafts the cherubim.

1606   Lad of Athens, faithful be
        To thyself,
        And Mystery -
        All the rest is Perjury -

1607   How slow the Wind - how slow the Sea -
        How late their Feathers be!

1608   Candor - my tepid friend -
        Come not to play with me -
        The Myrrhs, and Mochas, of the Mind
        Are it's iniquity -

1609   Who has not found the Heaven - below -
        Will fail of it above -
        For Angels rent the House next our's,
        Wherever we remove -

1610   Where Roses would not dare to go,
        What Heart would risk the way,
        And so I send my Crimson Scouts
        To sound the Enemy -

1611   By homely gifts and hindered words
        The human heart is told
        Of nothing -

"Nothing" is the force
That renovates the World -   5

1612   Witchcraft was hung, in History,
        But History and I
        Find all the Witchcraft that we need
        Around us, Every Day -

1613   The Lassitudes of Contemplation
        Beget a force -
        They are the spirit's still vacation
        That him refresh -
        The Dreams consolidate in action -   5
        What mettle fair

1614   Blossoms will run away -
        Cakes reign but a Day,
        But Memory like Melody,
        Is pink eternally -

1615   It would not know if it were spurned,
        This gallant little flower -
        How therefore safe to be a flower
        If one would tamper there.

        To enter, it would not aspire -   5
        But may it not despair
        That it is not a Cavalier,
        To dare and perish there?

1616   This Me - that walks and works - must die
        Some fair or stormy Day -
        Adversity if it may be
        Or wild prosperity
        The Rumor's Gate was shut so tight   5

Before my mind was born
Not even a Prognostic's push
Could make a Dent thereon -

1617   To her derided Home
A Weed of Summer came -
She did not know her station low
Nor Ignominy's name -
Bestowed a summer long   5
Upon a fameless flower,
Then swept as lightly from disdain
As Lady from her Bower -

Of Bliss the Codes are few -
As Jesus cites of Him -   10
"Come unto me" the Moiety
That wafts the Seraphim -

1618   There came a Wind like a Bugle -
It quivered through the Grass
And a Green Chill upon the Heat
So ominous did pass
We barred the Windows and the Doors   5
As from an Emerald Ghost -
The Doom's Electric Moccasin
That very instant passed -
On a strange Mob of panting Trees
And Fences fled away   10
And Rivers where the Houses ran
Those looked that lived - that Day -
The Bell within the steeple wild
The flying tidings told -
How much can come   15
And much can go,
And yet abide the World!

1619   We wear our sober Dresses when we die,
               But Summer, frilled as for a Holiday
               Adjourns her Sigh -

1620   The Bobolink is gone - the Rowdy of the Meadow -
               And no one swaggers now but me -
               The Presbyterian Birds can now resume the Meeting
               He gaily interrupted that overflowing Day
               When opening the Sabbath in their afflictive Way   5
               He bowed to Heaven instead of Earth
               And shouted Let us pray -

1621   Morning is due to all -
               To some - the Night -
               To an imperial few -
               The Auroral Light -

1622   The Summer that we did not prize
               Her treasures were so easy
               Instructs us by departure now
               And recognition lazy -
               Bestirs itself - puts on it's Coat   5
               And scans with fatal promptness
               For Trains that moment out of sight
               Unconscious of his smartness -

1623   The Heart has many Doors -
               I can but knock -
               For any sweet "Come in"
               Impelled to hark -
               Not saddened by repulse,   5
               Repast to me
               That somewhere, there exists,
               Supremacy -

1624 Pass to thy Rendezvous of Light,
   Pangless except for us -
   Who slowly ford the Mystery
   Which thou hast leaped across!

1625 Expanse cannot be lost -
   Not Joy, but a Decree
   Is Deity -
   His Scene, Infinity -
   Whose rumor's Gate was shut so tight   5
   Before my Beam was sown,
   Not even a Prognostic's push
   Could make a Dent thereon -

   The World that thou hast opened
   Shuts for thee,   10
   But not alone,
   We all have followed thee -
   Escape more slowly
   To thy Tracts of Sheen -
   The Tent is listening,   15
   But the Troops are gone!

1626 Climbing to reach the costly Hearts
   To which he gave the worth,
   He broke them, fearing punishment
   He ran away from Earth -

1627 The Spirit lasts - but in what mode -
   Below, the Body speaks,
   But as the Spirit furnishes -
   Apart, it never talks -
   The Music in the Violin   5
   Does not emerge alone
   But Arm in Arm with Touch, yet Touch
   Alone - is not a Tune -
   The Spirit lurks within the Flesh

Like Tides within the Sea
That make the Water live, estranged
What would the Either be?
Does that know - now - or does it cease -
That which to this is done,
Resuming at a mutual date
With every future one?
Instinct pursues the Adamant,
Exacting this Reply,
Adversity if it may be, or wild Prosperity,
The Rumor's Gate was shut so tight
Before my Mind was sown,
Not even a Prognostic's Push
Could make a Dent thereon -

1628   Immured in Heaven!
What a Cell!
Let every Bondage be,
Thou sweetest of the Universe,
Like that which ravished thee!

1629 To try to speak, and miss the way
 And ask it of the Tears,
 Is Gratitude's sweet poverty -
 The Tatters that he wears -

 A better Coat if he possessed   5
 Would help him to conceal,
 Not subjugate, the Mutineer
 Whose title is "the Soul -"

1630 A Drunkard cannot meet a Cork
 Without a Revery -
 And so encountering a Fly
 This January Day
 Jamaicas of Remembrance stir   5
 That send me reeling in -
 The moderate drinker of Delight
 Does not deserve the Spring -
 Of Juleps, part are in the Jug
 And more are in the Joy -   10
 Your connoisaeur in Liquors consults the Bumble Bee -

1631 'Tis not the swaying frame we miss -
 It is the steadfast Heart,
 That had it beat a thousand years,
 With Love alone had bent -
 It's fervor the electric Oar,   5
 That bore it through the Tomb -
 Ourselves, denied the privilege,
 Consolelessly presume -

1632 Quite empty, quite at rest,
 The Robin locks her Nest, and tries her Wings -
 She does not know a Route

But puts her Craft about
For *rumored* springs -
She does not ask for Noon -
She does not ask for Boon -
Crumbless and homeless, of but one request -
The Birds she lost -

5

1633   Within that little Hive
Such Hints of Honey lay
As made Reality a Dream
And Dreams, Reality -

1634   Each that we lose takes part of us;
A crescent still abides,
Which like the moon, some turbid night,
Is summoned by the tides.

1635   Arrows enamored of his Heart -
Forgot to rankle there
And Venoms he mistook for Balms
Disdained to rankle there -

1636   Circumference thou Bride of Awe
Possessing thou shalt be
Possessed by every hallowed Knight
That dares - to Covet thee

1637   There are two Mays
And then a Must
And after that a Shall
How infinite the compromise
That indicates I will

5

∾ 1884

1638   Declaiming Waters none may dread -
        But Waters that are still
        Are so for that most fatal cause
        In Nature - they are full -

1639   Few, yet enough,
        Enough is One -
        To that etherial throng
        Have not each one of us the right
        To stealthily belong?   5

1640   Who is it seeks my Pillow Nights,
        With plain inspecting face -
        "Did you" or "Did you not," to ask -
        'Tis "Conscience," Childhood's Nurse -

        With Martial Hand she strokes the Hair   5
        Upon my wincing Head -
        "All" Rogues "shall have their part in" what -
        The Phosphorous of God -

1641   Though the great Waters sleep,
        That they are still the Deep,
        We cannot doubt.
        No vacillating God
        Ignited this Abode   5
        To put it out.

1642   A World made penniless by that departure
        Of minor fabrics begs
        But sustenance is of the spirit
        The Gods but Dregs -

1643   We send the wave to find the wave,
        An errand so divine

The messenger enamored too
Forgetting to return,
We make the sage decision still   5
Soever made in vain,
The only time to dam the sea
Is when the sea is gone.

1644   Sunset that screens, reveals -
        Enhancing what we see
        By menaces of Amethyst
        And Moats of Mystery.

1645   Morning, that comes but once,
        Considers coming twice -
        Two Dawns upon a Single Morn
        Make Life a sudden price -

1646   The Auctioneer of Parting
        His "Going, going, gone"
        Shouts even from the Crucifix,
        And brings his Hammer down -
        He only sells the Wilderness,   5
        The prices of Despair
        Range from a single human Heart
        To Two - not any more -

1647   Not knowing when the Dawn will come,
        I open every Door,
        Or has it Feathers, like a Bird,
        Or Billows, like a Shore -

1648   A Flower will not trouble her, it has so small a Foot,
        And yet if you compare the Lasts,
        Her's is the smallest Boot -

1649   Back from the Cordial Grave I drag thee
          He shall not take thy Hand
          Nor put his spacious Arm around thee
          That none can understand

1650   The Pedigree of Honey
          Does not concern the Bee -
          A Clover, any time, to him,
          Is Aristocracy -

1651   As from the Earth the light Balloon
          Asks nothing but release -
          Ascension that for which it was,
          It's soaring, Residence.
          The spirit looks upon the Dust   5
          That fastened it so long
          With indignation,
          As a Bird
          Defrauded of it's Song.

1652   Oh Future! thou secreted peace
          Or subterranean Wo -
          Is there no wandering route of grace
          That leads away from thee -
          No circuit sage of all the course   5
          Descried by cunning men
          To balk thee of thy sacred Prey -
          Advancing to thy Den -

1653   So give me back to Death -
          The Death I never feared
          Except that it deprived of thee -
          And now, by Life deprived,
          In my own Grave I breathe   5
          And estimate it's size -

It's size is all that Hell can guess -
And all that Heaven was -

1654 Still own thee - still thou art
What Surgeons call alive -
Though slipping - slipping - I perceive
To thy reportless Grave -

Which question shall I clutch -   5
What answer wrest from thee
Before thou dost exude away
In the recallless sea?

1655 Talk not to me of Summer Trees
The foliage of the mind
A Tabernacle is for Birds
Of no corporeal kind
And winds do go that way at noon   5
To their Etherial Homes
Whose Bugles call the least of us
To undepicted Realms

1656 The Sun in reining to the West
Makes not as much of sound
As Cart of man in road below
Adroitly turning round
That Whiffletree of Amethyst   5

1657 Betrothed to Righteousness might be
An Ecstasy discreet
But Nature relishes the Pinks
Which she was taught to eat -

1658 Show me Eternity, and I will show you Memory -
   Both in one package lain
   And lifted back again -

   Be Sue, while I am Emily -
   Be next, what you have ever been, Infinity -   5

1659 I held it so tight that I lost it
   Said the Child of the Butterfly
   Of many a vaster Capture   .
   That is the Elegy -

1660 But that defeated accent
   Is louder now than him
   Eternity may imitate
   The Affluence of time

1661 Not Sickness stains the Brave,
   Nor any Dart,
   Nor Doubt of Scene to come,
   But an adjourning Heart -

1662 The going from a world we know
   To one a wonder still
   Is like the child's adversity
   Whose vista is a hill,
   Behind the hill is sorcery   5
   And everything unknown,
   But will the secret compensate
   For climbing it alone?

1663 Upon his Saddle sprung a Bird
   And crossed a thousand Trees
   Before a Fence without a Fare
   His Fantasy did please

And then he lifted up his Throat
And squandered such a Note
A Universe that overheard
Is stricken by it yet -   5

1664   In other Motes,
        Of other Myths
        Your requisition be.
        The Prism never held the Hues,
        It only heard them play -   5

1665   The farthest Thunder that I heard
        Was nearer than the Sky
        And rumbles still, though torrid Noons
        Have lain their Missiles by -
        The Lightning that preceded it   5
        Struck no one but myself -
        But I would not exchange the Bolt
        For all the rest of Life -
        Indebtedness to Oxygen
        The Happy may repay,   10
        But not the obligation
        To Electricity -
        It founds the Homes and decks the Days
        And every clamor bright
        Is but the gleam concomitant   15
        Of that waylaying Light -
        The Thought is quiet as a Flake -
        A Crash without a Sound,
        How Life's reverberation
        It's Explanation found -   20

1666   Some Arrows slay but whom they strike,
        But this slew all *but* him,
        Who so appareled his Escape,
        Too trackless for a Tomb -

1667   Parting with Thee reluctantly,
That we have never met,
A Heart sometimes a Foreigner,
Remembers it forgot -

1668   Apparently with no surprise
To any happy Flower
The Frost beheads it at it's play -
In accidental power -
The blonde Assassin passes on -   5
The Sun proceeds unmoved
To measure off another Day
For an Approving God -

1669   Oh what a Grace is this -
What Majesties of Peace -
That having breathed
The fine - ensuing Right
Without Diminuet Proceed!   5

1670   The Jay his Castanet has struck
Put on your muff for Winter
The Tippet that ignores his voice
Is impudent to nature
Of Swarthy Days he is the close   5
His Lotus is a chestnut
The Cricket drops a sable line
No more from your's at present

1671 Take all away from me, but leave me Ecstasy,
And I am richer then, than all my fellow men -
Is it becoming me, to dwell so wealthily, when at my very door
Are those possessing more, in boundless poverty?

1672 A Letter is a joy of Earth -
It is denied the Gods -

1673 Go thy great way!
The Stars thou meetst
Are even as Thyself -
For what are Stars but Asterisks
To point a human Life? 5

1674 Is it too late to touch you, Dear?
We this moment knew -
Love Marine and Love Terrene -
Love celestial too -

1675 Of God we ask one favor, that we may be forgiven -
For what, he is presumed to know -
The Crime, from us, is hidden -
Immured the whole of Life
Within a magic Prison
We reprimand the Happiness 5
That too competes with Heaven -

1676 A chastened Grace is twice a Grace -
Nay, 'tis a Holiness.

1677   Their dappled importunity
        Disparage or dismiss -
        The Obloquies of Etiquette
        Are obsolete to Bliss -

1678   Some one prepared this mighty show
        To which without a Ticket go
        The nations and the Days -
        Displayed before the simplest Door
        That all may examine them - and more   5

1679   The Ditch is dear to the Drunken man
        For is it not his Bed - his Advocate - his Edifice -
        How safe his fallen Head
        In her disheveled Sanctity -
        Above him is the sky -   5
        Oblivion bending over him
        And Honor leagues away -

1680   The Ecstasy to guess,
        Were a receipted Bliss
        If Grace could talk -

1681   "Red Sea," indeed! Talk not to me
        Of purple Pharaoh -
        I have a Navy in the West
        Would pierce his Columns thro' -
        Guileless, yet of such Glory fine   5
        That all along the Line
        Is it, or is it not, marine -
        Is it, or not, divine -
        The Eye inquires with a sigh
        That Earth sh'd be so big -   10
        What Exultation in the Woe -
        What Wine in the fatigue!

1682   Extol thee - could I - Then I will
          By saying nothing new
          But just the fair - averring -
          That thou art heavenly -
          Perceiving thee is evidence   5
          That we are of the sky
          Partaking thee a guaranty
          Of immortality

1683   Why should we hurry - Why indeed
          When every way we fly
          We are molested equally
          By immortality
          No respite from the inference   5
          That tragedy begun
          Though where it's labors lie
          A bland uncertainty
          Besets the sight
          This mighty night   10

1684   The immortality she gave
We borrowed at her Grave -
For just one Plaudit famishing,
The Might of Human Love -

1685   Of Glory not a Beam is left
But her Eternal House -
The Asterisk is for the Dead,
The Living, for the Stars -

1686   The gleam of an heroic act
Such strange illumination
The Possible's slow fuse is lit
By the Imagination

1687   Beauty crowds me till I die
Beauty mercy have on me
But if I expire today
Let it be in sight of thee -

1688   Endanger it, and the Demand
Of tickets for a sigh
Amazes the Humility
Of Credibility -

Recover it to nature   5
And that dejected Fleet
Find Consternation's carnival
Divested of it's meat

1689   To tell the Beauty would decrease
To state the spell demean
There is a syllableless Sea
Of which it is the sign
My will endeavors for it's word   5
And fails, but entertains
A Rapture as of Legacies -
Of introspective mines -

1690   The Blunder is in estimate
Eternity is there
We say as of a Station
Meanwhile he is so near

He joins me in my Ramble   5
Divides abode with me
No Friend have I that so persists
As this Eternity

1691   Volcanoes be in Sicily
        And South America
        I judge from my Geography
        Volcano nearer here
        A Lava step at any time   5
        Am I inclined to climb
        A Crater I may contemplate
        Vesuvius at Home

1692   Of this is Day composed
        A morning and a noon
        A Revelry unspeakable
        And then a gay unknown
        Whose Pomps allure and spurn   5
        And dower and deprive
        And penury for Glory
        Remedilessly leave

1693   Summer begins to have the look
        Peruser of enchanting Book
        Reluctantly but sure perceives
        A gain upon the backward leaves

        Autumn begins to be inferred   5
        By millinery of the cloud
        Or deeper color in the shawl
        That wraps the everlasting hill

        The eye begins it's avarice
        A meditation chastens speech   10
        Some Dyer of a distant tree
        Resumes his gaudy industry

                                                       □

Conclusion is the course of all
Almost to be perennial
And then elude stability   15
Recalls to immortality -

1694   Speech is one symptom of affection
And Silence one -
The perfectest communication
Is heard of none

Exists and it's indorsement   5
Is had within -
Behold said the Apostle
Yet had not seen!

1695   I see thee clearer for the Grave
That took thy face between
No mirror could illumine thee
Like that impassive stone -

I know thee better for the act   5
That made thee first unknown
The stature of the empty nest
Attests the Bird that's gone

1696   There is a solitude of space
A solitude of sea
A solitude of Death, but these
Society shall be
Compared with that profounder site   5
That polar privacy
A soul admitted to itself -

1697   The ones that disappeared are back
The Phebe and the crow
Precisely as in March is heard

The curtness of the Jay -
Be this an Autumn or a Spring   5
My wisdom loses way
One side of me the nuts are ripe
The other side is May.

1698   Lightly stepped a yellow star
To it's lofty place
Loosed the Moon her silver hat
From her lustral Face
All of evening softly lit   5
As an Astral Hall
Father I observed to Heaven
You are punctual -

1699   Peril as a Possession
'Tis good to bear
Danger disintegrates satiety
There's Basis there -
Begets an awe   5
That searches Human Nature's creases
As clean as Fire

1700   Glory is that bright tragic thing
That for an instant
Means Dominion
Warms some poor name
That never felt the Sun   5
Gently replacing
In oblivion -

1701   The butterfly obtains
But little sympathy
Though favorably mentioned
In Entomology -

                                                 □

Because he travels freely
And wears a proper coat
The circumspect are certain
That he is dissolute

Had he the homely scutcheon
Of modest Industry
'Twere fitter certifying
For Immortality -

1702   Fame is a fickle food
Upon a shifting plate
Whose table once a
Guest but not
The second time is set
Whose crumbs the crows inspect
And with ironic caw
Flap past it to the
Farmer's corn
Men eat of it and die

1703   The wind drew off
Like hungry dogs
Defeated of a bone
Through fissures in
Volcanic cloud
The yellow lightning shone -
The trees held up
Their mangled limbs
Like animals in pain
When Nature falls upon herself
Beware an Austrian

1704   I know of people in the Grave
Who would be very glad
To know the news I know tonight
If they the chance had, had

'Tis this expands the least event   5
And swells the scantest deed
My right to walk upon the Earth
If they this moment had

1705   These are the days that Reindeer love
And pranks the northern star
This is the Sun's objective
And Finland of the year

1706   Today or this noon
She dwelt so close
I almost touched her
Tonight she lies
Past neighborhood   5
And bough and steeple
Now past surmise

1707   Judgment is justest
When the Judged
His action laid away
Divested is of every Disk
But his sincerity   5

Honor is then the safest hue
In a posthumous Sun
Not any color will endure
That scrutiny can burn.

1708   I did not reach Thee
But my feet slip nearer every day
Three Rivers and a Hill to cross
One Desert and a Sea
I shall not count the journey one   5
When I am telling thee

                                                     □

Two deserts but the year is cold
So that will help the sand
One desert crossed -
The second one   10
Will feel as cool as land
Sahara is too little price
To pay for thy Right hand

The Sea comes last - Step merry feet
So short we have to go   15
To play together we are prone
But we must labor now
The last shall be the lightest load
That we have had to draw

The Sun goes crooked -   20
That is Night
Before he makes the bend
We must have passed the Middle Sea
Almost we wish the End
Were further off   25
Too great it seems
So near the Whole to stand

We step like Plush
We stand like snow
The waters murmur new   30
Three rivers and the Hill are passed
Two deserts and the Sea!
Now Death usurps my Premium
And gets the look at Thee -

1709   The Sun retired to a cloud
         A Woman's shawl as big
         And then he sulked in mercury
         Upon a scarlet log -
         The drops on Nature's forehead stood   5
         Home flew the loaded bees
         The South unrolled a purple fan
         And handed to the trees

1710   I watched her face to see which way
She took the awful news
Whether she died before she heard
Or in protracted bruise
Remained a few slow years with us   5
Each heavier than the last
A further afternoon to fail
As Flower at fall of Frost -

1711   He went by sleep that drowsy route
To the surmising Inn -
At daybreak to begin his race
Or ever to remain -

1712   Witchcraft has not a pedigree
'Tis early as our Breath
And mourners meet it going out
The moment of our death -

1713   With sweetness unabated
Informed the hour had come
With no remiss of triumph
The autumn started home -
Her home to be with Nature   5
As competition done
By influential kinsmen
Invited to return
In supplements of Purple
An adequate repast   10
The heavenly reviewing
Her residue be past -

1714   In snow thou comest
Thou shalt go with the resuming ground

The sweet derision of the crow
And Glee's advancing sound

In fear thou comest
Thou shalt go at such a gait of joy   5
That men anew embark to live
Upon the depth of thee -

1715   A word made Flesh is seldom
And tremblingly partook
Nor then perhaps reported
But have I not mistook
Each one of us has tasted   5
With ecstasies of stealth
The very food debated
To our specific strength -

A word that breathes distinctly
Has not the power to die   10
Cohesive as the Spirit
It may expire if He -

"Made Flesh and dwelt among us"
Could condescension be
Like this consent of Language   15
This loved Philology

1716   That she forgot me was the least
I felt it second pain
That I was worthy to forget
Was most I thought upon

Faithful was all that I could boast   5
But Constancy became
To her, by her innominate
A something like a shame

1717   Guest am I to have
Light my northern room

Why to cordiality so averse to come
Other friends adjourn
Other bonds decay   5
Why avoid so narrowly
My fidelity -

1718   Rather arid delight
        If Contentment accrue
        Make an abstemious ecstasy
        Not so good as joy -

        But Rapture's Expense   5
        Must not be incurred
        With a tomorrow knocking
        And the Rent unpaid -

1719   'Tis easier to pity those when dead
        That which pity previous
        Would have saved
        A Tragedy enacted
        Secures applause   5
        That Tragedy enacting
        Too seldom does

1720   Winter under cultivation
        Is as arable as Spring

1721   Down Time's quaint stream
        Without an oar
        We are enforced to sail
        Our Port a secret
        Our Perchance a Gale   5
        What Skipper would
        Incur the Risk
        What Buccaneer would ride

Without a surety from the Wind
Or schedule of the Tide -

1722   Nature can do no more
She has fulfilled her Dyes
Whatever Flower fail to come
Of other Summer days
Her crescent reimburse
If other Summers be
Nature's imposing negative
Nulls opportunity -

1723   As we pass Houses musing slow
If they be occupied
So minds pass minds
If they be occupied

1724   The event was directly behind Him
Yet He did not guess
Fitted itself to Himself like a Robe
Relished His ignorance
Motioned itself to drill
Loaded and Levelled
And let His Flesh
Centuries from His soul

1725   If I could tell how glad I was
I should not be so glad -
But when I cannot make the Force
Nor mould it into word
I know it is a sign
That new Dilemma be
From mathematics further off
Than from Eternity

1726   The right to perish might be thought
An undisputed right
Attempt it, and the Universe
Upon the opposite
Will concentrate it's officers -   5
You cannot even die
But nature and mankind must pause
To pay you scrutiny -

1727   Sometimes with the Heart
Seldom with the soul
Scarcer once with the might
Few - love at all

1728   The Hills erect their Purple Heads
The Rivers lean to see
Yet man has not of all the Throng
A Curiosity

1729   To do a magnanimous thing
And take one's self by surprise
If one's self is not in the habit of him
Is precisely the finest of Joys -

Not to do a magnanimous thing   5
Notwithstanding it never be known
Notwithstanding it cost us existence once
Is Rapture herself spurn -

1730   His mind of man, a secret makes
I meet him with a start
He carries a circumference
In which I have no part

Or even if I deem I do   5
He otherwise may know

Impregnable to inquest
However neighborly -

1731   The Look of thee, what is it like
        Hast thou a hand or Foot
        Or mansion of Identity
        And what is thy Pursuit

        Thy fellows are they realms or Themes   5
        Hast thou Delight or Fear
        Or Longing - and is that for us
        Or values more severe -

        Let change transfuse all other Traits
        Enact all other Blame   10
        But deign this least certificate
        That thou shalt be the same -

1732   They talk as slow as Legends grow
        No mushroom is their mind
        But foliage of sterility
        Too stolid for the wind -

        They laugh as wise as Plots of Wit   5
        Predestined to unfold
        The point with bland precision
        Portentously untold

1733   Of Yellow was the outer Sky
        In Yellower Yellow hewn
        Till Saffron in vermillion slid
        Whose seam could not be shown -

1734   Eden is that old fashioned House
        We dwell in every day
        Without suspecting our abode
        Until we drive away

                                                       □

How fair on looking back the Day   5
We sauntered from the Door
Unconscious our returning
But discover it no more

1735   A - Cap of Lead across the sky
Was tight and surly drawn
We could not find the mighty Face
The Figure was Withdrawn -

A Chill came up as from a shaft   5
Our noon became a well
A Thunder storm combines the charms
Of Winter and of Hell

1736   Advance is Life's condition
The Grave but a Relay
Supposed to be a terminus
That makes it hated so -

The Tunnel is not lighted   5
Existence with a wall
Is better we consider
Than not exist at all -

1737   When we have ceased to care
The Gift is given
For which we gave the Earth
And mortgaged Heaven
But so declined in worth   5
'Tis ignominy now
To look upon -

1738   Not any sunny tone
From any fervent zone
Find entrance there

Better a grave of Balm
Toward human nature's home   5
And Robins near
Than a stupendous Tomb
Proclaiming to the gloom
How dead we are -

1739   Conferring with myself
My stranger disappeared
Though first upon a berry fat
Miraculously fared
How paltry looked my cares   5
My practise how absurd
Superfluous my whole career
Beside this travelling Bird

1740   'Twas comfort in her Dying Room
To hear the living Clock
A short relief to have the wind
Walk boldly up and knock
Diversion from the Dying Theme   5
To hear the children play
But wrong the more
That these could live
And this of our's must *die*

1741   A lane of Yellow led the eye
Unto a Purple Wood
Whose soft inhabitants to be
Surpasses solitude
If Bird the silence contradict   5
Or flower presume to show
In that low summer of the West
Impossible to know -

1742   In Winter in my Room
I came upon a Worm
Pink lank and warm
But as he was a worm
And worms presume   5
Not quite with him at home
Secured him by a string
To something neighboring
And went along -

A Trifle afterward   10
A thing occurred
I'd not believe it if I heard
But state with creeping blood
A snake with mottles rare
Surveyed my chamber floor   15
In feature as the worm before
But ringed with power
The very string with which
I tied him - too
When he was mean and new   20
That string was there -

I shrank - "How fair you are"!
Propitiation's Claw -
"Afraid he hissed
Of me"?   25
"No Cordiality" -
He fathomed me -
Then to a Rhythm *Slim*
Secreted in his Form
As Patterns swim   30
Projected him.

That time I flew
Both eyes his way
Lest he pursue
Nor ever ceased to run   35
Till in a distant Town
Towns on from mine
I set me down
This was a dream -

1743 On my volcano grows the Grass
   A meditative spot -
   An acre for a Bird to choose
   Would be the general thought -

   How red the Fire rocks below   5
   How insecure the sod
   Did I disclose
   Would populate with awe my solitude

1744 To their apartment deep
   No ribaldry may creep
   Untumbled this abode
   By any man but God -

1745 Unto a broken heart
   No other one may go
   Without the high prerogative
   Itself hath suffered too

1746 Those final Creatures, - who they are -
   That faithful to the close
   Administer her ecstasy,
   But just the Summer knows.

1747 That Love is all there is
   Is all we know of Love,
   It is enough, the freight should be
   Proportioned to the groove.

1748 As subtle as tomorrow
   That never came,
   A warrant, a conviction,
   Yet but a name.

1749   By a departing light
We see acuter, quite,
Than by a wick that stays.
There's something in the flight
That clarifies the sight   5
And decks the rays

1750   Consulting summer's clock,
But half the hours remain.
I ascertain it with a shock -
I shall not look again.
The second half of joy   5
Is shorter than the first.
The truth I do not dare to know
I muffle with a jest.

1751   Did life's penurious length
Italicize it's sweetness,
The men that daily live
Would stand so deep in joy
That it would clog the cogs   5
Of that revolving reason
Whose esoteric belt
Protects our sanity.

1752   God is indeed a jealous God -
He cannot bear to see
That we had rather not with Him
But with each other play.

1753   Had I known that the first was the last
I should have kept it longer.
Had I known that the last was the first
I should have mixed it stronger.
Cup, it was your fault,   5

Lip was not the liar.
No, lip it was your's,
Bliss was most to blame.

1754   He was my host - he was my guest,
I never to this day
If I invited him could tell,
Or he invited me.

So infinite our intercourse   5
So intimate, indeed,
Analysis as capsule seemed
To keeper of the seed.

1755   Her face was in a bed of hair,
Like flowers in a plot -
Her hand was whiter than the sperm
That feeds the sacred light.
Her tongue more tender than the tune   5
That totters in the leaves -
Who hears may be incredulous,
Who witnesses, believes.

1756   If all the griefs I am to have
Would only come today,
I am so happy I believe
They'd laugh and run away.

If all the joys I am to have   5
Would only come today,
They could not be so big as this
That happens to me now.

1757   Is Immortality a bane
That men are so oppressed?

1758   Love can do all but raise the Dead
          I doubt if even that
          From such a giant were withheld
          Were flesh equivalent

          But love is tired and must sleep,   5
          And hungry and must graze
          And so abets the shining Fleet
          Till it is out of gaze.

1759   One crown that no one seeks
          And yet the highest head
          It's isolation coveted
          It's stigma deified

          While Pontius Pilate lives   5
          In whatsoever hell
          That coronation pierces him
          He recollects it well.

1760   Proud of my broken heart, since thou did'st break it,
          Proud of the pain I did not feel till thee,

          Proud of my night, since thou with moons dost slake it,
          Not to partake thy passion, *my* humility.

          Thou can'st not boast, like Jesus, drunken without companion
          Was the strong cup of anguish brewed for the Nazarene

          Thou can'st not pierce tradition with the peerless puncture,
          See! I usurped *thy* crucifix to honor mine!

1761   That it will never come again
          Is what makes life so sweet.
          Believing what we dont believe
          Does not exhilirate.

          That if it be, it be at best   5
          An ablative estate -
          This instigates an appetite
          Precisely opposite.

1762 The joy that has no stem nor core,
   Nor seed that we can sow,
   Is edible to longing,
   But ablative to show.

   By fundamental palates   5
   Those products are preferred
   Impregnable to transit
   And patented by pod.

1763 The mob within the heart
   Police cannot suppress
   The riot given at the first
   Is authorized as peace

   Uncertified of scene   5
   Or signified of sound
   But growing like a hurricane
   In a congenial ground.

1764 The most important population
   Unnoticed dwell.
   They have a heaven each instant
   Not any hell.

   Their names, unless you know them, 5
   'Twere useless tell.
   Of bumble bees and other nations
   The grass is full.

1765 The parasol is the umbrella's daughter,
   And associates with a fan
   While her father abuts the tempest
   And abridges the rain.

   The former assists a siren   5
   In her serene display;
   But her father is borne and honored,
   And borrowed to this day.

1766 The waters chased him as he fled,
   Not daring look behind;
   A billow whispered in his Ear,
   "Come home with me, my friend;
   My parlor is of shriven glass,   5
   My pantry has a fish
   For every palate in the Year," -
   To this revolting bliss
   The object floating at his side
   Made no distinct reply.   10

1767 The words the happy say
   Are paltry melody
   But those the silent feel
   Are beautiful -

1768 There comes an hour when begging stops,
   When the long interceding lips
   Perceive their prayer is vain.
   "Thou shalt not" is a kinder sword
   Than from a disappointing God   5
   "Disciple, call again."

1769 This docile one inter
   While we who dare to live
   Arraign the sunny brevity
   That sparkles *to* the Grave

   On her departing span   5
   No wilderness remain
   As dauntless in the House of Death
   As if it were her own -

1770 Through those old grounds of memory,
   The sauntering alone
   Is a divine intemperance

A prudent man would shun.
Of liquors that are vended   5
'Tis easy to beware
But statutes do not meddle
With the internal bar.
Pernicious as the sunset
Permitting to pursue   10
But impotent to gather,
The tranquil perfidy
Alloys our firmer moments
With that severest gold
Convenient to the longing   15
But otherwise withheld.

1771   'Twas here my summer paused
        What ripeness after then
        To other scene or other soul
        My sentence had begun.

        To winter to remove   5
        With winter to abide
        Go manacle your icicle
        Against your Tropic Bride

1772   Softened by Time's consummate plush,
        How sleek the woe appears
        That threatened childhood's citadel
        And undermined the years.

        Bisected now, by bleaker griefs,   5
        We envy the despair
        That devastated childhood's realm,
        So easy to repair.

1773   My life closed twice before it's close;
        It yet remains to see
        If Immortality unveil
        A third event to me,

                                                        □

So huge, so hopeless to conceive   5
As these that twice befell.
Parting is all we know of heaven,
And all we need of hell.

1774   A face devoid of love or grace,
       A hateful, hard, successful face,
       A face with which a stone
       Would feel as thoroughly at ease
       As were they old acquaintances -   5
       First time together thrown.

1775   Upon the gallows hung a wretch,
       Too sullied for the hell
       To which the law entitled him.
       As nature's curtain fell
       The one who bore him tottered in, -   5
       For this was woman's son.
       "'Twas all I had," she stricken gasped -
       Oh, what a livid boon!

1776   The reticent volcano keeps
       His never slumbering plan;
       Confided are his projects pink
       To no precarious man.

       If nature will not tell the tale   5
       Jehovah told to her
       Can human nature not proceed
       Without a listener?

       Admonished by her buckled lips
       Let every prater be   10
       The only secret neighbors keep
       Is Immortality.

1777   To lose thee - sweeter than to gain
All other hearts I knew.
'Tis true the drought is destitute,
But then, I had the dew!

The Caspian has it's realms of sand,   5
It's other realm of sea.
Without the sterile perquisite,
No Caspian could be.

1778   High from the earth I heard a bird;
He trod upon the trees
As he esteemed them trifles,
And then he spied a breeze,
And situated softly   5
Upon a pile of wind
Which in a perturbation
Nature had left behind.
A joyous going fellow
I gathered from his talk   10
Which both of benediction
And badinage partook.
Without apparent burden
I subsequently learned
He was the faithful father   15
Of a dependent brood.
And this untoward transport
His remedy for care, -
A contrast to our respites.
How different we are!   20

1779   To make a prairie it takes a clover and one bee,
One clover, and a bee,
And revery.
The revery alone will do,
If bees are few.   5

1780   Sweet is the swamp with it's secrets,
Until we meet a snake;
'Tis then we sigh for houses,
And our departure take
At that enthralling gallop   5
That only childhood knows.
A snake is nature's treason,
And awe is where it goes.

1781   The distance that the dead have gone
Does not at first appear;
Their coming back seems possible
For many an ardent year.

And then, that we have followed them,   5
We more than half suspect,
So intimate have we become
With their dear retrospect.

1782   How dare the robins sing,
When men and women hear
Who since they went to their account
Have settled with the year! -
Paid all that life had earned   5
In one consummate bill.
And now, what life or death can do
Is immaterial.
Insulting is the sun
To him whose mortal light   10
Beguiled of immortality
Bequeath him to the night.
Extinct be every hum
In deference to him
Whose garden wrestled with the dew,   15
At daybreak overcome!

1783   Death is like the insect
Menacing the tree,
Competent to kill it,
But decoyed may be.

Bait it with the balsam   5
Seek it with the saw,
Baffle, if it cost you
Everything you are.

Then, if it have burrowed
Out of reach of skill -   10
Wring the tree and leave it.
'Tis the vermin's will.

1784   The grave my little cottage is,
Where "keeping house" for thee
I make my parlor orderly
And lay the marble tea.

For two divided, briefly,   5
A cycle, it may be,
Till everlasting life unite
In strong society.

1785   Sweet hours have perished here,
This is a timid room -
Within it's precincts hopes have played
Now fallow in the tomb.

1786   Which misses most -
The hand that tends
Or heart so gently borne,
'Tis twice as heavy as it was
Because the hand is gone?   5
Which blesses most
The lip that can,
Or that that went to sleep

With "if I could" endeavoring
Without the strength to shape?   10

1787   Were nature mortal lady
       Who had so little time
       To pack her trunk and order
       The great exchange of clime—

       How rapid, how momentous—   5
       What exigencies were—
       But nature will be ready
       And have an hour to spare.

       To make some trifle fairer
       That was too fair before—   10
       Enchanting by remaining,
       And by departure more.

1788   Fame is a bee.
       It has a song—
       It has a sting—
       Ah, too, it has a wing.

1789   The saddest noise, the sweetest noise,
       The maddest noise that grows,—
       The birds, they make it in the spring,
       At night's delicious close,

       Between the March and April line—   5
       That magical frontier
       Beyond which summer hesitates,
       Almost too heavenly near.

       It makes us think of all the dead
       That sauntered with us here,   10
       By separation's sorcery
       Made cruelly more dear.

                                                  □

It makes us think of what we had,
And what we now deplore.
We almost wish those siren throats   15
Would go and sing no more.

An ear can break a human heart
As quickly as a spear.
We wish the ear had not a heart
So dangerously near.   20

1. Distribution by Year

The number of poems is tabulated per year, with the earliest known manuscript of a poem determining the year in which the poem is counted.

Year	Numbers	Total
1850	1	1
1852	2	1
1853	3	1
1854	4	1
1858	5-47	43
1859	48-129	82
1860	130-183	54
1861	184-271	88
1862	272-498	227
1863	499-793	295
1864	794-891	98
1865	892-1120	229
1866	1121-1130	10
1867	1131-1142	12
1868	1143-1153	11
1869	1154-1164	11
1870	1165-1192	28
1871	1193-1240	48
1872	1241-1275	35
1873	1276-1313	38
1874	1314-1351	38
1875	1352-1385	34
1876	1386-1416	31
1877	1417-1458	42
1878	1459-1481	23
1879	1482-1516	35
1880	1517-1542	26

1881	1543-1567	25
1882	1568-1594	27
1883	1595-1628	34
1884	1629-1670	42
1885	1671-1683	13
1886	1684-1685	2
Undated	1686-1789	104
Total		1,789

2. Editorial Notes

This reading edition is based on *The Poems of Emily Dickinson,* Variorum Edition (Cambridge, Mass.: Belknap Press of Harvard University Press, 1998). When multiple sources exist for a poem, the following table identifies the one selected for the present edition, cited by poem number and italic letter (with the date of the manuscript in parentheses if later than the initial year of the poem); also recorded are the adoptions from Dickinson's revisions and alternative readings. When no choice of sources exists, no letter is cited, though it is always *A* or, when not a holograph, [*A*].

The first words of a number of lines have been capitalized, and one emendation, beyond those recorded in *Poems* (1998), has been made (891). Three other changes have been made or noted (128, 853, 1683).

1852

2   [*A*]

1853

3   *B* (1858)

1854

4   *A*

1858

5   *B* (1859)
9   *B* (1859)
11   *B* (cf. *C* form)
14   *B* (1862) (cf. *C* form)
16   *D* (1859)
18   *C*
20   *B*
24   *B*
32   *B*
35   *B*
38   *B*
42   *B*

43   *B*
44   *B*

1859

49   [*A.1*]
57   *B* (1861)
60   *B*
61   *B*
66   *B*
67   *B*
78   *B*
80   *C* (1864)
82   *B*
87   *B*
88   *C*
95   *B*
96   *B*
97   *B*
98   *C* (cf. *D, E* form)
99   *B*
105   *B*
106   *B*
110   *B*
112   *C* (cf. *D* form)
115   *B*
117   *B*

120	*B*
121	*B*, with the revision for line 5 adopted (cf. *A*)
122	*C*
123	*B*
124	*F* (1862)
125	*B*
128	*B*, with line 18, omitted in *Poems* (1998), restored
129	*B*

1860

131	*B* (1861)
132	*B* (1861)
135	*B* (1861)
136	*B*
137	*B*
140	*B*
141	*B*
143	*B*
144	*B*
145	*B*
150	*Ḃ*
151	*B*
153	*B*
155	*B*
162	*B*
164	*B*
166	*B*
172	*B* (1862)
173	*B*
174	*B*
178	*B*
181	*B*
182	*B*

1861

185	*C* (1863)
187	*C* (1863), with the alternatives for lines 4 and 10 adopted (cf. *B*)
191	*B* (1863)
192	*B* (1865)
193	*A* (cf. [*B*] indefinite sequence)
194	*B* (1865)
195	*B* (1863)

197	*B* (1862)
202	*C*
204	*B* (1862)
207	*B*, with the alternative for line 16 adopted (cf. [*A*])
208	*B*
217	*B* (1862)
219	*B* (cf. *C* customized)
226	*B*
227	*B*
229	*B*
230	*B*
233	*B*
236	*C* (1862)
237	*B*
240	*B* (1863)
243	*A*
244	*B*
253	*B*
255	*B*, with the alternative for line 4 adopted (cf. *A*)
258	*B*, with the alternative for line 3 adopted (cf. *A*)
260	with the alternatives for lines 4 and 7 adopted (underscored)
262	*B* (1862)
263	*B*, with the alternative for line 10 (underscored) not adopted (cf. *A*)
265	*B*

1862

273	*B* (1865)
277	*C*
278	[*A*.2]
279	with the alternative for line 7 adopted (underscored)
282	*B* (1865)
283	*C* (1863), with the alternative for line 21 adopted (cf. *B*)
284	*B* (1863)
285	*B* (1863)
286	*C* (1863, revised 1880s), with the revision for line 6 adopted
287	*B* (1865)
288	*B* (1863)

289   *B* (1865), with the alternative
for line 6 adopted (cf. *A*)

291   *E* (1883) (cf. *A*, *B* longer
version)

292   with the alternatives for lines
1 ("take") and 27 adopted
(underscored)

295   *B*, with the alternative for line
3 adopted (cf. *A*)

301   with the alternative for line
11 adopted (underscored)

303   with the alternative for line 2
adopted (underscored) and,
as the beginning of the line,
capitalized

304   *B*

305   with the alternative for line 6
adopted (underscored)

307   with the alternatives for lines
5, 6, 7, and 15 adopted
(underscored)

311   *B*

314   *B*

318   *B* (1865)

321   *C* (1866)

322   *B* (1863)

325   *C* (revised 1870s, revised text)
(revision of *C* later than *D*)

328   *B*

334   *C* (1863)

335   with the alternative for line 7
adopted (underscored)

336   *B*, with the alternative for line
15 adopted (cf. *A*)

346   *B*, with the alternative for line
11 adopted (cf. *A*)

352   *B*

359   *C*

362   *B*

369   with the alternative for line
23 adopted (underscored)

374   *B*

375   *B* (1863)

376   *B*

379   *B*, with the alternatives for
lines 15 and 16 adopted (cf.
A)

380   *B*

381   *B*

391   *B* (1865)

394   with the revision for lines 4
and 11 adopted

401   *C*, with the alternatives for
lines 4, 5, and 6 adopted (cf.
A) and that for 6, the
beginning of the line,
capitalized

403   *B*

407   *B* (1864)

408   *B* (1863)

409   *A*

418   *C*

420   *C*, with the alternatives for
lines 2 (underscored), 7, and
8 ("on far") adopted (cf. *A*,
B) and that for 8, the
beginning of the line,
capitalized

421   with the alternative for line 4
adopted (underscored)

422   *B* (1863)

430   *B*

437   *B*

440   *B* (1872)

442   *C*

457   *B*

477   *B*, with all the alternatives
adopted (cf. *A*)

478   *C* (1866)

482   *C* (1866)

494   *B*

495   *B*, with the alternatives for
lines 3 and 15-16 adopted (cf.
A)

496   *B*

1863

500   *A*

501   *C* (1865)

503   *B* (1865)

504   *B* (1864), with the
alternatives for lines 6, 9 (in
part), 16, 20, and 22 adopted
(cf. [*A*])

505	B (1864), with the alternatives for lines 2 and 3 adopted (cf. [A])	644	B
506	B (1865)	657	B
510	B	721	B
528	B	724	B
529	B	725	with the beginning of line 7 capitalized
534	B	729	B (1865)
540	B	735	B
542	B	738	C (1865), with the alternative for lines 7-8 adopted (cf. B); (cf. A longer version)
549	B	744	D
557	B	748	B
559	B	752	B
565	B	755	B
566	B	771	B
568	B	772	B
569	B	773	B
571	C (1878), with revision for line 7 adopted (underscored)	785	with the revision for lines 5 and 6 adopted (underscored)
572	C	787	C, with the alternatives for lines 6 (cf. B) and 20 (cf. A, B) adopted and that for 20, the beginning of the line, capitalized
573	B (1865)		
576	B (1864)		
577	B		
579	C		
590	B		

505 B (1864), with the alternatives for lines 2 and 3 adopted (cf. [A])
506 B (1865)
510 B
528 B
529 B
534 B
540 B
542 B
549 B
557 B
559 B
565 B
566 B
568 B
569 B
571 C (1878), with revision for line 7 adopted (underscored)
572 C
573 B (1865)
576 B (1864)
577 B
579 C
590 B
592 B, with the alternative for line 8 adopted (cf. A)
593 B, with the alternatives for lines 5 and 35 adopted (cf. [A])
594 C (1871)
600 C, with the alternative for line 12 ("showing") adopted (cf. A, B)
604 with an alternative for line 26 ("Arguments") adopted (underscored)
606 C (1866) (cf. A longer version)
608 B, with an alternative for line 8 ("decide") adopted (cf. A)
615 with the revision for line 8 adopted
618 B
630 B, with the alternative for line 14 adopted (cf. A)
635 C (1865) (cf. A longer version)
638 B, with the alternative for line 3 adopted (cf. A)

644 B
657 B
721 B
724 B
725 with the beginning of line 7 capitalized
729 B (1865)
735 B
738 C (1865), with the alternative for lines 7-8 adopted (cf. B); (cf. A longer version)
744 D
748 B
752 B
755 B
771 B
772 B
773 B
785 with the revision for lines 5 and 6 adopted (underscored)
787 C, with the alternatives for lines 6 (cf. B) and 20 (cf. A, B) adopted and that for 20, the beginning of the line, capitalized

1864

794 B (1865)
795 B (1865)
796 E (1883)
797 B (1865)
798 B (1865)
799 B (1865)
803 B (1865)
804 D (1883)
806 C (1865)
807 C (1865)
809 B (1865), with the alternative for line 7 adopted (cf. A)
810 B (1865)
811 B (1865)
813 B (1865)
814 C (1865)
815 B (1865)
816 B (1865)
817 B (1865)
818 B (1865)

819 E (1867)
820 A
822 B
846 A
852 C (1865)
853 Line 8 does not stand apart, though so stated in *Poems* (1998)
855 B, with the alternative for line 6 adopted (cf. *A*)
861 A
862 B
867 B
876 B
878 B
881 (revised mid-1870s), with the revision adopted for lines 4, 6 ("this"), 6 ("specific" underscored), 8 ("fled" underscored), and 9 (underscored)
888 B
890 B
891 with an emendation: *after* 20] *a line standing apart deleted* (And then Return - and Night - and Home -)

1865

894 B
895 F (1883) (cf. *A* longer version)
897 C
919 B
923 B
933 B
935 E (1882)
937 C
940 B
946 C
949 B
951 B
956 B
962 B
964 B
966 C (1866)
972 B
974 B (1867)

986 B
991 C (1866)
995 B
996 A
1014 B
1016 B
1022 B (1872, revised 1873 or 1874), with the revision for lines 7 (both) and 8 adopted; (revision of *B* later than C)
1039 B
1066 with the beginning of line 6 capitalized
1078 B
1081 C (1866)
1086 B
1090 B
1096 C (1872)
1098 B
1099 C (1866)
1102 B
1103 B
1104 C (1866)
1110 B (1867)
1113 B
1120 C

1866

1122 A
1124 [A]
1125 B
1126 A, with both alternatives for line 1 adopted (cf. [B])
1130 C

1867

1138 A (cf. [B] indefinite sequence)
1141 A
1142 B

1868

1143 with the alternatives for lines 2, 3, and 6 ("seconds") adopted (underscored)
1147 B

1869

1154	(revised text)
1158	A
1160	A
1163	A
1164	B

1870

1166	C
1169	A
1171	A/B
1172	B
1174	with the revision for line 23 adopted and the beginning of lines 10 and 12 capitalized
1175	C
1176	with the alternative for line 3 adopted (underscored)
1180	C
1183	D (1871), with the alternative for lines 11-12 adopted (cf. *B*, *C*)
1192	with the beginning of lines 2 and 4 capitalized

1871

1194	E (1878)
1196	B
1197	with the beginning of line 6 capitalized
1201	with the beginning of lines 2, 4, 5, 6, and 7 capitalized
1208	C (1873)
1214	B (1873)
1216	B, with the revision for line 3 adopted; (revision of *B* later than *C*)
1219	B
1223	A
1227	D
1229	C
1234	D
1235	with the alternative for line 5 adopted (underscored)
1236	B

| 1237 | B (1872) |
| 1239 | B (revised 1872), with alternatives for line 10 ("withdraws" and "worthless"), 13 ("function"), and 15 as well as the revision for lines 2 and 3 (both underscored) adopted (cf. *C*), but with the revision for line 7 (underscored) not adopted (cf. *C*); with an adopted alternative for line 10, the beginning of the line, capitalized |

1872

1242	A
1243	with the beginning of line 7 capitalized
1244	with the alternative for line 5 adopted (underscored) and, as the beginning of the line, capitalized
1245	with the alternative for line 2 adopted (underscored)
1247	with the alternative for line 6 adopted (underscored)
1255	(revised text)
1256	C as the first stanza, B as the second, with the alternative for line 6 (*B*) adopted (underscored)
1257	B
1266	B
1267	B
1268	A, with the alternatives for lines 2 and 4 adopted (cf. *B*) and with the revision for line 6 adopted and, as the beginning of the line, capitalized
1269	with the revision for line 3 adopted (underscored)
1270	B
1274	A
1275	C

1873

1277	B
1278	C
1279	D (1876)
1280	A (revised text), with the canceled reading "Distance" restored for line 6 (cf. [B])
1282	with the revision for line 4 adopted
1284	with the beginning of line 6 capitalized
1285	C
1286	B, with the alternatives for lines 5 and 6 adopted (cf. [C], D)
1287	with the alternative for line 2 adopted (underscored)
1288	[B]
1296	B
1298	C, with the revision for line 5 adopted (underscored)
1300	B
1304	B
1305	B
1311	B, with the alternative for line 4 adopted (underscored)

1874

1314	C
1317	B
1319	with the revision for line 2 adopted
1322	[B]
1329	B
1333	with the revision for line 6 ("summons") adopted
1337	with the alternative for line 7 ("mountain") adopted (underscored)
1341	A (revised text) (cf. C form)
1342	[B]
1343	with the alternatives for lines 5 and 6 adopted (underscored)
1349	B
1350	F

1351	B, with the alternative for line 4 ("Carriage was") adopted (cf. A)

1875

1352	[A]
1353	B
1354	B
1356	B/C
1357	D
1358	[B]
1361	A
1364	B
1365	with the underscored revision for lines 4 ("To Denizen denied"), 5 ("closing"), 7 ("And she will point you sighing"), and the underscored alternative for line 8 ("To her rescinded Bud") adopted.
1367	with the alternatives for lines 3 and 5 adopted (underscored) and that for 3, the beginning of the line, capitalized
1368	A
1369	C (1876)
1372	E (1878)
1380	F (1876)
1381	B (cf. C form)
1382	B
1383	F (1877)
1384	E (1876)

1876

1386	D
1387	A
1388	A
1394	B
1395	B
1396	B
1400	B

1404	with the alternative for line 11 adopted (underscored) and the beginning of line 12 capitalized
1405	with the alternative for line 8 adopted (underscored)
1411	C (revised text) as the first stanza, E as the second
1413	with both alternatives for line 6 adopted (underscored)
1416	C (1878)

1877

1419	B
1422	C
1423	A
1424	A
1425	B
1426	B
1428	B
1432	B (cf. C customized)
1433	[A]
1434	B
1440	with the alternative for line 4 adopted (underscored)
1441	B, with the alternative for line 11 adopted (cf. A)
1442	with the alternative for line 3 adopted (underscored)
1448	with the beginning of lines 4, 9, and 12 capitalized
1451	C
1453	D, with the revision for line 1 (both), 2, and 4 (implied) adopted
1454	D
1455	A, with the revision for lines 3 and 7-8 adopted (cf. [B])
1456	A, with the alternative for line 2 adopted (cf. B)

1878

1459	C
1461	with the beginning of lines 2 and 4 capitalized
1462	C (1880)

1463	C
1470	with the alternative for line 12 adopted (underscored)
1474	with the alternative for line 3 adopted (underscored)
1476	with the alternative for lines 5-6 adopted (underscored)
1477	[B]
1480	with the alternative for line 4 adopted (underscored)
1481	B

1879

1483	with the revision for line 6 adopted
1484	C
1487	C
1488	D
1489	G (1883)
1503	B
1504	B
1505	B (1883)
1506	C
1509	[B]
1516	A (cf. B customized)

1880

1520	B
1521	B
1523	with the alternative for line 3 adopted (underscored) and the beginning of line 6 capitalized
1524	[A.1], with the beginning of lines 3 and 4 capitalized
1525	C
1527	[A]
1533	with the beginning of lines 3 and 4 capitalized
1534	with the beginning of lines 6 and 8 capitalized
1535	with the beginning of line 6 capitalized
1537	B
1538	A
1539	C

1540 [C]
1542 [B]

1881

1544 B
1545 B
1546 A
1547 B
1553 with the revision for lines 7 and 8 adopted
1557 with the beginning of line 2 capitalized
1560 with the alternative for line 4 adopted (underscored)
1562 B (cf. [A] longer version)
1563 C
1564 B

1882

1569 A, with the alternatives for lines 3 and 7 adopted (underscored)
1570 F
1571 B, with the alternative for line 8 adopted (cf. C) and, as the beginning of the line, capitalized; (cf. C customized)
1572 A
1573 A (cf. B customized)
1574 C
1577 C
1583 [B]
1592 with the alternative for line 4 adopted (underscored) and the beginning of line 8 capitalized
1594 C

1883

1596 C
1597 D
1598 D (1884)
1599 C
1600 B (cf. C form)
1601 A, with the alternative for line 12 (entire) adopted (cf. B)

1602 C
1604 A, with the alternative for line 3 adopted (cf. [B])
1606 B
1607 with the beginning of line 2 capitalized
1609 B
1610 with the revision for line 2 and 4 adopted
1616 B, with the alternative for line 8 adopted (cf. C, D, and the poems "Expanse cannot be lost" and "The spirit lasts but in what mode")
1617 B, with the revision for lines 9 and 10 adopted and that for 9, the beginning of the line, capitalized
1622 with the beginning of line 6 capitalized
1624 B (1885)
1626 A (cf. B customized)
1627 B
1628 B

1884

1629 B
1630 A
1635 with the beginning of line 4 capitalized
1636 A
1637 [A.1]
1638 B
1639 B
1641 F (1885)
1642 B
1643 [B]
1644 B
1647 B (cf. C customized)
1650 C (cf. A longer version)
1660 with the beginning of line 2 capitalized
1663 A
1665 B
1666 C
1670 with the beginning of line 4 capitalized

1885

1671	F
1672	A (cf. B form)
1673	B
1675	B
1679	with the beginning of line 2 capitalized
1682	with the beginning of lines 2 and 8 capitalized
1683	with the alternative for line 6 (underscored) adopted for "this which is"—not just "which is" as proposed in *Poems* (1998)—and the beginning of lines 3, 4, 5, 6, and 7 capitalized

1886

1684	B

Undated

1693	[A]
1786	[A]

Index of First Lines

The first lines of poems are indexed by poem numbers. No attempt has been made to reproduce exact punctuation or capitalization.

To hang our head ostensibly   160
To hear an oriole sing   402
To help our bleaker parts   1087
To her derided home   1617
To him who keeps an orchis' heart   31
To his simplicity   1387
To interrupt his yellow plan   622
To know just how he suffered would be dear   688
To learn the transport by the pain   178
To lose if one can find again   30
To lose one's faith surpass   632
To lose thee sweeter than to gain   1777
To love thee year by year   618
To make a prairie it takes a clover and one bee   1779
To make one's toilette after death   471
To make routine a stimulus   1238
To mend each tattered faith   1468
To my quick ear the leaves conferred   912
To my small hearth his fire came   703
To offer brave assistance   492
To one denied to drink   1058
To own a Susan of my own   1436
To own the art within the soul   1091
To pile like thunder to it's close   1353
To put this world down like a bundle   404
To see her is a picture   1597
To see the summer sky   1491
To tell the beauty would decrease   1689
To the bright east she flies   1603
To the stanch dust   1434
To their apartment deep   1744
To this world she returned   815
To try to speak and miss the way   1629
To undertake is to achieve   991
To venerate the simple days   55
To wait an hour is long   884
To whom the mornings stand for nights   1055
Today or this noon   1706
"Tomorrow" whose location   1417
Too cold is this   1137
Too few the mornings be   1201
Too happy time dissolves itself   1182
Too little way the house must lie   902
Too scanty 'twas to die for you   1023